Nationalism
in Uzbekistan

Nationalism in Uzbekistan

A Soviet Republic's Road to Sovereignty

James Critchlow

Westview Press
BOULDER • SAN FRANCISCO • OXFORD

ALP 6710-6/2

This Westview softcover edition is printed on acid-free paper and bound in library-quality, coated covers that carry the highest rating of the National Association of State Textbook Administrators, in consultation with the Association of American Publishers and the Book Manufacturers' Institute.

Published in 1991 in the United States of America by Westview Press, Inc., 5500 Central Avenue, Boulder, Colorado 80301-2847, and in the United Kingdom by Westview Press, 36 Lonsdale Road, Summertown, Oxford OX2 7EW

Library of Congress Cataloging-in-Publication Data
Critchlow, James.
   Nationalism in Uzbekistan : a Soviet republic's road to sovereignty / by James Critchlow.
      p.   cm.
   Includes bibliographical references and index.
   ISBN 0-8133-8403-6
   1. Uzbek S.S.R.—History—Autonomy and independence movements.
2. Nationalism—Uzbek S.S.R.   3. Soviet Union—Ethnic relations.
I. Title.
DK948.86.C75   1991
958'.7—dc20   91-27668
                                                                 CIP

Printed and bound in the United States of America

The paper used in this publication meets the requirements of the American National Standard for Permanence of Paper for Printed Library Materials Z39.48-1984.

10   9   8   7   6   5   4   3   2   1

In memory of Pat

and for Ann, Jane, and Alanna

Contents

Contents

Tables

Preface

In June 1990, the government of the republic of Uzbekistan declared its political independence. It followed this action in early 1991 by refusing, at least for a time, to sign a "union" treaty with Moscow because it held that the wording of the draft originally proposed by Mikhail Gorbachev was inconsistent with its newly sovereign status. As described in greater detail later in this book, Islam Abdughanievich Karimov, the President of Uzbekistan (and still First Secretary of its Communist Party), declared his republic's willingness to continue an association with a Soviet "Union," but only on a basis of equality in which Uzbek sovereignty would be fully recognized, and the prerogatives of the central government, such as responsibility for defense, would be delegated by voluntary consent of the constituent republics.

Only a few years earlier, Uzbekistan had been regarded as a classic example of a non-Russian Soviet republic subservient to Moscow in all things. What happened to bring it so rapidly to its new status of independence? Clearly, the new climate created by perestroika and glasnost is part of the explanation. Another part is the Kremlin's preoccupation with more militant forms of separatism in the Baltic and Caucasian republics. But the internal forces in Uzbekistan which spearheaded its relatively quiet drive for independence did not emerge overnight: they have been at work beneath the surface for decades, beginning even in Stalin's day. A reversion in Moscow to hard-line politics, as manifested by the anti-Gorbachev coup of August, 1991, can slow political evolution, but it cannot reverse it.

This book traces the growth of nationalism in Uzbekistan since its creation as a new political entity in 1925, with special emphasis on events of recent years. My aim is to provide background for assessing the rapid political change which has prevailed in Uzbekistan during the late 1980s and early 1990s, as Central Asia has followed other non-Russian areas of the Soviet Union in dissolving or altering its old ties with the center in Moscow. Obviously, the present pace of events is so breathtaking that no book-length work can be up-to-date these days in reflecting details of last-minute change. This volume is offered as the best possible alternative, a benchmark for measuring the nature and extent of Uzbekistan's transformation at various steps of the way.

This is not an attempt to write a comprehensive history of modern Uzbekistan, nor a treatise on its economy, nor a Kremlinological analysis of its politics, tasks which the author cheerfully leaves to others. Rather, the more modest purpose is to touch on all of those things, and others, as they affect Uzbek ethnic awareness, to distill something of the "soul" of present-day Uzbek nationalism by examining the attitude of Uzbeks, especially the elites, toward some of the issues which inform the collective consciousness. I hope that this will contribute to the understanding of a new political entity which shows promise of becoming an independent actor on the international stage.

Part of the book's claim to originality stems from the fact that it is based on Uzbek vernacular sources which have not been systematically developed by other researchers. These offer a unique insight into the mentality of Uzbek writers. Even in the pre-perestroika period, Uzbek-language media were less inhibited in expressing nationalist views than were parallel sources in the Russian language. This is doubtless explained by the relative inaccessibility of materials in Uzbek to Russians and other non-natives. Although even the vernacular media were not entirely free from censorship, they were the expression of Uzbeks dealing with other Uzbeks, with greater opportunities for candor and esoteric communication.

Two broad classes of issues have given stimulus to Uzbek nationalism: economic and cultural. The central economic issue has been imposition by Moscow of a cotton "monoculture" under which the Soviet planning organs in Moscow forced Uzbekistan to become the country's primary cotton base. Under this system, the Uzbeks saw themselves as little better than cotton slaves to Moscow. Reckless expansion of cotton acreage, particularly in the 1960s and 1970s, stunted growth of other sectors of the economy and did enormous harm to the environment, leading to popular grievances in such emotional areas as living standards and health. The central cultural issue has been "russification," the practical consequence of decades of Soviet policy which held that the Russian "elder brother," his language and his culture, were superior to that of the Uzbeks and other non-Russian peoples; the Uzbeks saw this as a threat to the survival of their own identity and centuries-old Islamic culture. These two issues, and the conflicts which they engendered, are the *leitmotiv* of this book.

The work is organized in three parts. Part I, "The Rise of Uzbek Nationalism," describes, in historical perspective, the development of Uzbek nationalism from the early days of Soviet rule through approximately 1988. Its first chapter, "Who Are the Uzbeks?" focuses on the early days of Soviet rule when "Uzbek" first came to be regarded as the designation of a nation in the European sense of the word. Previously, "Uzbek" had been merely a conglomerate name for various Turkic tribes of nomadic origin. The chapter discusses the impact of Soviet policy and institutions in creating, for the first time ever, a sense of "Uzbek" national identity that came to be internalized by members of the Uzbek nationality. The second chapter, which is based mainly on a survey of the Uzbek-language press in the later 1960s and early 1970s, is entitled "Prelude to Perestroika: Signs of Emerging Nationalism." It describes early efforts by Uzbek intellectuals to take advantage of the relatively lax policies of the Brezhnev period by making their republic into an emotional national symbol, while at the same time attempting to undo russifying trends of the Stalin era. The third chapter examines the post-Brezhnev reaction to Uzbek nationalism, particularly under Andropov and in Gorbachev's early years, which took the form of action against the Uzbek elites through a campaign aimed ostensibly at stamping out "corruption" that actually masked a much broader political objective.

Part II focuses on particular issues of the more recent period: the cotton "monoculture," the environmental crisis typified by disappearance of the Aral Sea, irritation with the presence of a domineering Russian "elder brother," Russian and Stalinist rewriting of Uzbek history and attempts to correct it, the tactics of resistance to central authority, the uproar caused by violent deaths of Uzbek youths while serving in the Soviet military, and the "Islamic factor." The focus is on exploitation by the Uzbek elites of these issues to mobilize mass support against the central authority in Moscow.

Part III, "Problems of Sovereignty," details some of the challenges facing Uzbekistan, and especially the Uzbek elites, as the republic sets out on its new course. Chief of these is that of survival in the face of the impending collapse of the Soviet economy. Another is the problem of the heterogeneous composition of Uzbekistan's population--Russians, Tajiks and other non-Uzbek minorities--and the continuing menace of internal ethnic unrest. These vastly complicate the problems of those attempting to govern an increasingly independent Uzbekistan.

An afterword, "The Shape of Things to Come," looks at prospects for the future evolution of Uzbekistan as an increasingly independent member of the world community. It addresses the central question of whether the new Uzbek nationalism, as personified by the elite class engendered during the Soviet period, has been able over the decades to sink deeply enough into the fabric of society to provide a basis for stable rule. Also considered are possible outcomes if Uzbekistan were to fail as a nation, creating a political vacuum in the region.

Much of the material is derived from articles published in serial literature, but in substantially updated and revised form.

The book is written from the vantage of years of trying to answer my own and other people's questions about Uzbekistan. I believe that it will serve a triple purpose:

1. For the general student, to offer a diversity of information in easily accessible form about this still relatively obscure but increasingly important part of the world.
2. For those specializing in Soviet affairs, to assist in acquiring knowledge of the specifics of the Muslim part of the USSR.
3. For those with a special interest in Soviet Islam, to provide source materials for further study.

Frequent references in this book to the terms "elite" and "elites" may raise questions about the author's definition of them. In highly stratified Soviet society there is a fairly sharp dividing line between those who wield power and influence and those who do not. The former, corresponding roughly to Milovan Djilas' "New Class," are what I have in mind. In his study, *Privilege in the Soviet Union*, Mervyn Matthews suggested considering as "elites" those who had a monthly income of more than approximately 500 rubles.[1] I do not pretend to that degree of precision, and beg the reader's indulgence: I hope that my definition of "elite" will be clear from the context.

Transliteration. In transliterating Uzbek words, I have generally relied on the Edward Allworth's table,[2] with some modifications. In particular, where Western readers are accustomed to a different spelling (e.g. Samarkand instead of Samarqand) I have used the more familiar form. Words from other languages encountered in Russian texts are transliterated as from the Russian (e.g. "Dzhanibekov").

James Critchlow

Notes

1.   Mervyn Matthews, *Privilege in the Soviet Union: A Study of Elite Life-Styles Under Communism,* London (George Allen & Unwin) 1978, p. 22.

2.   Edward Allworth, *Nationalities of the Soviet East: Publications and Writing Systems,* New York (Columbia University Press) 1971, p. 378.

Acknowledgments

My thanks are due to the University of Illinois at Urbana-Champaign for providing me with my first academic home after years in government and to the admirable staff of that institution's Slavic Library. The Smithsonian's Kennan Institute for Advanced Russian Studies kindly provided me with a grant that enabled me to do research on Uzbek materials at the Library of Congress. Since 1987, I have been privileged to be affiliated with the Harvard University Russian Research Center, and have been continuously grateful for the fellowship and advice that I have received there: from Adam Ulam, director, from Marshall Goldman, associate director, and from friends and associates too numerous to mention. In a very grim sense, this book might not have seen the light of day without the ministrations of the amiably indomitable Mary Towle, the center's administrative officer, resourceful Michele Wong Albanese, staff assistant, and that wizard of desktop publishing, Margaret Buckley, to all of whom I am enormously indebted.

A special word of appreciation about some of those who have encouraged me to pursue the interest which led to this book: the late Professor Alexandre Bennigsen, who first inspired me in that direction with his infectious enthusiasm for the topic, and Professors Edward Allworth of Columbia University, Teresa Rakowska-Harmstone of Carleton University, Donald Carlisle of Boston College, and William Fierman of Indiana University. There have been many others, but those five stand out.

I must acknowledge the kindness of S. Enders Wimbush, director of Radio Liberty, in granting me permission to adapt material from numerous articles which originally appeared in *Report on the USSR,* also that of Frank Cass Publishers and of Norton Dodge of the Cremona Foundation for similarly agreeing to let me make use of one article each from the *Journal of Communist Studies* and *The Soviets in Asia.*

Finally, a grateful nod to Rebecca Ritke of Westview Press, who was willing to take on editorial responsibility for the project despite having sat through one of my courses at the University of Illinois.

The shortcomings of the work are uniquely my own.

J.C.

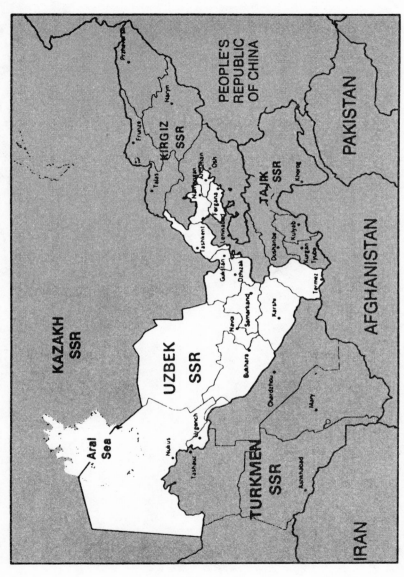

Uzbekistan. *Source*: Central Intelligence Agency.

PART ONE

The Rise of Uzbek Nationalism

1

Who Are the Uzbeks?

Anyone who has visited the Soviet republic of Uzbekistan has been struck by the distinctive appearance of the land and its people: by the graceful Islamic architecture of the older buildings, by the fragrance of Eastern spices in the bazaars, by the serenity of the teahouses, and by the dignified bearing of the Uzbeks themselves, coifed in their traditional *doppilar*, skullcaps.

The Uzbeks occupy a commanding position in the politics of Soviet Central Asia. The most populous of the USSR's various Muslim nationalities, they are increasingly asserting control over their own republic, to the virtual exclusion of Moscow's representatives who once held sway there as proconsuls. Ethnically, the Uzbeks are descended from a conglomerate of nomadic Turkic tribes; over a period of many centuries their ancestors invaded the region from the Eurasian steppes to the north, many settling in the warmer southern climate and intermingling with the native Iranian stock. Even today, many Uzbeks are bilingual, speaking both their own language, which is closely related to Turkish, and Tajik, an Iranian tongue of the Indo-European family that differs little from the Farsi of Iran or the Dari of the Afghan cities. The result of the Uzbeks' mixed heritage is a proliferation of facial types, ranging from Mongolian to Mediterranean.

As a "nationality" in the modern sense, the Uzbeks are essentially a product of the early Soviet period. The name "Uzbek" reaches back into the middle ages, but chiefly as a tribal classification.[1] In 1869 a dictionary of "Turko-Tatar dialects," intended for use by Russian officials and traders, defined "Uzbek" as "the proper name of a tribe of Tatars (sic) comprising the main population of the khanate of Khiva" and described the word as "a sobriquet adopted by the nomads of

3

Central Asia together with their clannic names."[2] A volume of the Russian Brockhaus-Efron Encyclopedia issued in St. Petersburg in 1902 referred to "Uzbeks" as a "conglomerate of tribes in which the Turkic element is mixed with Mongol." The entry asserted that "the name itself has more of a politico-historical than ethnic meaning," and that "pure" Uzbeks, judging from the fact that they had no fewer than 80 clannic names, "were composed of the most diverse branches of the Turkic tribe."[3] In its most recent edition, the Large Soviet Encyclopedia, while referring to the Uzbeks as a "nation" (*natsiya*), indicated that their formation as such was incomplete prior to the 1917 revolution.

Uzbekistan: A Modern Geographic Concept

In 1924, the Soviet government in Moscow, now dominated by Stalin in the aftermath of Lenin's recent death, ordered a "national delimitation" of the vast territory of the former Russian imperial province of Turkestan. The many tribal and local groups native to the region were conglomerated by administrative fiat into a much smaller number of "nationalities." "Nationality" was in fact a European concept imported to the territory by outsiders operating in the framework of the new Soviet regime.

Lines were drawn on the map to establish five "republics," each named after the "nationality" most prominent in its population: Uzbekistan, Tajikistan, Kyrghyzystan (more often in English called Kirghizia), Turkmenistan and Karakalpakistan, the latter now an "autonomous" enclave in the northwest corner of Uzbekistan. (Kazakhstan, the large area to the north inhabited mainly by nomadic Kazakhs and Russian settlers, had already become a separate republic.)

"Uzbekistan," the land of the Uzbeks, emerged from the delimitation as a tract of land almost the size of California that extended nearly a thousand miles from the Aral Sea in the West to the Ferghana Valley in the East. Its population was 4.26 million. Since 1924 the population has more than quintupled, mainly due to high Muslim birth-rates, and is now in excess of 20 million.

Uzbekistan is bounded to the north by Kazakhstan, to the west by Turkmenistan, to the south by Turkmenistan, Afghanistan--with which it shares its only foreign border--and Tajikistan, and to the east by

Kirghizia. The terrain includes mountain ranges and low-lying deserts broken by fertile river-valleys. During the summer growing-season, there is practically no rainfall. Melted snow from the foothills of the Himalayas to the East flows westward into the rivers and toward the Aral, forming the lifeline for human habitation.

The Uzbeks, although new as a nation, are obsessed with tracing their complex ethnic heritage, which they call by the Arabic name *miras* (or *meras*). Alexander of Macedonia passed through this land in the fourth century B.C. on his way to conquer India. He paused in Maracanda, an ancient city near the present site of Samarkand, long enough to form local alliances and to marry Roxana, daughter of a local chieftain. He has survived, under the local name Iskander, as a strong figure in *miras*, a demi-god of sorts.

In Alexander's day, the inhabitants of the region were mainly Iranian. Turkic tribes had not yet begun to arrive on the scene. They did so later, roaming in from the steppes to north and east, a movement that continued for centuries. Many were assimilated to the predominantly Iranian culture of the cities. Some of those cities, like Bukhara and Samarkand, became, thanks to the growth of European trade with China and India, important way-stations on the main East-West caravan route, the Great Silk Road.

In the late seventh century there occurred an event that was to leave its mark on the region forever. Arab invaders overran the area by crossing the Amu River (Amu-Darya) from the South. They called it *Mavera-an-Nahr*, "land across the river." The Arabs stayed only briefly, but long enough to implant the Islamic religion so firmly that it has survived to the present day, despite determined efforts to stamp it out by Russian missionaries in the last century and Soviet ideologists in this one. In the wake of the Arabs, an important Islamic civilization flourished on what is now the territory of Uzbekistan, linking it spiritually and intellectually with the entire Muslim world, from North Africa and the Middle East to South Asia and the East Indies. In the ninth century, in the westerly region of the Khorezmian oasis, site of the city of Khiva today, was born a mathematician known to the world as "al-Khorezmi"; he is credited with having invented algebra, its name derived from the Arabic word *al-jabr* in the title of his treatise. The scholar Avicenna, in the East called "Ibn Sina," was born a few decades later near Bukhara, and wrote a medical textbook so advanced that centuries later it was still being used, in Latin translation, throughout Europe. A contemporary of Avicenna's, the

Khorezmian scholar al-Biruni, also made major contributions to the world of learning of his time; his travelogue of a trip through India is still in print today, in English and other languages. Men like these wrote in Arabic or Persian, and it is doubtful that they even understood the alien Turkic dialects on which modern Uzbek is based, but today's Uzbeks insist on referring to them as "our fellow countrymen" and base much of their pride in the national *miras* on that assumed relationship.

Civilized progress was broken off in the early thirteenth century by the arrival of Mongol invaders, who devastated the cities, proverbially leaving "not one stone upon another." With the Mongols came Turkic warriors as allies, some of them staying on to rule the territory. This mixed Turko-Mongol caste succumbed quickly to the civilizing influence of Islam. Central Asian Muslims went to China to serve as financial administrators in the Mongol Empire of Kublai Khan; one of them, a man from Tashkent named Ahmad, was implicated in corruption and sexual scandals.[4] When Marco Polo and his brother passed through Bukhara only a century after it had been destroyed by the Mongol Jenghis Khan, they found it to be a "very great and noble city."[5]

One of the Turko-Mongol rulers, Tamerlane, made his seat in Samarkand, but led his troops to conquests as far away as India, Syria and southern Russia. His imposing blue-domed mausoleum, the Gur Emir, is today a major tourist attraction in Samarkand. Another descendant of warriors, Babur, marched his men through Afghanistan to India, where he founded the Mogul (Mongol) Empire which was still in place when the British Raj arrived. Babur is revered by today's Uzbeks as a warrior and man of letters who wrote his major work not in Arabic or Persian but in the eastern variant of Turkish: his *Baburname*, memoirs, is considered one of the great classics of "Uzbek" literature. (Both Tamerlane and Babur are celebrated in contemporary Uzbek historical novels. This "glorification of the past" was long condemned by Moscow loyalists, who saw in it, with some justification, an effort to build up past military heroes as symbols of today's Uzbek nationalism.)

Then, in the late sixteenth century, a long night of depression descended on Central Asia as caravan travel was made obsolete by competition from the newly discovered, and safer, sea-routes around the Cape of Good Hope. Disappearance of the caravans relegated the region to isolation and stagnation. Its Islamic society, which had inspired such great works of creativity, now came under the sway of cruel and despotic rulers with narrow, bigoted mullahs as their henchmen.

Russian Conquest

It was not until the last century that the oasis cities, the future nuclei of today's Uzbekistan, were jolted fatefully from their torpor by the advent of the Russians. Although the Russian presence is a relatively recent one, it has left indelible scars on the landscape and in the minds of the inhabitants. The virtual disappearance of the Aral Sea, once greater in area than Lake Michigan and the largest body of water between the Caspian Sea and the Pacific, is a permanent reminder of what the Russians have done.

The invasion of Central Asia was the culmination of three centuries of Russian eastward expansion. In 1552, Tsar Ivan IV captured the city of Kazan on the Volga from its rulers, Muslim Tatars who made up still another branch of the farflung Turkic family. Kazan's defeat was followed by a dynamic movement of Russian explorers and traders across Siberia until they reached the Pacific Coast and Alaska, and, briefly, California and the Hawaiian Islands.

For a time, however, this eastward movement bypassed the Islamic region of Central Asia, where in general only adherents of the faith were welcome. Russia's commercial interests there were served by intermediary Volga Tatar merchants, who as Muslims were acceptable visitors. Indeed, the Tatar merchants made a practice of sending their sons to study in the *madrasas*, religious seminaries, of Bukhara, regarded as one of the holiest cities in all Islam. But for non-Muslim visitors, the territory was off-limits. As recently as the past century, there were well-documented cases of hapless European travelers to Bukhara who ended up in the Emir's foul dungeons or became victims of his executioners.

This equilibrium began to tilt in the eighteenth century as land-hungry settlers from European Russia encroached on the Kazakh nomads' grazing lands in the steppes north of the oases. To protect the settlers from reprisals by the nomads, an advancing string of Russian forts was established. By the mid-nineteenth century, Russian troops were poised to strike into the heart of the Muslim territory. Internal dissensions among the defenders paved the way for the invaders. In 1865, Tashkent fell, becoming the center of Russian administration in the region of oases and deserts which extended west to the Caspian. By

1885, the last organized resistance was crushed with the defeat of the Turkmen tribes in the western desert.

The territory was made by the Russians into the "Turkestan Government-General," headed by a succession of military generals, with Tashkent as its capital. Within the territory but retaining nominal independence, the Emirate of Bukhara and the khanates of Khiva and Kokand were allowed to continue under their native rulers, as Russian protectorates. (Russian dissatisfaction with the situation in Kokand soon led to liquidation of the khanate there, but Bukhara and Khiva retained their autonomous status until after the Russian Revolution of 1917.)

Russian goals were primarily economic and strategic: to make money and block any attempt by the British to expand their sphere of influence from their imperial base in India. Even in areas outside the protectorates where they governed directly, the Tsar's administrators conceded a considerable measure of autonomy to the native society, in which religious courts operating under the *shariat*, Islamic law, played the major role. To help keep down unrest in the population, some governors-general even prevented proselytizing attempts by Russian Orthodox missionaries.

In general, Russians living in Central Asia shrank from learning the language or entering into the native life. They preferred to rule through native surrogates. This policy helped to spawn a new class of indigenous elites who derived their status from Russian power, not from their position in their own society, and who were often feared or despised by their fellow-countrymen. At the same time, this new native class never fully enjoyed the confidence of the Russians, for there were those among them who were more than ready to betray or quietly undercut their new rulers. The native elites of the tsarist period were forerunners of the Soviet-era elites on which the Communist regime depended to spread its message and implement its policies, and with which it experienced many of the same problems.

Russian occupation brought to Central Asia an infusion of capital and a rush of technological innovation. Railroads revolutionized the mobility of people and goods, and telegraph wires laid along the railroad right-of-way revolutionized communication. These developments did much to break down the isolation of the region, opening it to contact with the Russian metropolis. For native intellectuals and businessmen, they also facilitated new ties with other Muslim countries, especially Persia and the Ottoman Empire, both in a state of ferment as reformers attempted to change old ways.

The Russian arrival happened to coincide with an increase in the world cotton price. Small-scale cotton-farming had been practiced for centuries in the oasis areas, using irrigation techniques said to have been learned from the Chinese. Raising cotton, a water-intensive crop, was impossible without irrigation in the arid Central Asian climate. Now, under the influence of the cotton boom Russian business interests rushed to expand cotton production, attempting at the same time to introduce massive irrigation schemes. In doing so, they often acted on their own and without sufficient knowledge of the land. The result, in some cases, was to create vast tracts of swampland, a microcosmic forerunner of the environmental disasters of the later Soviet period.

The new emphasis on cotton disrupted the society. A stratum of prosperous native businessmen arose, middle-men who dealt with the *dehqan*s, the local peasants, as brokers for Russian economic interests. The *dehqan*s were encouraged to borrow money to expand production, only to lose their farms when bad years made it impossible to repay their debts. Thus, while one segment of society was becoming ever richer, another was becoming poorer. Ultimately, the infidel Russians were seen as the culprits, despite their good works in some areas, such as improvement of public health conditions.

In Central Asia, as in other Muslim areas of the Russian Empire, discontent gave rise to reform movements. The most important reformers were the *jadid*s, who sought to modernize the traditional Muslim schools in order to give the natives a better chance to compete in the new world of science and technology. The *jadids*' efforts to introduce secular subjects into the religious curriculum of the schools were resented by the conservative Islamic clergy, who regarded their actions as heresy and a challenge to the established order. The *jadid*s were also viewed askance by Russian conservatives as trouble-makers whose orientation toward pan-Turkism and pan-Islamism was threatening the equilibrium of the Empire. (Chapter 10 on the "Islamic factor" discusses the *jadids*' continuing influence in Uzbek public life.)

In fact, the jadids were for the most part willing to work within the framework of the Empire. Reform, not revolution, was their immediate goal. In this they made common cause with Russian liberals, and they had little to do with the country's radical revolutionaries.

9

The Revolution in Central Asia

By 1917, there was still no serious revolutionary movement among Central Asian Muslims. There had been disturbances, some of them bloody, like the massive 1916 rebellion which broke out when the tsarist government tried to draft Central Asians as labor troops in World War I, but these were evidently spontaneous outbursts, not the result of conspiratorial revolutionary organization. Revolutionary sentiment in the territory existed mainly among Russians and other immigrants who were allied with movements in the metropolis.

The Central Asians were therefore not prepared for the tide of revolution that swept into the region from Russia proper. With the outbreak of civil war between Reds and Whites, the Tashkent Soviet, which had been organized with workers of that city's railroad yards as its core and was generally supportive of the Bolsheviks, emerged as the most powerful political force in the territory. When White forces in Siberia cut communications lines between the Tashkent Soviet and Bolshevik headquarters in Russia proper, the Soviet began to operate on its own in a way that discredited the new revolutionary regime in native eyes. The Muslim population was made to bear the brunt of wartime shortages, suffering severe privation. A Muslim autonomous government set up in Kokand was brutally attacked by forces of the Tashkent Soviet, with much destruction to that city and its population. One result of this action was to stimulate the "Basmachi" movement of Muslim armed resistance to the Soviets.

It was only in November 1919 that the White blockade was broken and representatives of the Soviet regime were able to reach Tashkent. There they set about trying to undo the damage to Soviet prestige wrought by two years of excesses committed by the local Soviet. On receiving a report on the situation from their representatives, Lenin and his fellow Bolshevik leaders were particularly concerned that their cause had been harmed not only in Central Asia but in the eyes of the Asian-African world at large.

Among palliative measures taken was the removal from office of those in the Tashkent Soviet who had been responsible for the situation. Some were transferred to other parts of the country. At the same time, a drive was launched to recruit Muslims to support the regime. Muslims were urged to join the Party, and ideological standards of membership were relaxed. As a result, many signed up whose sympathy for Marxism and the Soviet goals was doubtful in the extreme. It has been suggested, as we shall see later, that their true motivation was to manipulate the new regime in order to further their own nationalist goals.[6]

Such was the situation when the Soviet republic of Uzbekistan emerged from the "national delimitation."

Early Days of Uzbekistan

The national delimitation of 1924 was in many ways a giant ethnic oversimplification. Many members of the emergent nationalities had only a tenuous relationship to their national classification. In the case of the "Uzbeks," many were more apt to think of themselves primarily in other terms, as members of tribes with names like Barlas or Lokait, or as inhabitants of localities, such as the Bukharans or Samarkandis. Moreover, because the various population groups of the territory were widely dispersed, the delimitation had left many inhabitants isolated from the republic of the nationality that included their group. Politically, the most sensitive case was that of Uzbekistan's neighboring republic of Tajikistan. While all of the region's other major nationalities were Turkic, the Tajik nationality was Iranian, its members descended from the original inhabitants of Central Asia. The Tajiks had existed for centuries in a state of tension with the Turkic tribes, who had come to the region at various times as invaders, displacing the Iranians from fertile river valleys. The 1924 delineation left many Tajiks living in Uzbekistan (and a lesser number of Uzbeks in Tajikistan), a situation that was potentially destabilizing to the border between the two republics, and an irritant to good relations. There were even accusations that the leaders of Uzbekistan had used their influence in Moscow to appropriate areas that were principally settled by Iranians and should have become part of Tajikistan, including the two ancient cities of Samarkand and Bukhara. The subordinate political position of Tajikistan was underlined by the fact that it remained for years an "autonomous" (lower-ranking) republic, part of Uzbekistan. Only in 1929 did it achieve full "union" status, placing it on a par with Ukraine, Uzbekistan and other union republics.

Whatever the basis, or lack of it, for creation of an Uzbek "nationality," there can be little doubt that all of the indigenous

Muslim inhabitants of the territory now known as Uzbekistan have a strong attachment to their homeland and its Islamic culture.

Various reasons have been advanced for the Soviet decision to create separate republics in the old Turkestan Government-General. Was it the old principle of "divide and conquer," to break up the unity of the territory, or merely for greater efficiency in mobilizing the population to support the goals of Communism? There was undoubtedly a mixture of motives, but central to the scheme, in addition to the manifest goal of fragmenting anti-Soviet resistance, was the idea of promoting "modernization"--an essential component of social and economic development, or in Marxist-Leninist terms, of "socialist construction."

In the early 1920s, Lenin, with the help of his Georgian Bolshevik colleague Stalin as Commissar for Nationalities, went to great lengths to win the non-Russians of the old Empire to the Communist cause. One of the inducements was federalism, a system which granted autonomy, and even the theoretical right to secession, to the nationalities, within a central framework. Each Soviet republic had its own territory, its own administrative apparatus, and its own Party organization. For a time, republics were even able to have their own armed forces and conduct their own relations with foreign countries. However, there were many strings attached to this autonomy, the most inhibiting of which was Lenin's principle of "democratic centralism," effectively subordinating all activity to the party leadership in Moscow.

Like its tsarist predecessor, the new regime lacked cadres of its own to rule in Central Asia. Under the slogan *korenizatsiya* (nativization), the republics were urged to establish, with help from the center, programs for the crash-training of natives to man important posts in the structure. There followed a boom of "nation-building," with the new native cadres involved in setting up schools, newspapers, publishing houses, scientific centers, and other organizations in the name of their republics.

After Lenin's death in January 1924, his successor Stalin continued his liberal nationality policy for a time. But the policy of wholesale recruitment of Central Asian intellectuals into the ranks of the Communist Party in the 1920s had had an adverse effect on discipline. Many of the new members had joined the Party opportunistically, or in order to pursue goals which were often at variance with those of the Party leadership.[7] Chapter 10 of this book, dealing with Islam, describes how recalcitrance among Tashkent Party members delayed for five years the implementation of a campaign of anti-religious agitation decreed by the leadership.)

By the end of the decade, however, Stalin had consolidated power sufficiently to reverse course. He increased pressure on the republics. In order to put through his programs of radical change, he needed a disciplined and responsive apparatus of Party and state workers. In Central Asia, he attacked the problem of industrialization by effectively abandoning the Leninist policy of *korenizatsiya* and appointing outsiders to key economic posts, under whom a largely non-native class of industrial workers was formed. In agriculture, however, which accounted for the lion's share of Central Asian output, he needed to rely on native cadres to penetrate the peasant masses, which had remained aloof to outsiders. Collectivization of agriculture was meeting with strong opposition in Central Asia, as elsewhere in the country. There was also grass-roots resistance to social change, especially to the Party's efforts to stamp out religion and to "emancipate" women.

To insure loyalty and conformity to Moscow's unpopular directives, Stalin staged periodic purges of so-called "bourgeois nationalists" in the Party and state apparat. Many of the leading Central Asian Communists, men who had appeared to be loyal servants of Stalin, fell victim. In Uzbekistan, the purges culminated in 1937 with the arrest of its two most prominent leaders. Akmal Ikramov, head of the Party, and Faizulla Khojaev, head of the government, were locked up on bizarre charges of having tried to detach Uzbekistan from the Soviet Union and make it a British protectorate. At a Moscow show trial, where they shared the defendant's bench with Nikolay Bukharin and other leading "Old Bolsheviks," they were sentenced to be shot.

The liquidation of Ikramov and Khojaev shocked the Uzbeks profoundly, for their names had long been synonymous with Communist power in the republic. Their main transgression seems to have been that each, on at least one occasion, had talked back to Stalin. Whatever the case, their demise gave rise to a new generation of native hacks and toadies, robot-like executors of Stalin's every whim. In this atmosphere, the least sign of non-conformity was apt to brand a person as a "nationalist," consigning him to death or disappearance in the gulag.

World War II brought a brief respite. As he had in Russia proper, Stalin reversed policy, attempting to mobilize support for the war effort by appealing in the name of national traditions. The drive against religion was eased. In the Muslim regions, official religious institutions were sanctioned for the first time since the Revolution. A Mufti was named in Tashkent to minister to the spiritual needs of Muslims of "Central Asia and Kazakhstan." While this was in part a cynical move to control religion by channeling it through state-approved institutions, it represented recognition of the importance of religion to the Central Asian peoples.

Meanwhile, masses of Central Asians were recruited for the Red Army. Many fought with distinction. Yet the unpopularity and illegitimacy of the Soviet regime in Central Asian eyes became apparent when large numbers who fell into German captivity enlisted in a "Turkestan Legion" organized to fight against the Soviets, under the slogan of "liberation" of their homeland.[8]

Although the German invasion never reached Central Asia, the region was directly affected by the war. Millions of individuals from the European part of the country were evacuated there to escape German occupation. Entire factories were relocated, bringing their personnel with them. All of this further disrupted native society and strengthened the alien presence in the region.

Consolidation of "Uzbek" as a Nationality

If *korenizatsiya* had gone out the window as Stalin assigned his own outsiders to the Party and government apparatus in the national republics, with unchecked power to rule from behind the scenes, there was still a need for native leadership cadres. The idea of national autonomy had suffered under Lenin from the impediment of "democratic centralism," and under Stalin it became a mockery. Still, the "Leninist nationality policy" continued to be honored in principle, if more in the breach than in the observance, and the institutions of federalism remained in place. These institutions were now hamstrung by terror and other instruments of Stalinist coercion, but they continued as a base for recruitment and promotion of native cadres.

Under Stalin and his successors, Uzbek nationality, however artificial its original premises, has been shaped and consolidated by the federal institutions of the Soviet system. For nearly seven decades, citizens of Uzbekistan have been carrying passports in which their identity is stamped as "Uzbek." They have been going to school in the "Uzbek" language. They have been consumers of "Uzbek" newspapers, and "Uzbek" radio and television programs. The offices with which they have dealt, in a system where the citizen turns instinctively to officialdom to provide for his or her needs, have said "Uzbek" on the door, even when the top people inside were Russians. When they have traveled outside of Uzbekistan, or when their sons have served in the Soviet Army, they have been treated as "Uzbeks." In this way, the idea of being "Uzbek" has become internalized in the minds of those who compose the nationality. Perhaps most importantly in political terms, "Uzbek" institutions have provided a power base for the Uzbek elites who staff them, even when they have had to kowtow to Russian overseers.

With the weakening of central authority during the early years of Gorbachev's tenure, the local institutions in Uzbekistan, as in other republics, realized a new measure of autonomy. Officials who were once perceived as "transmission belts" of Moscow policy emerged as spokesmen for Uzbek national interests. Nationalism was particularly strong in the cultural institutions, among writers and artists, and in the scientific establishment.

In later chapters, this book will examine, through recent events in Uzbekistan, the role of nationalism, coalescent around the Uzbek identity and spearheaded by the Uzbek elites, as the bulwark of confrontation with Moscow and the driving force of political action for increased national autonomy.

Notes

1. For a more complete discussion of the historical antecedents of the Uzbek nationality, see Edward Allworth, *The Modern Uzbeks*, Stanford (Hoover Institution Press) 1990, especially the early chapters.

2. Lazar' Budagov, *Sravnitel'nyy slovar' Turetsko-tatarskikh narechiy*, St. Petersburg 1869, Vol. I, p. 131. (Facsimile published 1960 by the USSR Academy of Sciences.)

3. F. A. Brockhaus and I. A. Efron, *Entsiklopedicheskiy slovar'*, St. Petersburg 1902, Vol. 34, pp. 608-10.

4. Morris Rossabi, *Khubilai Khan: His Life and Times*, Berkeley (University of California Press) 1988, pp. 119, 179-84.

5. George B. Parks (ed.), *The Book of Ser Marco Polo, the Venetian*, New York (Macmillan Modern Readers' Series) 1927, pp. 4, 62.

6. This argument is developed in Alexandre A. Bennigsen and S. Enders Wimbush, *Muslim National Communism in the Soviet Union: A*

Revolutionary Strategy for the Colonial World, Chicago (University of Chicago Press) 1979.

7. For a detailed treatment of this problem, see Bennigsen and Wimbush, *Muslim National Communism*.

8. Alexander Dallin, *German Rule in Russia: 1941-1945*. New York (St. Martin's Press) 1957.

2

Prelude to Perestroika: Signs Of Emerging Nationalism

The dramatic weakening of Soviet power in Uzbekistan, which was symbolized in 1990 by that republic's declaration of "sovereignty," was foreshadowed by a chain of events that had begun long earlier. This chapter describes the emergence of Uzbek nationalism in the period beginning with Stalin's death in 1953 and ending with the accession of Gorbachev in 1985.[1]

Following the victory over the Germans, Stalin quickly reimposed his repressive policies. It was only after his death in 1953 that respite came to Central Asia. Stalin's successors, in their convoluted internecine struggle for power, made concessions to the non-Russian republics in an attempt to gain their political support. There was talk of increasing the autonomy of the republics and of upgrading the status of their languages, even to the point of requiring Russian overseers in the local ministries to learn and use them. Nikita Khrushchev's ally Nuriddin Akramovich Muhiddinov, who as First Secretary of the Uzbek Communist Party helped Khrushchev to rally support against the "anti-Party group" in 1957, was rewarded in December of that year by promotion to full membership in the Politburo (then called "Presidium"), the only Uzbek ever to reach that eminence. (One of Muhiddinov's successors as First Secretary, Sharaf Rashidov, made it only to alternate member.) Later on, when Khrushchev felt more sure of his power, he went back on his conciliatory policy toward the nationalities and again tightened the screws. Muhiddinov was unceremoniously demoted, and after Brezhnev succeeded Khrushchev, was eventually sent off to be Soviet ambassador to Syria. (He was still around in the perestroika period, as head of Uzbekistan's commission charged with preserving antique monuments, a post lacking in political power but with enormous cultural prestige, given its relationship to *miras*.)

In both the late Khrushchev period and throughout Brezhnev's tenure in office, Soviet policy was directed toward eventual assimilation of the non-Russians to a single Soviet nationality. In essence, this meant russification of the peoples and their cultures. For a time, the candid slogan of "merging of peoples" dominated policy, so offensive to the nationalities that in Brezhnev's latter years it began to be replaced by the slightly less obnoxious one of inter-nationality "rapprochement."

Despite its overtly assimilationist policies, the post-Stalin period gave birth to a paradoxical development: at the republic level, a gradual political evolution, buttressed by social processes, was greatly strengthening the hand of the native elites. In the new nations of Central Asia, this promoted a republic-based nationalism which had never before existed.

The Patrimonial Society

After the traumas of the 1920s and '30s, of militant atheism and *hujum*, of industrialization and collectivization (which for nomads in Central Asia meant forced sedentarization and an abrupt change from ancient ways of doing things), of the purges of "bourgeois nationalists," and then in the 1940s the upheavals brought by World War II and Stalin's turbulent last years, Soviet Central Asia entered into a period of unprecedented tranquility. Social change was still on the agenda of the regime in Moscow, but the first priority was economic: if growth continued and plans were met, other matters could be deferred. A theme of the latter Brezhnev period introduced a new permissiveness toward Islam: if a person worked well at his job, then religion was "a matter of individual consciousness."[2]

This relatively peaceful period ushered in a patrimonial era[3] of native first secretaries, republican Party leaders whose ability to do their jobs to Moscow's satisfaction earned them long terms in office. Table 2.1 shows the roster in 1982.

TABLE 2.1 Roster of Central Asian First Secretaries in 1982

Republic	CP First Secretary	Entry in Office
		Uzbekistan
Kazakhstan	Dinmukhamed Kunaev	1960
Kirghizia	Turdiakun Usubaliev	1961
Turkmenistan	Mukhamednazar Gapurov	1969
Tajikistan	Jabar Rasulov	1961

Source: Compiled by the author from various Soviet press sources.

In its day, this had been something of a fresh generation, compared with its predecessors. All had joined the Party in 1939 or later, missing the worst of the purges of the 1930s and the campaign against "bourgeois nationalists." Two were war veterans. All had completed higher education, at either Party or technical institutions. Of the five, Kunaev had become a member of the Politburo, and Rashidov a candidate member. Rashidov, a wounded veteran of World War II who became a journalist, had twice during his term in office been distinguished as "Hero of Socialist Labor," the Soviet Union's highest civilian honor, and regularly had himself acclaimed by his own propaganda apparatus for his novels and other writings.[4]

The patrimonial character of their reign acquired a peculiar resonance in societies where tribal memories were recent, where the rank-and-file looked instinctively for leadership to a chieftain and his council of elders (*aqsaqals*, "white beards"). The concept of patrimonial authority was further bolstered by the virtual sanctification, in the current vernacular literature, of medieval charismatic leaders: in the case of Uzbekistan, figures like Tamerlane and Babur. An addition of more recent figures to the pantheon of the patrimonial cult came with the rehabilitation of Communist and other leaders executed under Stalin. In Uzbekistan, Faizulla Khojaev and Akmal Ikramov became "scions of the Uzbek people" once more, and were given the rare distinction of having their "selected works" published.[5]

The long tenure of the Central Asian first secretaries enabled them to put their personal stamp on the republican machinery as in a fiefdom, appointing their followers to senior posts at republican, oblast and rayon levels. Thus, Kunaev's brother became President of the Kazakh Academy of Sciences. In Uzbekistan, officials from First Secretary Rashidov's native Jizzakh (Dzhizak) oblast seemed to do well in their careers. In turn, the protégés of these top republican leaders became entrenched in their sub-fiefdoms, creating their own entourages.

Signs of Emerging Nationalism

This period of relative tranquility and stability created unprecedented opportunities for nationalism in the Central Asian republics. Members of the republican intelligentsias were able to assert national interests in ways that under Stalin would have invited instant repression. Moscow's presence in the republics was still powerful, and caution was still the order of the day, but the three decades between Stalin and Gorbachev paved the way for the later surge of nationalism that was to push forth, at first hesitantly, under glasnost.

The amorphous and unsettled condition of Soviet politics that followed in the early years after Khrushchev's ouster, before Brezhnev in turn had consolidated his power, was comparatively favorable for the non-Russian nationalities to pursue a quiet separate evolution. Talk of the future "merging" of nationalities all but disappeared from official pronouncements. Typical of a lack of firmness on national questions was a conference held in Volgograd in November 1968 to discuss the future complexion of Soviet society; it was adjourned after the participants, representatives of a variety of nationalities, including Russians, conceded "the lack of solution of a number of problems."[6] At the same time, the Party's tolerance did not apply to nationalists who challenged its policies too bluntly and openly, as shown by a series of arrests in the Ukraine.

In post-Khrushchevian Uzbekistan, Moscow's main concern was to expand cotton production. The First Secretary, Sharaf Rashidov, was given extensive liberty to run the republic as he saw fit, in return for his effectiveness in delivering ever more cotton to the center. Rashidov's one-man dictatorship, which lasted nearly a quarter-century, countenanced many abuses, especially of his enemies, but it also opened the way for Uzbek intellectuals to write and publish, especially in the late 1960s and early 1970s, works glorifying the Uzbek nation--a foretaste of what was to come under perestroika. Toward the end of

Rashidov's reign (1959-1983) there was a conservative backlash, but only after the ground had been laid for the nationalist resurgence of the Gorbachev era.

Uzbek intellectuals were not alone in their nationalist activities. All of the Muslim republics of the Soviet Union were being swept by a new tide of self-assertiveness and particularism. The 1970 all-union census listed more than 30 million Soviet citizens who belonged to traditionally Muslim ethnic groups. The Muslims were, then as now, the Soviet Union's fastest growing population group, the major contributor to the trend of differential birth-rates that was on the way to making the Russians a minority "in their own country."

The Muslim community, then accounting for more than one Soviet citizen in eight, was fairly compactly distributed. Its heartland consisted of six of the USSR's 15 union republics, located along the southern marches of the country from the Azerbaijan SSR in the west to the five Central Asian republics across the Caspian to the east: the Uzbek, Kazakh,[7] Tajik, Turkmen and Kirghiz SSRs. To the north and west of these lay two other major Muslim political units separated from the rest by a narrow isthmus of the Russian SFSR: the Tatar and Bashkir Autonomous SSRs. With the exception of the Iranian Tajiks, all of these major nationalities shared a common Turkic ethnic and linguistic character in addition to past Islamic ties. Other, less numerous Muslim peoples occupied autonomous SSR's and oblasts in Central Asia, the Caucasus and in certain areas of the Russian SFSR.[8]

Both Soviet and Western writers have referred to the persistence of Islamic customs in Central Asia among believers and non-believers alike.[9] For example, pig-breeding in the Muslim republics was at a negligible level compared with the rest of the country.[10] It was widely reported that the Muslim ritual of circumcision, which was the target of sharp criticism by the Soviets, was still being practiced almost universally, even by native officials high in the regime. Marriages between Muslim men and non-Muslim women, sanctioned by tradition, were not uncommon, but the marriage of Muslim women to non-Muslims, proscribed by the *shariat*, was still rare in the extreme.[11]

The Muslim nationalities also clung to their own native languages: the 1970 census revealed that they were still among the least susceptible to linguistic assimilation. Of those resident in their own union republics, the percentage who had kept the mother tongue of their nationality continued in all cases to be higher than 98. In fact, there was a general increase in this percentage compared with the 1959 census.

The Muslim's political leverage was enhanced by geopolitics: flanked on one side by their kinsmen in Xinjiang and on the other by the Islamic nations of the Middle East, these peoples had the advantage of a strategic position between two regions in which Soviet interests were at stake. Indeed, it appeared that Moscow was purchasing their loyalty, as Lenin once had, at the price of strengthening their national institutions and their new national elites.

The climate of those years fostered the emergence of a distinct personality for the Muslim republics and their elites. An undoubted concomitant was the creation of a new variant of Soviet communism more attractive for export to the Afro-Asian world than the European-oriented, Russian-based Marxism-Leninism of tradition. Yet to the extent that this trend developed its own *élan*, Soviet Muslim communism was showing signs of being no longer a tame adjunct to Soviet strategy; in it were the seeds of a new ideological challenge and incipient threat to the "democratic centralism" on which all Soviet administration was based.

This challenge was finding ever more direct expression in the writing of Uzbek and other Muslim authors. The idea of the distinctiveness of Central Asian communism began to compete with "proletarian internationalism" as a theme. It was implicit, for example, in verse published in 1969 by an Uzbek poet, in which he alluded to the ancient glories of Samarkand and Bukhara and traced their influence on the present content of regional communism. This was his concluding stanza:

> My cradle was the territory of great Asia,
> The cradle that rocked Ulugh Bek and Avicenna,
> The light in whose eyes has spanned a thousand years.
> This is the world that led the caravan of history,
> This Samarkand, this Bukhara: these two universes.
> This is the cradle of communism in the bosom of the East![12]

De-Russification: The Tide Turns

The evolution of Uzbek society in the 1960s, and especially after Khrushchev's removal in 1964, was characterized by a current of de-russification in such areas as language, cadres, and history. There were some efforts to expunge Russian vocabulary from the Uzbek language, reversing the earlier trend, and preferential treatment began to be given to the use of Uzbek for communications; at the same time, the proportion of Russian cadres in local institutions, even the sacrosanct party apparat, was reduced. This represented a kind of return to *korenizatsiya*, this time at the initiative not of Moscow but of the Central Asians themselves.

Especially telling was the work during this period of Uzbek historians, who re-emphasized the ancient roots of their communities and their cultural debt to traditional Islamic, particularly Arabic and Persian influence, while downgrading the Russian contribution. Writers hinted that a new, Eastern form of Communism had been brought into being. In much of this literature, the Uzbek republic began to supplant the USSR as the primary object of patriotic loyalty. A poem, "Thou, Uzbekistan," which appeared on the front page of an Uzbek-language newspaper for January 1, 1970, was featured more prominently than New Year's greetings from party and state organs in Moscow, which were carried on the same page:

Thou, Uzbekistan

I wished to speak about happiness,
To sing a joyous ode,
To think of tomorrow and today,
To hold a fabulous feast;
In my eyes thou appearst,
Thou at last art the one, the eternal object of learning,
    Thou, Uzbekistan.

Child of toil art thou, sound of heart,
And thy enviers are distraught and downcast,
    with every year;
At every step art thou paradise, an Eden, a garden,
Thy nights unending myriads of candelabra,
Thou art despot to enemy, solace to friend,
Danger afar, art thou a bower of calm,
    Thou, Uzbekistan.

Thy hand holds the key to treasures of riches,
In thy garden and desert a happy year's song,
Left and right thy gold and thy silk;

23

How many the peoples enrapt in thy path,
Thou art fruit and wine and water and cake,
Thou art twin rivers of love,
   Thou, Uzbekistan.

Thou art thine own machine-builder, thine own
   live-stock-breeder,
Thine own scholar, thine own cultural worker.
Thou art volunteer soldier, noble guide,
A storehouse of cotton priceless, without peer,
Thy soul Lenin's child forever,
   Thou, Uzbekistan.[13]

The condescending and degrading image of the superior Russian "elder brother" leading primitive Soviet Asians out of obscurity, which had been in vogue since Stalin's day, was now recalled only rarely in local media. The elder brother's siblings were on the rise. Acknowledgement of Russian assistance now tended to specify material, not spiritual contributions. Above all, the centralist statement of the 1961 Party Program that "the boundaries between the union republics are increasingly losing their significance" had lost much of its own significance. The current trend was in the opposite direction.

De-russification became overt and official, implemented through such devices as conferences held in Uzbekistan and other Muslim republics to discuss "speech culture." Commenting on one such conference organized in 1969, an Uzbek writer revealed that its purpose was to rectify linguistic injustices of an earlier period, when numerous native words were purged from the Uzbek language in favor of Russian ones (see Table 2.2). Noting the substantial measure of de-russification that had already taken place prior to the conference, the author, possibly with tongue in cheek, advanced in justification that the Russians themselves had purified their language through elimination of such foreign borrowings as *aeroplan* and *gelikopter*.[14]

In pressing for de-russification, the Uzbeks were not alone among Soviet Muslims. A Tatar poet complained in print of continuing outside pressure to have his language replace its traditional geographic names derived from Arabic with their Russian equivalents, e.g. Russian *Kair* for *Qahira* (Cairo) and *Indiya* for *Hindstan*. [15]

TABLE 2.2 The De-Russification of Uzbek

Uzbek Word	Russian Word	English Equivalent
	Group A	
khiyaban	prospekt	avenue
javan	shkaf	cabinet (as for books)
buyurtma	zakaz	order (for goods)
buyurtmachi	zakazchik	customer
zarbdar	udarnik	shock-worker
namzad	kandidat	candidate
	Group B	
qamus	entsiklopediya	encyclopedia
darilfunun	universitet	university
jarrah	khirurg	surgeon
jarrahlik	khirurgiya	surgery
tababat (tibbiyat)	meditsina	medicine
katib	sekretar'	secretary
	Group C	
muallif	avtor	author
an"ana	traditsiya	tradition
inqilab	revoliutsiya	revolution
inqilabchi	revoliutsioner	revolutionary
mafkura	ideologiya	ideology
daha	geniy	genius

Explanation:

A: "Forgotten" Uzbek words restored to usage instead of Russian equivalents once a standard part of Uzbek vocabulary.

B: Uzbek words once relegated to "obsolescence" but now revived for use together with Russian words as "literary synonyms."

C: Uzbek words eliminated from the dictionary during a "certain" period when "the culture of speech suffered considerable damage" and now rehabilitated -- used interchangeably with Russian equivalents.

Source: A. Osman, "Ozbek adabii tilining ba"zi masalari" (Certain Problems of the Uzbek Literary Language), *Sovet Ozbekistani*, May 24, 1969, p. 3.

Efforts to purify the national languages were accompanied by more extensive use of them in public communication, at the expense of Russian. A 1969 comparative study of selected periodicals in Muslim areas showed that in recent years those printed in the vernacular languages had been exceeding their Russian-language counterparts in circulation growth-rates, reversing the earlier russifying trend (see Tables 2.3 and 2.4). The trend was later reversed by a higher authority which controlled paper allocations to publishers, but only after readers' appetites had been whetted. By 1970, the Uzbek, Kazakh, Azerbaijan, Kirghiz, Tajik and Turkmen SSRs alone were publishing 132 journals and 477 newspapers in their own local languages with combined circulations of 6.6 and 7.5 million respectively.[16]

TABLE 2.3 Comparison of Average Monthly Circulation Figures for Newspapers: Uzbek Language (*Sovet Ozbekistani*) and Russian Language (*Pravda Vostoka*), 1956-65

	Language	
Year	Uzbek	Russian
1956	170,000	140,000
1957	175,000	140,000
1961	271,000	146,000
1962	279,000	146,000
1963	305,000	155,000
1964	400,000	160,000
1965	382,400	161,000

Available years only. Both papers issued six times weekly.

Source: "Paper Allocation Rivalry and National Pressures in the USSR," *Radio Liberty Research Paper*, New York, 1969.

TABLE 2.4 Comparison of Average Monthly Circulation Figures for Literary Journals: Azeri Language (*Azerbaijan*) and Russian Language (*Literaturnyy Azerbaidzhan*), 1960-68

	Language	
Year	Azeri	Russian
1960	6,670	3,125
1963	9,000	3,200
1964	14,500	3,400
1965	18,000	3,100
1966	19,400	4,000 (6 mo.)
1967	22,800	3,400
1968 (10 mo.)	29,000	2,500

Available years only. Azeri journal has 200 pages; Russian, 150 pages.

Source: "Paper Allocation Rivalry and National Pressures in the USSR," *Radio Liberty Research Paper*, New York, 1969.

The New Soviet Muslim Elite

Of even more profound and enduring significance to the political future of Uzbekistan was the attrition of European cadres in key Party and government organs. Things had changed remarkably since a study had noted that "in the Uzbek Central Committee Secretariat during the 1940s, Russians and other European party secretaries and department heads constituted three-fourths of the total, and no change in this proportion was apparent in the 1950s."[17] By 1966 (Seventeenth Uzbek Party Congress) the number of Russians and other Europeans in these posts was not three-fourths but approximately one-fourth of the total,[18] and remained fairly constant in ensuing years. Between 1958 and 1966, the number of Europeans in the Uzbek Central Committee dropped from 31 percent to less than 20 percent. A similar trend was evident in other Muslim republics; even in Kazakhstan, where European immigration

the Central Committee.[19]   Such important Central Committee
departments as administrative organs, propaganda and agitation,
culture and education were now commonly being directed by Asian cadres
(except in Kazakhstan). The European foothold was largely reduced to
the traditional proconsular post of second secretary, the party organs
departments of Central Committees, the republican committees of state
security, and local military commands.[20]

This was a far cry from the situation in the last years of
Khrushchev's tenure (1962-1964) when establishment of a Central Asian
Bureau (later defunct) of the Central Committee of the CPSU,
paralleling a similar body that had existed in Stalin's day, moved a
Western observer to comment: "The new bureau, standing between
Moscow and the authorities of the union republics and visibly controlled
by Russians, cannot possibly fail to diminish the already meager powers
left in the hands of the Muslim Communist officials."[21]

A steady increase in the native graduates of higher education,
bolstered by the Muslim demographic advantage, added to pressures for
a return to *korenizatsiya*. Between 1962-1963 and 1968-1969, the number
of Muslims enrolled in higher education doubled, compared to a
corresponding increase of only about 50 percent for Russian students; the
number of Muslims enrolled was of the order of half a million.[22] At that
rate, Muslims could catch up with Russians in per capita student
population within the next few years. Another index of the vigor with
which Muslim elites were growing was the increase in the number of
scientific workers: from 17,000 to 48,000 for the principal Muslim
nationalities between 1960 and 1969, well above the equivalent growth-
rate for Russians.[23] An American scholar who spent five months at
Tashkent University in 1969 reported a sense of injustice among Russians
and other Slavs at the privileges accorded to the Uzbeks:

> Though the Uzbeks and other Turks feel sure of their social and legal
> equality, some Slavs feel that they are discriminated against by the
> Uzbeks. Because the Uzbeks are in the majority, and many of the
> high civil posts are held by Uzbeks, there is a tendency for Uzbeks to
> be preferred for positions over other peoples. A Russian school
> teacher told me that she resented the fact the Uzbeks seemed to get
> better jobs.[24]

The new elites could be said to owe their status to the Soviet regime, which had given them modern professional training and an economic and social structure in which to use it. At the same time, they suffered from a paradox of Soviet society: the system encouraged minority education but restricted the occupational mobility of the Uzbek and other Muslim graduates toward the center. Members of the native elites had a vested interest in the system, but to the extent that it confined their advancement to the level of the republic, they could succeed best by pushing to improve that republic's position.

Resurrection of the Pre-Revolutionary Past

It was in the republican educational and cultural establishments that Uzbek power first came into its own. Modern Soviet communications facilities were being used, as never before, for mass glorification of pre-Russian and pre-communist roots. With the national languages providing a convenient means of esoteric communication, the rallying cry was *miras*, a word that appeared regularly in the indigenous press, frequently in headlines ("Let Us Study Our *Miras*!"). Typically, an Uzbek article pegged to a conference on translations recalled that Uzbek literary development had been influenced since early days by translations from Persian and Arabic, beginning with the *Thousand and One Nights*, long before Russian works began to be translated into the language--a far cry from the once familiar image of dark stagnation until the advent of the Russian "elder brother."[25] The downgrading of Russian influence also favored the West at times, as when an Uzbek newspaper announced that 1970 Uzbek theatrical repertories would include plays "Western European, Russian and from the fraternal peoples"--in that order.[26]

Other pointed expressions of *mirasism* were observance of the 2,500th anniversary of Samarkand (with associated complaints in the press about neglect of local religious monuments), the holding of a Tashkent conference on Lenin and the Culture of the Peoples of the East (in November 1969), and the promulgation (in the same month) of a Law on Preservation of Monuments for the Uzbek SSR.[27]

These events were reminders that in the perspective of their total recorded history, the Uzbeks had been exposed only briefly to Russian and communist influence. In the new atmosphere, Uzbek historiography no longer accepted unquestioningly, as it had been forced to in Stalin's

29

day, that annexation of the Muslim territories by Russia had been a "progressive" phenomenon. One scholar even went so far as to refer pointedly to the "national liberation struggle" of the Uzbek people and to name the Russians as one of their traditional enemies, without the customary qualification that Soviet rule had removed the basis for historical enmities. He referred in that context to tsarist-era uprisings in which much Russian blood had been spilled by Muslim insurgents:

> The question of the people's liberation struggle and its reflection in literature may be defined and investigated at all phases of our literary history... It was not possible that the popular liberation movements conducted by our people against the twin oppressions of the tsarist colonizers and rural exploiters (events of 1892 and 1898, popular uprising of 1916) and the revolutionary struggles of 1905 and 1917 should not find expression in literature.[28]

In a similar vein, a Kazakh writer lamented in 1969 that Chinese communist encroachment on his land (then a matter of friction between China and the Soviet Union) was only the latest in a series of invasions through the ages, including those of the "white tsar" from the north:

> Oh, land, my cradle, noble country of my forefathers, Motherland! Who has not been lured to you, who has not wished to tramp your fertile slopes! The Jungarian invaders from the east, Kokand from the south, the White Tsar who violated your peace from the north, and Hitler with his sudden onslaught from the west... [29]

Pressing Moscow for Greater Autonomy

While Uzbek writers sought sources of national legitimacy in the memory of distant struggles against invaders, they simultaneously invoked the earlier history of the Soviet period to legitimize their quest for greater autonomy from the center. They referred persistently to the Soviet constitutional provision of sovereignty for the union republics as more than just a paper concept, making frequent allusions to the "right of secession."

On November 5, 1969, on the eve of that year's official observance of the October Revolution, newspapers in the five capitals of the Central Asian republics (including Kazakhstan) appeared with a "joint issue" dedicated to the fiftieth anniversary of a letter written by Lenin in which he called, *inter alia*, for "elimination of vestiges of Great Russian chauvinism" in Soviet Turkestan.[30] The letter, a "personal message" from Lenin to members of the Turkestan Commission which had been sent to the region in 1919 to try to repair the alienation of Muslims by the excesses of the Tashkent Soviet, had presaged the high tide of permissiveness toward Muslim particularism and nationalism under Soviet rule.[31] This bit of history was underscored on the same day by an Uzbek scholar's article in Tashkent's Uzbek-language daily, in which he recalled that in its early period the Turkestan Autonomous Soviet Socialist Republic (i.e. before the 1924 "national delimitation") "was given the right to organize armed forces and have direct relations with foreign countries." The same author stressed the distinct roots of Communism among the Muslims of Turkestan ("the first Soviet state in the East"), the "voluntary" nature of Turkestan's federal ties to the Russian SFSR, and Lenin's insistence that representatives of the center should be deferential toward Party and state organs in Turkestan.[32]

Allusions like these, to the permissive period of the 1920s before the idea of "national autonomy" was made a mockery by Stalin, began to recur in the Uzbek press with a peculiar intensity. Against the background of other assertive trends, they were clearly more than empty rituals.

Emphasis on sovereign rights received a new dimension when a publication of the Uzbek Academy of Sciences quoted an official document on settlement of differences "between socialist states." Significantly, the context was an article on the rights of the Uzbek Soviet republic. In other words, this was tantamount to a proposal that henceforth disagreements between Moscow and the union republics should be considered no differently from disagreements between Moscow and the Warsaw Pact countries. Settlement of differences would have to be "voluntary," presumably for both partners. If this fell short of true national freedom, it was a far cry from the Stalinist tradition of abject subservience:

Any disagreement between socialist nations which may arise in the course of events, due to differences in the level of their economic development, social structure and international situation, and related to their national idiosyncrasies, can and must be settled successfully on the basis of proletarian internationalism, and by means of comradely discussion and voluntary fraternal co-operation.[33]

During this period, the concept of *gosudarstvennost'* (statehood) began to receive wide development in Soviet literature dealing with the union republics, both in the republics themselves and in Moscow. In the relatively liberal climate which prevailed during the Prague spring of 1968, Moscow's State Publishing House for Juridical Literature brought out an anthology devoted to the "national *gosudarstvennost'* of the union republics," in which jurists from each union republic stressed its separate institutional life. A foreword described portentously how Lenin had revised his own ideas about the national question, abandoning his early opposition to federalism and self-determination as harmful to the class struggle and accepting the realization, after the October Revolution, that federation was the only way to halt dismemberment of the Soviet state.[34]

A further building-block in elaboration of the Uzbek case for national autonomy appeared in the form of a major policy declaration on the legal status of the Uzbek SSR, published in mid-1969 in the form of an article in the Party journals *Ozbekistan Kommunisti* (Uzbek) and *Kommunist Uzbekistana* (Russian). Like other Uzbek declarations on the rights of the republics, it gave prominence to the assertion that Lenin had "resolutely defended the right of the peoples to self-determination up to and including secession and formation of an independent state." The article recalled that the Bolsheviks' 1917 "Declaration of Rights of the Peoples of Russia" had specified that "the policy of playing off one people against another which was carried out by tsarism was to be replaced by a policy of voluntary and honest union of the peoples of Russia, founded on complete mutual trust." The article also quoted at length from the Soviet government's appeal of November 20, 1917, "To All Toiling Muslims of Russia and the East":

Henceforth your beliefs and customs, your national and cultural institutions are declared free and inviolate. Organize your national life freely and without hindrance. That is your right. Know that your rights, like the rights of all the peoples of Russia, are protected by the entire might of the Revolution and its organs, the Soviets of Workers, Soldiers and Peasants Deputies.[35]

The article made the usual qualification about the guiding role of the Communist Party (thus avoiding the recent "error" of the 1968 Czechoslovak revisionists) but left open the question of whether this referred to the Soviet Party or the Uzbek Party, then headed by the powerful--and increasingly autonomous--Sharaf Rashidov.[36]

Identifying Lenin with "the right of the peoples to self-determination" became a standard practice of Uzbek political writing, which used Leninist quotations to buttress every argument for national rights. In 1970, observance of the 100th anniversary of Lenin's birth provided a splendid peg for this device. Typical was a front-page editorial citing Lenin's opposition to compulsory teaching of Russian. In all of this, Lenin emerged as a kind of supranational idol (indeed, portraits of him in local media always seemed to emphasize his Tatar cheekbones and make his eyes look Asian) who had come to replace the Russian "elder brother" as the bearer and guide of national revolution. "Lenin's noble teaching about heritage" was even invoked as the authority for promoting such *miras*-oriented activities as the study of the shashmaqam, a classical Bukharan musical instrument.[37]

This relatively permissive period also witnessed the first public utterance of complaints about Moscow's economic exploitation of Uzbekistan, complaints that in the later time of Gorbachev and glasnost were to swell into a mighty chorus. An early harbinger was an article by an Uzbek economist who noted that, although Uzbekistan was the country's major producer of raw cotton, two-thirds of its requirements for manufactured cotton textiles had to be supplied from other parts of the Soviet Union. In other words, Uzbekistan's cotton had to be exported and then reimported, with the central government profiting on each transaction, in the classic colonial pattern.[38]

Out of Isolation

The above developments coincided with a new climate of exposure to outside influence. Looking back at the Prague spring after the 1968 Soviet occupation of Czechoslovakia, a Party spokesman admitted that Eastern European revisionism had not been without its impact on the Uzbeks. Writing from an orthodox viewpoint, he denounced the "separatism and self-isolation" which had been engendered by other "models of socialism."[39]

The opening of Uzbekistan and its sister Muslim republics to outside influence was by no means limited to contact with other Communist countries. As part of Moscow's policy of using the Muslim republics as a showcase of Asian communism, visits by foreign delegations, especially from the Middle East and other Third World nations, were a regular feature of life in such cities as Tashkent and Baku. The Muslim republics were also host to large numbers of Asian, African and Latin American students. Between 1958 and 1968, more than 30 international conferences and meetings were convened in Uzbekistan, such as the 1966 Indo-Pakistan peace conference in Tashkent and Samarkand's UNESCO-sponsored symposium on Timurid culture, held in September 1969.[40] Uzbekistan was said to be exporting goods to 90 foreign countries, maintaining cultural ties with 91 countries, and assigning 600 of its specialists to work in developing countries.[41] The republic was also the target of American broadcasts in Uzbek, by both Radio Liberty and the Voice of America.

The conservative backlash that affected the Soviet Union in the wake of the Sinyavsky-Daniel trial and the invasion of Czechoslovakia was to put a damper on manifestations of Uzbek nationalism, but for a few years in the late 1960s and early 1970s the Uzbeks had had a historic opportunity to air, with circumspection, their grievances and to voice their aspirations for greater independence. This was an important phase in preparing public opinion for the new opportunities that were to come, eventually, with Gorbachev.

In Uzbekistan, the Gorbachev period opened inauspiciously. After Brezhnev's death in 1982, Moscow, under Brezhnev's shortlived successor Yuriy Andropov, had already begun to take notice of the freewheeling activities of the Uzbek elites. A drive launched to correct the situation faltered under the next incumbent, Konstantin Chernenko. But when Gorbachev was elected General Secretary in 1985, he resumed the drive against the elites with a vengeance.

Notes

1. Portions of this and the following chapter are adapted (in updated and substantially rewritten form) from my two articles "'Corruption,' Nationalism and the Native Elites in Soviet Central Asia," *Journal of Communist Studies*, June 1988, pp. 142-161, and "Signs of Emerging Nationalism in the Muslim Soviet Republics, " in Norton T. Dodge (ed.), *The Soviets in Asia*, Mechanicsville, Maryland (Cremona Foundation) 1972. Thanks are due to the publishers, Frank Cass and Co. Ltd., London, and the Cremona Foundation, Mechanicsville, for their kind permission to draw from this material.

2. See T. S. Saidbaev, *Islam i obshchestvo*, Moscow (*Nauka*) 1978, p. 226.

3. Max Weber described *Patrimonialismus* as a decentralized form of patriarchal society in which the ruler's retainers held sway over territories allocated to them, in a relationship of mutual dependence with the ruler. In a patrimonial system, officeholders are there primarily to perform personal services for the ruler, not as professional specialists. See Max Weber, *Wirtschaft und Gesellschaft*, Tübingen (J. C. B. Mohr [Paul Siebeck]) 1925, pp. 682-83, 693.

4. The late Arkadiy Belinkov, a prominent Moscow literary critic who defected in 1968, told the author that in his circle it was "common knowledge" that Rashidov's works were actually written by a Russian, Yuriy Karasev, a well-known translator of Uzbek literature into Russian. I am indebted to another emigre friend for the information that Rashidov had a Russian mistress in Moscow, a relative of my source, whom he visited regularly over a period of years.

5. The two Uzbeks were sentenced to death and shot after the 1938 trial of the "Bloc of Rights and Trotskyites," whose most famous defendant was Nikolay Bukharin. They were accused of conspiring to separate Uzbekistan from the USSR with British help. The Russian defendants at the trial remained without rehabilitation, suggesting that Khojaev and Ikramov must have been the object of a special lobbying by Uzbek interests.

6. V. S. Markov, "Sovetskiy narod--novaya istoricheskaya obshchnost' lyudey" (The Soviet People is a New Historical Community of Human Beings), *Voprosy filosofii*, Moscow, No. 3, 1969, pp. 156-58.

7. Kazakhstan, the largest of these republics, is regarded by Soviet geographers as separate from Central Asia, despite the fact that its Turkic native population is closely related to the Kirghiz, Uzbeks, and others. It was once the object, especially in its northern and western regions, of intensive immigration from the European SSR. By the 1959 census, the Republic's population was more than one-half European. In later years the demographic trend reversed, due not only to higher Asian birthrates but also to a mass movement of Europeans out of the republic. (See Ann Sheehy, "1989 Census Data on Internal Migration in the USSR," Radio Liberty *Report on the USSR*, November 10, 1989, p. 7.)

8. See Geoffrey Wheeler, "The Muslims of Central Asia," *Problems of Communism*, Vol. 16 (1967), No. 5, p. 74 for a listing of Muslim nationalities by ethnic classification.

9. One of the most comprehensive Soviet treatments is L. I. Klimovich, *Islam* (second edition), Moscow 1965, pp. 214-85.

10. *Narodnoe khozyaystvo v 1969 g.* (USSR Statistical Yearbook for 1969), Moscow 1970, p. 371.

11. An article by a Soviet scholar mentioned a study of mixed marriages in Ashkhabad, capital of the Turkmen SSR, where "during the period under

study the percentage of marriages of mixed nationalities was generally low, only male Turkmens contracted mixed marriages, and not a single case was registered of a multinational marriage involving Turkmen women." L. N. Terent'eva, "Opredelenie svoey natsional'noy prinadlezhnosti podrostkami v natsional'nosmeshannykh sem'yakh" (Determination of National Affiliation by Minors in Nationally Mixed Families), *Sovetskaya etnografiya*, No. 3, 1969, p. 25n.

12. Jamal Kamal, "Samarqandu Bukhara bu. . ." (Samarkand and Bukhara, These . . .), *Sharq yulduzi*, Tashkent, No. 9, 1969, p. 117. For more on the tendency of recent Central Asian verse to seek avenues of expression that placed it at variance with the direction of official Soviet poetry, still dominated by socialist-realist vestiges of Stalinism, see Edward Allworth, "An Old Mood Returns to Central Asian Literature," *Literature East and West*, June 1967, pp. 149-154. Allworth traced this trend to cultural linkages with the pre-Russian, pre-Soviet past: he discerned "subtle echoes of traditional ghazals and rubais whose elegant structural formalities have fallen into disuse . . . in recent decades," and "a vocabulary encrusted by medieval writers with layers of meaning (that) enriches contemporary language with charged words."

13. Source: Mirtemir (pseudonym of Mirtemir Tursanov), *"Ozbekistansan"* (Thou, Uzbekistan), *Sovet Ozbekistani*, Tashkent, January 1, 1970. This poem was run *above* a message of New Year's greetings from Moscow which appeared on the same page. My own prose translation.

14. A. Osman, "Ozbek adabiy tilining ba"zi masalari," (Certain Problems of the Uzbek Literary Language), *Sovet Ozbekistani*, May 24, 1969.

15. Gustav Burbiel, "Like the Proverbial Phoenix, the Rich and Resilient Tatar Writing Re-emerges as a National Tool," *MidEast*, October 1969, p. 45.

16. *Pechat' SSSR v 1970 g.*, Moscow 1971, pp. 158-60, 188-90.

17. Michael Rywkin, "Central Asia and the Price of Sovietization," *Problems of Communism*, Vol. 13 (1964), No. 1, p. 11.

18. Institute for Study of the USSR, Prominent Personalities in the USSR, Metuchen, New Jersey (The Scarecrow Press) 1968, pp. 759 *ff.* for 1966 data. *Ozbekistan madaniyati*, Tashkent, March 6, 1971 for 1971 figures.

19. Ibid. and Rywkin, *Russia in Central Asia*, New York (Collier Books) 1963, p. 121.

20. Institute for Study of the USSR, *Prominent Personalities*.

21. Rywkin, "Central Asia and the Price of Sovietization," p. 14.

22. *Narodnoe khozyaystvo SSSR v 1969 g.*, Moscow 1971, p. 690.

23. Ibid., p. 697.

24. David C. Montgomery, "An American Student in Tashkent," *Asian Affairs*, February 1972, p. 35.

25. Gulnara Ghafurova, "Tarjima Haqida Mulahazalar" (Thoughts About Translation), *Ozbekistan madaniyati*, Tashkent, November 25, 1969.

26. "Sahna kuzguisida," ("In the Mirror of the Stage"), *Ozbekistan madaniyati*, January 9, 1970.

27. For a detailed contemporary compilation of such manifestations, see David Nissman, "Recent Developments in the Study of the Uzbek Central Asian Heritage," *Radio Liberty Research Paper* No. 35, March 1970.

28. Ghulam Karimov (Doctor of Philological Sciences), "Tarih, khalq va adabiyat" ("History, the People and Literature"), *Ozbekistan madaniyati*, April 1, 1969.

29. Tel'man Zhanuzakov (Doctor of Philological Sciences), "Shekaradaghi Shaiqas" ("Combat on the Border," an account of a Sino-Soviet border clash), *Qazaq edebiyeti*, Alma-Ata, August 23, 1969.

30. The newspapers were *Pravda Vostoka*, Tashkent; *Kazakhstanskaya Pravda*, Alma-Ata; *Kommunist Tadzhikistana*, Dushanbe; *Sovetskaya Kirgiziya*, Frunze; and *Turkmenskaya iskra*, Ashkhabad. In fact, the "joint issue" was a split run which permitted inclusion of local news from each republic. The information here is based on the Tashkent edition.

31. Alexandre Bennigsen and Chantal Lemercier-Quelquejay, *Islam in the Soviet Union*, New York (Praeger) 1968, p. 98. The Turkestan Commission "overhauled administrative policy in a sense favorable to the Muslims." Bennigsen writes further, "In addition, thanks to the pledges of wide autonomy and of respect for the cultural and religious institutions of Islam, the Turkestan Commission managed to win numerous adherents to the new regime from among the jadid left wing, from the most revolutionary-minded of the Young Bukharans and from the Young Khivans." For a detailed contemporary account by a Soviet writer, see G. Safarov, *Kolonial'naya revolyutsiya*, Moscow (Gosizdat) 1921.

32. A. Eshanov (Ishanov), "Lenin ziyasi bilan" ("With Lenin's Light"), *Sovet Ozbekistani*, November 5, 1969.

33. *Fan va Turmush*, Tashkent, August 1969, p. 15.

34. D. L. Zlatopol'skiy (ed.), *Natsional'naya gosudarstvennost' soyuznykh respublik*, Moscow 1968, pp. 5 *ff*.

35. Ya. Nasriddinova, "Ozbekistan Sovet milliy davlatining barpa bolishi wa rivajlanishi" ("The Creation and Development of the Soviet National State of Uzbekistan"), *Ozbekistan Kommunisti*, Tashkent, 1969, No. 6, pp. 3-19. The "author" was at that time Chairman of the Presidium of the Uzbek Supreme Soviet. She was later implicated in a local scandal involving charges of bribery and transferred to a minor ministerial position in Moscow. Her name figured during the perestroika period in further accusations of past "corruption" in Uzbekistan.

36. Ibid.

37. Nissman, *Recent Developments*, pp. 1-2.

38. A. Aminova, "Strukturnye sdvigi v ekonomicheskikh svyazyakh Uzbekistana" ("Structural Shifts in Uzbekistan's Economic Relations"), *Kommunist Uzbekistana*, Tashkent, No. 1, 1972, pp. 55 *ff.*

39. Ch. Abutalipov, "Marksistsko-Leninskoe uchenie o proletarskom internatsionalizme i sovremennost'" ("Marxist-Leninist Teaching on Proletarian Internationalism and the Present Day"), *Kommunist Uzbekistana*, No. 11, 1972.

40. Zlatopol'skiy, *Natsional'naya gosudarstvennost'*, 207.

41. Ibid.

3

The Post-Brezhnev Crackdown: "Corruption," Nationalism and the Elites

For the Uzbeks, and especially for their Communist elites, the post-Brezhnev era began with a far-reaching purge, accompanied by criminal prosecutions. The crackdown on the republic reached a new pitch of intensity in February 1986 with Mikhail Gorbachev's angry references to Uzbekistan in his speech at the Twenty-Seventh Party Congress in Moscow. In those days before the emergence of independence movements in Baltic and other republics, Uzbekistan and the Uzbek elites bore the brunt of the wrath that Moscow directed against wayward non-Russian nationalists. Later, the center was to have its attention distracted by other nationalisms, by the failure of perestroika to make early headway against the economic crisis, and by the general deterioration of the Soviet system, which further weakened its campaign against the Uzbek elites.

In Uzbekistan, the drama of the post-Brezhnev period was the clash of wills between the center on the one hand, led, in time, by Gorbachev himself, and on the other hand the native elites who occupied leadership positions in the republic's Soviet institutions. Goaded into counter-action by Moscow's attacks, the elites were at the cutting edge of Uzbek nationalism. They battled Moscow against daunting odds, playing skillfully on popular dissatisfaction with the ethnic discrimination and economic failures of Soviet rule. When Moscow sought to arouse public opinion against them as alleged exploiters of the Uzbek masses, the elites turned the tables by mobilizing national grievances against the center (as described in the

39

next chapters). In their struggle, the elites capitalized on their ability to circumvent censorship controls and appeal to the Uzbek masses through the network of vernacular media.

The battle was precipitated by the Moscow leadership's attempts, following Leonid Brezhnev's death in 1982, to purge the existing elites and tighten central control of cadre policy. The formal reason given for these efforts was the need to root out "negative phenomena" that had reached intolerable proportions during the Brezhnev era. Of these, the most serious from Moscow's standpoint were the various aspects of local "corruption" involved in the so-called "cotton affair," which soon came to be known to Russians as the "Uzbek affair." At the same time, it appears that Moscow's overarching goal was to halt the processes of de-colonization and de-russification, which had jeopardized central control.[1] The function of "corruption" in the Uzbek context, thus, was much broader than the mere personal gain of individuals.

When Brezhnev died, a purge was already looming in the party and state institutions of the four Soviet Central Asian republics and Kazakhstan. From that time--and especially after Mikhail Gorbachev's accession--the elites of those institutions were the target of a profound shakeup, featuring dismissals, expulsions from the Party, arrests and an undetermined number of death sentences. These moves in Uzbekistan and the other Central Asian republics were distinguished from the post-Brezhnev tightening in other parts of the country by two salient factors: 1) their greater scope and intensity, and 2) their close relationship to ethnic issues.

Moscow's concern with the incipient threat of growing nationalism in Uzbekistan, particularly among the elites, was confirmed beyond a doubt in the latter part of 1986, after the Uzbek and all-union Party congresses, when the focus expanded to include "ideological shortcomings." The concept of *miras* was particularly targeted, in the form of attacks on "idealization of the past." A number of vernacular literary works came under fire, including a historical novel lionizing Babur, the sixteenth-century Ferghana native who went on to found the Mogul Empire on the Indian subcontinent. Its author, a leading Uzbek establishment writer, was accused of rewriting history to "sow nostalgia for the patriarchal system and present Islam almost as the guardian of national culture."[2] Another work attacked on many occasions and by many regime spokesmen was a novel whose hero, the obkom first secretary of Bukhara (thinly disguised in the plot as "Shahristan"), is praised for ignoring higher orders and appropriating water from the Amu-Darya to make the desert in his oblast bloom (to the possible detriment of downstream areas).[3] Perhaps the most significant attack on nationalism among the intelligentsia, however, was criticism of the late Professor Ibrahim Muminov, a former vice-president of the Uzbek Academy of Sciences who was closely involved with the *miras* movement, particularly through his editorship of numerous volumes of the Uzbek Soviet Encyclopedia published in Tashkent in the 1970s, Rashidov's heyday. This campaign ended before it could bear major results, perhaps in part because by that time Moscow's political grip was already weakening to the point where Uzbeks could, and did, disregard it.

There can be little doubt that the top leadership was genuinely concerned about irregularities in the Central Asian republics, where they were clearly widespread. At the same time, there were indications that the campaign masked a determined effort not merely to eliminate wrongdoing but to achieve a fundamental transformation of the traditionally Islamic native societies, on a scale far beyond anything ever before achieved, even by Stalin.[4] The campaign sought to break the hold of the networks of local officials who over the years had built a power base that, despite nominal subservience to central authority, enabled them to stave off change from outside. The efficacy of these networks was recognized in the complaints of Moscow loyalists that personnel policies in the area, specifically the "nomenklatura" system which was still in force, had been perverted by "nepotism," "local favoritism," "kinship," "personal devotion," "obsequiousness," and "protectionism," all of this accompanied by a "stifling of criticism and self-criticism."[5] Thus, while societal transformation at all levels was the ultimate design, the elites had become the immediate target, for until they could be made to collaborate effectively--in deed as well as word--in bridging the policy-implementation gap between directives of the central authority and the masses, far-reaching change was doubtful.

At the heart of the "cotton affair" were charges that Uzbek officials at all levels of the republic had been defrauding the central government through an elaborate system of bribetaking and padding reports. According to a prosecutor of Uzbekistan, who happened to be a Russian, in that republic alone the state paid more than one billion rubles in 1978-1983 for cotton that was never produced, according to the "most modest" expert estimates.[6]

41

The cotton affair began to unfold in earnest when, in 1983, the prosecutor's office in Moscow sent a team of investigators headed by Tel'man Khorenovich Gdlyan to look into reports of bribetaking in Bukhara. Gdlyan and his associates had soon spread their net throughout Uzbekistan and begun to arrest and interrogate large numbers of suspects. Their efforts extending over several years eventually would lead to the conviction of the late Brezhnev's son-in-law, Yuriy Churbanov, a former deputy USSR Minister of Internal Affairs. Gdlyan and his colleague Nikolay Ivanov became Soviet celebrities: heroes in the minds of some, villains in the view of others. They were both elected to the Congress of People's Deputies from Moscow constituencies. To many Uzbeks, they were unspeakable pointmen for an ethnic vendetta emanating from Moscow. Ironically, the police careers of both Gdlyan and Ivanov ended when a special commission found them guilty of using illegal methods to extract confessions and many of their victims were acquitted (although the guilt of others has apparently never been questioned). But by then, the bad feeling which they had aroused between Uzbekistan and the central authorities had polarized relations.

Speaking at the Moscow Party Congress in 1986, at the height of the Gdlyan-Ivanov investigations, Gorbachev singled out the Uzbek republic for special opprobrium as the place where "negative processes have been manifest in their most acute form."[7] Later, he added Turkmenistan and "a number of oblasts" of Kazakhstan (presumably those with predominantly native populations) to the list of republics where problems had been encountered "in extremely ugly forms." Of the non-Muslim republics, only Moldavia shared this inglorious ranking, together with--in last place--certain parts of the RSFSR.[8] Yet Uzbekistan, the republic with the country's largest Muslim population, was first and foremost of those on whom Moscow's lightning descended.

In Uzbekistan, as in other Muslim republics, the principal victims of the drive against corruption and its related national and regional autarky were indigenous personnel, although local Russian officials were also implicated. The various charges that provided the *leitmotiv* of the campaign were catalogued under such headings as "violation of Party and state discipline," "violation of Soviet laws and norms of morality," "overreporting and malicious thefts," "bribery," "abuses of office," "padding and deception," "cheating," "speculation," etc.[9]

42

It was clear that massive corruption could not have occurred without the concupiscence of the highest echelons of the republics, and that the houses would have to be cleaned from the top. Moscow was assisted in this to some extent by natural forces. By the end of 1986, all five of the long-tenured patrimonial leaders of the Central Asian republics were out of office.

• First to go was Tajikistan's Rasulov, who died in April 1982 of a sudden heart attack.[10]

• In 1983, Uzbekistan's active Rashidov also died suddenly, under circumstances suggesting that his heart attack had been brought on by pressure from Moscow, with rumors even reaching the foreign press corps in Moscow that he had committed suicide; by 1986, Rashidov had been publicly condemned for "encouraging nepotism and protectionism," a decree promulgated at the top level in Moscow to honor his memory had been withdrawn, and his body was removed from its ceremonial resting place in Tashkent.[11] Soon, the term "sharafrashidovshchina" had become a synonym in the Soviet press for official wrongdoing.

• Kirghizia's Usubaliev was retired in 1985; although he had reached a normal retirement age (66), dissatisfaction with his stewardship became evident when almost immediately most of the top Party secretaries of the republic who had served under him were replaced.[12]

• Then, in early 1986, Turkmenistan's Gapurov, although only 63, retired on pension in the wake of official criticism of the state of affairs in his republic.[13]

• Last but by no means least, after being the target of open sniping in *Pravda* and other central newspapers, Kazakhstan's Kunaev was replaced in December 1986 by a Russian, an action that triggered student riots in the capital city of Alma-Ata. Predictably, he was soon dropped from the Politburo in Moscow and charged with personal involvement in corruption.

Some of these events were apparently fortuitous, the result of aging, but they paved the way for broad changes. The scope of the purge was reflected not only in changes at the first-secretary level of the republics, but throughout the hierarchy.

In Uzbekistan, the most populous Central Asian republic and the hardest hit by the purge, only three of thirteen oblast first secretaries remained of those who had been in office at the time of Rashidov's death. Five of the incumbents were arrested, and one was sentenced to death.[14] Bukhara oblast, where Gdlyan had begun his investigation, was singled out as an egregious example of patronage: as a result of the former first secretary's making appointments out of "friendship and local favoritism," the oblast's top law-enforcement officials (prosecutor, internal affairs chief, and head of the "Department for Struggle Against Embezzlement of Socialist Property and Speculation") allegedly engaged in thievery and "large-scale" bribery.[15]

Mindful of the mini-cults of personality of party first secretaries that had allowed things to go awry, Moscow urged members to abstain in future from adulation of "first persons." Many lower-ranking secretaries were also eliminated. Between the two successive Uzbek party congresses held in 1981 and 1986, more than three-fourths of the full membership of the republican Central Committee changed. At the February 1986 All-Union Party Congress in Moscow, the Uzbek first secretary reported that half of those in Uzbekistan on the all-union and Uzbek nomenklatura lists had been replaced. Uzbeks as a nationality continued to be well represented in the Central Committee, but lost their majority in its ruling Bureau, as did also the Kazakhs in theirs. The ethnic coloration of the purge was demonstrated by efforts to replace native incumbents with Russians, especially in two highly visible jobs: the Party first secretaryships of the Kazakh republic and of Tashkent, capital of Uzbekistan and the country's largest Asian city.

Indeed, one of the most ominous aspects of the purge was the new policy of "interrepublican exchange of cadres" enunciated by Egor' Ligachev (then Party secretary in charge of personnel) at the Party Congress; from the context, it was clear that this was aimed at unseating those in posts traditionally earmarked for native incumbents in republics like Uzbekistan, and replacing them with Russian cadres. (The success of the Uzbek elites in stalling this policy is described in Chapter 8.)

"Corruption" in Perspective

As revelations of "corruption" continued to unfold, it became clear that the Uzbeks themselves viewed the phenomena by more than just abstract standards of public morality. For one thing, the chief target of "corruption" was the central economic apparatus in Moscow, perceived as a monster of tyranny and exploitation encroaching ruthlessly on Uzbek well-being. In that sense, Uzbeks could see themselves more as beneficiaries than victims of corruption. Moreover, it was evident from descriptions of concrete cases that not all corruption was venal. Some republican and local officials broke the rules not so much for personal gain as in the interest of their communities--for example, when they diverted funds for unauthorized but necessary public construction. Managers and party officials in rural areas were rebuked for allowing state-subsidized bread to be used as cheap livestock fodder, or for buying butter and delivering it to the state in fulfillment of milk quotas (practices which were by no means unique to Central Asia). In other cases, "abuses" took forms that would not be regarded as illegal or immoral in more flexible systems, as evidenced by Moscow-inspired charges that a "private-property psychology" was responsible.[16] Indeed, the record suggests that many of the irregular practices classed as "negative phenomena" were not new, that they had been quietly allowed to exist in the past because they helped to make the system work, by stimulating initiative, cementing working relationships, and easing popular dissatisfaction with the state-controlled sector of the economy by providing goods and services that would otherwise be unavailable.

Thus, elite "corruption" had its positive side. It was a factor in boosting the morale of the Uzbeks and other Central Asians, creating at the same time a kind of *de facto* autonomy that enhanced the role of the local population in handling its own affairs. Nancy Lubin wrote of this situation as a safety valve that helped to ward off the instability threatened by the failure of the offficial system to satisfy human material needs.[17]

Corruption was not new to Central Asia. In 1908, when it was still called Russian Turkestan, the tsarist government had dispatched to the territory an upright Baltic German and distinguished Senator, Count Konstantin Pahlen, to investigate, and act against, widespread accusations of malfeasance among Russian colonial administrators. After taking a full year to travel from place to place and complete his investigation, Pahlen found massive evidence of corruption among Russian officials. In the Transcaspian Province, situated roughly on the territory of the present-day Turkmen SSR, he wrote later, "It looked as if two-thirds of the entire administration were quite untrustworthy and profoundly corrupt."[18] A lieutenant-colonel in charge of the provincial governor's chancery had amassed a fortune of 300,000 rubles on a salary of 4,000 a year. In Pahlen's memoirs, the vocabulary of corruption was similar to that of today's Soviet media treatment: "embezzlement," "bribery," "extortion," "falsifying official returns," "unbelievable arbitrariness. . . ."

Pahlen blamed the Central Asian heat for "engendering a state of mental unbalance," and the life-style of the transplanted Russian officials--"wine, feminine society, cards"--which required much money. "In those parts of the world," he noted, "the power that is placed in the hands of any official allows the unscrupulous many opportunities of enrichment. . . ."[19] He also blamed the prevailing Asian mores.

In Uzbekistan, there also had been scandals earlier in the Soviet period: in the early 1970s, a chairman of the Uzbek Council of Ministers had been sentenced to a lengthy prison term on various accusations of malfeasance. But as native spokesmen were quick to point out, Soviet corruption was by no means a Central Asian monopoly, and when Brezhnev's son-in-law was arrested and later convicted, they found confirmation that the real culprits were not in Tashkent or Ashkhabad but in Moscow, at the top of a pyramid of payoffs. Still, there could be little doubt that Uzbek corruption, if occasionally inflated out of context by some of the media in Moscow, was widespread.

Lubin, whose book was based on her field work in Uzbekistan in 1978-1979, i.e. well before the beginning of the post-Brezhnev purge, was able to describe the full range of corrupt practices that later emerged in official revelations.[20] Thus, her list of sectors in which "embezzlement" and "plundering" were prevalent was headed by the cotton-cleansing (ginning) industry, two of whose senior officials were subsequently reported as sentenced to death in the Gorbachev period.[21]

In attempting to gauge the problem of corruption in the Soviet Union by Western yardsticks, one inevitably encounters the problem of values. J.S. Nye, noting that corruption "covers a wide range of behavior from venality to ideological erosion," has suggested an operational definition of it as "behavior which deviates from the formal duties of a public role because of private-regarding (personal, close family, private clique) pecuniary or status gains; or violates rules against the exercise of certain types of private-regarding influence."[22] Even so, behavior that is reprehensible by the norms of one society may be admissible by those of another.

Count Pahlen, in his Central Asian memoir cited above, was one of many writers on the subject who have pointed to the relatively greater permissiveness in this respect of traditional societies where public office, in particular, has often been viewed as conferring legitimate opportunity for enrichment.[23] In the Islamic Middle East, Marvin G. Weinbaum has commented, "opportunities for personal gain are expected very often to offset low salaries and poor working conditions, especially in the rural areas."[24]

In the speeches of Soviet leaders and in the Russian-language media, condemnations of Uzbek corruption commonly reflected political judgments based on moralistic reasoning. Western social scientists, in their analysis of corruption as a general phenomenon, tend to take a more nuanced approach, weighing costs against possible benefits. Nye, in the essay quoted above dealing with developing societies, a classification which largely fits the Muslim Soviet republics, lists among the possible benefits of corruption the stimulation of economic development (aiding capital formation, cutting red tape, encouraging entrepreneurship and incentives); national integration (elite integration, integration of non-elites); and governmental capacity (aggregation of power to govern through material incentives).

In the Uzbek context, if one reads between the lines of hostile media descriptions, the ethnic networks among officials had been providing two useful services, even while lining the pockets of some of their members:

1. By supporting the illegal or quasi-legal "second economy," they helped to remedy shortages of goods and services, and provided alternative sources of income for citizens.
2. Their activities gave members of the local nationality access to upward mobility in ways denied to them by the system. (One recalls here the American big-city machines of the nineteenth and early twentieth centuries, which helped many a poor immigrant to make a start despite ignorance of the prevailing language and culture.)

In some cases, "violations of discipline" seem to have been motivated by concern for the public interest. Yet even where "negative phenomena" were connected with self-enrichment pure and simple, as in the case of the corrupt Central Asian manager who siphoned off state funds for his own use, they might actually be stimulating economic growth, at least in the private sector; if he invested the money in private housing for his family and followers, it went into the pockets of individual entrepreneurs and black-market dealers who existed to provide services and materials that the state could not. Here one encounters political and ideological difficulties, of course, since such economic activity, even with legal funds, was viewed askance in a Soviet-type socialist economy, going well beyond even the carefully-circumscribed list of private services which became permissible under the "reforms" of the early Gorbachev era.

In general, the economic cost of corruption, due to diversion of resources from planned investment and other prescribed uses, could also be offset by hidden sociopolitical benefits. Writing of the Middle East, Weinbaum found that:

> The informal decision process offers a sometimes necessary antidote to the rigidities of formal bureaucratic structures. Tensions from rivalries and jealousies endemic to the system are mediated, if at all, by the security offered by family and friendship cliques, and clientele relationships.[25]

He observed that "in some countries at least, profit from or permissiveness in corrupt practices gives administrators a personal stake in the prevailing political order and regime leaders a powerful lever against possible political deviation."[26] Although based on extra-Soviet experience, this may help to explain why the top Soviet leadership was for many years complacent about corruption in Central Asia.

In concluding, after studying the relationship of ethnicity and economics in Uzbekistan, that illegal activity was a safety valve that helped to diminish ethnic tensions, Lubin warned that any major shift in Soviet policy could be destabilizing to the region.[27] She found that many economic sectors in Uzbekistan were controlled by Russians and other Europeans, and essentially closed to members of the local nationality. She attributed much of this to the Uzbeks' own unwillingness to compete with Russians in areas that they find uncongenial, or to acquire the language and other skills to do so. Aside from psychological considerations, there was the fact that official Soviet society, especially in the pre-perestroika period, was a normative one *par excellence*, and that norms breed discrimination.[28] In a Russocentric environment, the brown-skinned Uzbek in his *doppi* or skullcap, even if he was well-educated, spoke good Russian, and was indifferent to religion, was apt to feel subject to discrimination. Among his own people, operating in a language that very few Russians even began to comprehend, he was more assured of acceptance. (This situation was a microcosm of the Central Asians' larger unwillingness, despite massive unemployment in their own region, to take jobs in other parts of the USSR.)

Thus, when one took a close look at corruption in the Central Asian republics from the standpoint of local public interest, it resembled not so much an abstract evil as a mixture of positive and negative components. However, if the concealed benefits of corruption as a palliative for the ills of the system had in past decades been an incentive not to attempt decisive action against it, the Moscow leadership, first under Andropov and later under Gorbachev, gave signs of having concluded that the political costs were no longer acceptable, either in the short or the long run.

First, there was the fact that private activity, illicit or not, created and perpetuated alternative structures that competed with the system, depriving it of governing capacity and undermining its legitimacy. At the 1986 Uzbek Party Congress, First Secretary Usmankhojaev, as *de facto* spokesman for the Central Committee in Moscow, referred to the scale of "abuses and perversions" as "dangerous."[29] He devoted much of his lengthy report to documenting illegalities committed by Party members. At the same time, he registered concern at the "considerable share" of the population in some places who were living from earnings in the "individual sector." Around that time, the number of officially unemployed in Uzbekistan was set at one million.[30]

Second, the elites, while bilking the state economy, also conspired to frustrate the leadership's long-range goals of social integration. In the name of *miras*, they helped to keep the masses culturally aloof, immobile, and unwilling to relinquish traditional ways of doing things, whether in the realm of spiritual culture (Islam) or material (resistance to mechanized cotton-picking, a subject of recurring complaints, or clinging to the *ketmen*, a kind of hoe, to control irrigation). The result both limited the regime's access to Central Asian manpower for civilian and military uses, and allowed the burgeoning--given high rates of population increase--of a potential focus of unrest and instability.

This was further evidence that the political aspect, more than the immediate economic and social consequences of "corruption," was perceived as posing the main threat to central authority.

Moscow Presses the Attack

Moscow attacked the elites frontally by using the media to appeal to the masses in an attempt to undermine the elites' position. The "anti-corruption" campaign stressed themes calculated to make the elites odious in the public eye, such as alleged diversion by some of them of housing funds to private use. Instances of nepotism by the elite were also emphasized, among them use of influence to have children admitted to university or help in escaping military conscription. Concurrently, fanfare was given to steps aimed at stopping such unpopular local government practices--which could have existed in the past only with Moscow's connivance--as use of child labor for picking cotton or exposure of human beings to dangerous pesticides.

The consumerist and democratic themes of the Gorbachev leadership were deployed in the anti-elite campaign. Discredited officials were branded as responsible for failures to eliminate deficiencies in areas like housing, provision of consumer goods, and health care. Simultaneously, appeals went out to the rank-and-file of the Party and the citizenry in general to be outspoken in calling attention to the lapses of those in high places. In fact, this tactic by Moscow seems to have scored some initial successes: the response to its appeals was apparently enthusiastic, triggering "malicious" telephone calls and a spate of anonymous letters. At a Party plenum there were complaints that glasnost had encouraged people to "slander," and that a "considerable part" of the Party apparat was kept permanently busy looking into *anonimki*. [31]

In the long run, however, Moscow's attempt to turn the masses against their own elites failed. Whatever the former's resentment of a Central Asian "new class" that had benefited from a system that exploited them, they seem to have been willing to overlook socioeconomic differences and make common cause with their ethnic kin against the outsiders. They may have recognized that the elites, far from being totally dedicated to Moscow, were a defense against total domination by the center. History has recorded instances where other non-Russian leaders identified with unpopular policies--one thinks of Gomulka and Ceausescu--were able to manipulate national resentments to overcome social cleavage and rally a nation to face pressure from Moscow. Stalin, despite his persecution of Georgians while in office, became a posthumous symbol of national dissent, as witnessed by the 1956 Tbilisi student riots protesting the decision not to observe his death anniversary. In the Central Asian case, the legitimacy of the elites was actually enhanced, and their abuses overlooked, by Moscow's public attacks on them: there is evidence that they were regarded with favor by the masses because of their role in devising extra-legal solutions to pressing economic and social problems, and for forming a native buffer between the masses and an alien authority. Robin Hood, too, was called a criminal.

Deployment of administrative, political and popular pressures against the elites was clearly viewed by the top leadership only as a stopgap. Indeed, Ligachev's Congress speech had telegraphed Moscow's belief that the ultimate solution lay in housecleaning, in a thorough renovation of national cadres. The process of cadre transformation was initiated by attempting to bring in experienced Party workers from other republics, chiefly the RSFSR, as the nucleus of a new elite. As part of the process, local tampering with the sacrosanct nomenklatura system was condemned.

Another front on which Moscow attacked was in the area of training Party cadres. To insure that fresh cadres recruited from the local nationalities would display greater devotion to Moscow than their predecessors, new emphasis was given to training at such RSFSR institutions as the Academy of Social Sciences in Moscow[32] and the higher party schools of Moscow, Leningrad, Sverdlovsk, Saratov and Novosibirsk.[33]

Whether these measures might eventually have succeeded under more stable conditions is open to question. The course on which the Gorbachev leadership had now embarked, with a determination unmatched by any of its forerunners, involved transforming a Muslim society according to a secular Eurocentric model. If Atatürk managed to accomplish something of the kind in Turkey, it was because he had the advantage of being not an outsider but a son of his own people, a *ghazi* (fighter for Islam) to boot, and of operating at a time of revolutionary enthusiasm and *élan*. A measure of the seriousness attached by the Gorbachev leadership to the Central Asian problem was that it chose to tackle it precisely at a time when it was avowedly facing opposition on a variety of other fronts. The apparent reason was an assessment that time was running out, that with every year a mushrooming Asian population was developing further in directions that increased its divergence from the mainstream of Soviet society and diminished still further the chances of returning it to the fold.

In retrospect, it now seems clear that the turning-point for Soviet power in Uzbekistan, the beginning of the decline of Moscow's authority, was the offensive against the native elites led by Gorbachev at the Party Congress in 1986. Instead of conciliation and cautious political maneuvering, the impatient Gorbachev chose to attack the elites frontally. By threatening them and putting them on the defensive, he and the Moscow *apparat* transformed them from potential allies of Soviet power to its determined adversaries.

In any case, Moscow's actions became increasingly more impotent with the rapid retrenchment of Soviet power throughout the non-Russian areas, a trend that became a juggernaut in the face of the Gorbachev leadership's deepening economic crisis and the breakdown of political discipline. In Uzbekistan, this process was helped along by a chorus of grievances that became ever more insistent.

Notes

1. For a discussion of de-colonization and de-russification in all fourteen of the USSR's non-Russian "union" republics, see Gerhard Simon, *Nationalismus und Nationalitätenpolitik in der Sowjetunion*, Baden-Baden (Nomosverlag) 1986, pp. 17-18 and *passim. Now available in English as* Nationalism and Policy toward the Nationalities in the Soviet Union, *Boulder (Westview Press) 1991.*

2. *Pravda Vostoka*, October 5, 1986. The writer in question was Pirimqul Qadirov, author of *Yulduzli tunlar* (Starry Nights), Tashkent 1981.

3. Sadulla Karamatov, "Songgi barkhan" (The Last Dune), *Sharq yulduzi*, Nos. 3-5, 1983.

4. As Donald S. Carlisle put it, "the Stalinist solution was to accept the co-existence of traditional and modern society for the long term." See Carlisle, "The Uzbek Power Elite: Politburo and Secretariat (1938-83)," *Central Asian Survey*, Vol. 5 (1986), Number 3/4, p. 98.

5. See, for example, First Secretary Inamjan Usmankhojaev's report to Twenty-First Uzbek Congress, *Kommunist Uzbekistana*, No. 2, 1986, pp. 8-47.

6. "Qayta qurish: insan va huquq" ("Reconstruction: Man and Law," interview with Aleksei Vladimirovich Buturlin), *Ozbekistan adabiyati va san"ati*, February 6, 1987. It was characteristic of some of the recent personnel changes that the Slavic Buturlin occupied a sensitive job that had long been an Uzbek preserve.

7. Report of the Central Committee of the CPSU to the Twenty-Seventh Party Congress, *Kommunist*, Moscow, No. 4, 1986, p. 67.

8. Gorbachev's report to a plenum of the Central Committee of the CPSU, *Pravda*, January 28, 1987.

9. See *inter alia* Usmankhojaev's report to the Sixteenth Plenum of the Communist Party of Uzbekistan (*Pravda Vostoka*, June 26, 1984), also his report to the Twenty-First Congress of that Party.

10. "Communist Party Chief of Tajikistan Dies," *Radio Liberty Research* (*RLR*) 155/82, April 6, 1982.

11. See Ann Sheehy's "Former Premier of Uzbekistan Expelled from the CPSU," *RLR* 297/86, August 6, 1986, also her penetrating analyses, "Major Anti-Corruption Drive in Uzbekistan," *RLR* 324/84, August 30, 1984, and "Progress of Anti-Corruption Campaign in Uzbekistan Reviewed," *RLR* 457/84, November 11, 1984. Also *Literaturnaya gazeta*, June 10, 1987.

12. "New Kirghiz First Secretary Cleans House," *RLR*, 15/86, December 31, 1985.

13. "First Secretary in Turkmenistan Replaced," *RLR* 9/86 ("USSR This Week" section), December 27, 1985.

14. *Literaturnaya gazeta*, June 10, 1987.

15. "Raising Party and State Discipline and Work with Cadres to the Level of Present-Day Tasks," *Pravda Vostoka*, June 26, 1984 (translation in Foreign Broadcast Information Service, *Soviet Union*, July 11, 1984, pp. R1-20.)

16. Usmankhojaev, report to Twenty-First Uzbek Party Congress.

17. Lubin, *Labour and Nationality in Soviet Central Asia*, Princeton (Princeton University Press) 1984, pp. 224-42.

18. K. K. Pahlen, *Mission to Turkestan*, London (Oxford University Press) 1964, p. 127.

19. Ibid., pp. 156-57.

20. Nancy Lubin, *Labour and Nationality*, p. 191.

21. Uwe Englebrecht, Moscow correspondent of the Vienna *Die Presse*, reported in his paper's issue of September 1, 1986 that the former Uzbek Minister of Cotton Ginning, Usmanov, had been sentenced to death. Vakhobjan U. Usmanov was one of those dropped from the Uzbek Central Committee at the February 1986 Congress of the Communist Party of Uzbekistan. *Pravda* of July 3, 1984, announced the execution of Ata Ashirov, director of a cotton-ginning plant in Turkmenistan, for taking bribes to cover up falsification of crop figures.

22. J. S. Nye, "Corruption and Political Development: A Cost-Benefit Analysis," reprinted from the *American Political Science Review* in Arnold J. Heidenheimer (*ed.*), *Political Corruption*, New York (Holt, Rinehart and Winston) 1970, p. 567. Nye credits Edward C. Banfield for the second part of the definition.

23. For an example, see Bert F. Hoselitz, "Levels of Economic Performance and Bureaucratic Structures," in Joseph La Polombara (*ed.*), *Bureaucracy and Political Development*, Princeton (Princeton University Press) 1963, pp. 188-96.

24. Marvin G. Weinbaum, *Food, Development, and Politics in the Middle East*, Boulder (Westview Press) 1984, p. 97.

25. Ibid., p. 97.

26. Ibid., p. 98.

27. Lubin, *Labour and Nationality*, pp. 225-27.

28. The role of norms in "almost automatic consignment of other groups to inferior status" in a society is discussed in Nathan Glazer and Daniel P. Moynihan (introduction), *Ethnicity: Theory and Experience*, Cambridge, Massachusetts (Harvard University Press) 1975, pp. 13-14.

29. Ironically, Usmankhojaev himself, the man who was named by Moscow as First Secretary to clean up the corruption scandal in Uzbekistan and served in that capacity for more than two years, was later arrested on charges of corruption, and sentenced to a twelve-year prison term.

30. See "Soviet Is Reporting One Million Jobless in Uzbek Republic," *New York Times*, March 29, 1987, based on an article by the Uzbek economist R. Ubaydullaeva in *Sel'skaya zhizn'*, March 24, 1987.

31. *Pravda Vostoka*, October 7, 1986.

32. Ibid.

33. Reported by Usmankhojaev in speech at Twenty-Seventh CPSU Congress.

Uzbek Nationalism Today: Selected Themes

Introduction to Part Two

As the elites fought back against the center, their public strategy unfolded. It soon became evident that they were using the communications system, especially those media in their own language, to press economic and social issues in ways that went straight to the ethnic sensitivities of their co-nationals. The Central Asian masses were in this dispute a kind of Greek chorus to which both sides appealed for support: as we saw in the last chapter, Moscow and its henchmen by trying to summon moral outrage against the venality of (some) native officials, the local elites by playing on feelings of ethnic solidarity.

Although the media were paramount in the elites' resistance struggle, other means were also used. Ousted officials began mounting letter-writing campaigns (sometimes using anonymous denunciations), circulating petitions, and using their "connections" in various ways, such as gaining access to their own confidential dossiers.[1] Such efforts all too often succeeded, Moscow spokesmen complained, in getting them reinstated as Party members and appointed to important jobs, in revolving-door fashion. It was charged at a party plenum in October 1986, after the purge had been in progress for more than two years: "It is especially inadmissible that a number of compromised officials who were dismissed for negative reasons landed in cozy places in many republican organizations and institutions, including ideological ones. . ."[2]

The fact was that Moscow's purge goals were severely hampered by the lack of an adequate indigenous cadre reserve to serve as replacements for those in the nomenklatura who had been dismissed. This dearth of qualified replacements no doubt explained the continuing return of "compromised" officials to responsible posts. Moscow therefore ordered that priority be given to developing the reserve. In Uzbekistan and other republics of the region, this did not prevent local leaders from bypassing the official lists in favor of their own unlisted candidates; in one rayon of neighboring Kazakhstan, when 109 persons on the nomenklatura were removed "for various reasons," only eighteen were replaced from the reserve.[3]

Another case in Kazakhstan drew the wrath of *Pravda* in Moscow: a Kazakh raikom secretary whose sins had included protecting a local official who had absconded with 1,213 head of livestock was reinstated as a party member only twenty days after his expulsion.[4]

It was acknowledged that "compromised" people were successfully playing to feelings of local patriotism in their appeals for support. At the same time, deposed members of the hierarchy seem to have retained some of their former authority. Inamjan B. Usmankhojaev, who had succeeded Rashidov as Party first secretary in Uzbekistan and until his own ouster and arrest on corruption charges in January 1988 remained (ironically) the chief spokesman for the anti-corruption campaign in Uzbekistan,[5] expressed Moscow's dissatisfaction with the situation:

> Even shortcomings that have been exposed are being liquidated in some places timidly, with a backward look to past authorities. . . . Many people who have been justly summoned to assume Party and state responsibility for their ugly acts have not shrunk from creating a false public opinion as to the alleged massacring (*izbienie*) of cadres. Some "exes" (*byvshye*) who were until recently deceiving the Party and state, billing society and the workers, are today adopting the pose of persons who have been wronged and have suffered for the interests of the republic. There have been individual attempts, if veiled ones, to portray the struggle to restore order and justice almost as an anti-national campaign.[6]

There were still other forms of subtle resistance by those still in office. Moscow levied charges of "formalism" in local implementation of the anti-corruption campaign, as when officials were nominated for awards despite having been "compromised." The Uzbek first secretary also revealed that the high-priority campaign to promote learning of Russian was being "sidetracked," naming tow officials of the republican Academy of Sciences (one a Slav) who had closed down the department of Russian at the Institute of Language and Literature.[7] The Institute of Party History was a target of repeated censure, as for failure to produce works on "reasons for and means of overcoming negative phenomena" in Uzbekistan. Party committees were said to be winking at participation in Islamic rituals by Communists and Komsomol members.

But it was the media that tipped the balance of the struggle. "Glasnost" was a sword that cut both ways. Just as Moscow loyalists used local media to foment mass indignation at the misdeeds--real or claimed--of members of the local elites, so too did the elites use their continuing access to the same media to press their own cause.

Ironically, Moscow's campaign against the Uzbek elites served in the long run to weaken, not to strengthen, its grasp on Uzbekistan. Moscow not only undercut the elements on which it had always relied for support, but its campaign against those elements converted them into a powerful enemy, actually giving the elites greater legitimacy in the eyes of the Uzbek rank-and-file.

Notes

1. This practice has provoked numerous official complaints. See, for example, "Old Ties" in *Pravda*, October 11, 1986.

2. Ibid.

3. Yu. Kuznetsov, "How We Prepare the Cadre Reserve," *Partiynaya zhizn' Kazakhstana*, No. 1, 1985, p. 41.

4. "Old Ties," *Pravda*, October 11, 1986.

5. It is useful to bear in mind that representatives of the Central Committee in Moscow were conspicuous in their participation in preparations for republican Party meetings, like the one at which Usmankhojaev delivered the "report" in question. A parallel to the British monarch's "speech from the throne" at the opening of Parliament is suggested.

6. Usmankhojaev, report to Twenty-First Uzbek Party Congress.

7. Usmankhojaev, "Tasks of Party Organizations of the Republic to Further Increase the Effectiveness of Ideological Work in the Light of the Requirements of the Twenty-Seventh Congress of the CPSU," *Pravda Vostoka*, October 5, 1986.

4

The Cotton Monoculture

Until perestroika, nationalism among the non-Russian peoples of the Soviet Union had tended to center on ethnic issues. Were the local language and culture threatened by russification? Was there discrimination against the nationality in admission to higher education or white-collar employment? With perestroika, a new complex of issues arose, as the nationalities became more clearly aware of economic exploitation and environmental damage to their homelands caused by directives for reckless industrial and agricultural development imposed by leaders in Moscow who were oblivious or indifferent to the human costs.

In Uzbekistan and the two other cotton-growing republics of Tajikistan and Turkmenistan, the "cotton affair" and the purge which ensued heightened resentment of Moscow's high-handed politics, especially among the elites who bore the brunt of the center's wrath. Even those who did not suffer directly had good reason to resent outside interference in their homelands.

Cotton and Colonialism

Ironically, it was cotton--which had caused the trouble in the first place--that provided the elites with the opportunity to turn the tables. By the time of Brezhnev's death in 1982, the tragic economic and environmental consequences of decades of unbridled cotton expansion were being felt ever more acutely. Under Gorbachev's policy of glasnost, it became possible, as never before, to document and publicize them in the mass media. As new revelations burst forth nearly every day, once stealthy mutterings about the "cotton monoculture" grew into an open chorus of angry complaint.

Particular victims of the monoculture were women and children. In Soviet Central Asia, much of the work in raising cotton continues to be done by hand. Women and children have borne much of the brunt of this, with men reserving for themselves the physically less demanding managerial, administrative and distributive aspects of cotton production. During the growing season, women have been compelled to labor long hours in the hot sun with little shelter and inadequate food and drinking-water. One result has been an alarming incidence of female suicide, especially by self-immolation.[1] For years, entire classes of children were drafted from their schoolrooms to help with the cotton harvest, which often lasted into December; often they were required to live and work in harsh conditions with insufficient protection from the cold.

Emotional issues related to cotton, like the drying of the Aral Sea or the rise in infant and maternal mortality--all caused ultimately by cotton-delivery plans imposed on the republics by Moscow--stirred Central Asians deeply. They were also grist for the political mill. Central Asian officials, writers, and other members of the creative intelligentsia began to vie with each other in vilifying the system of forced cotton growing. "Monoculture" was no longer an esoteric economic concept: it had become a political slogan.

Central Asian discontent with Moscow over cotton-related issues goes back more than a hundred years, to the Russian occupation of Central Asia in the nineteenth century, which coincided with the industrial revolution and its sharply rising demand for cotton to be used in textile manufacturing. For the first time, the Russian Empire had a territory warm enough for effective cultivation of cotton. Although tsarist Russia remained a net importer of cotton, Central Asia became important as a domestic source of that commodity.

Cotton in the Soviet Period: The Squeeze

The Soviet rulers who took over after 1917 prized cotton as a raw material vital for industrialization. In November 1920, Lenin signed a decree calling for revitalization of cotton-growing on a "socialist" basis. This was the first of many exhortations to the cotton-republics to step up production for the state. A 1929 Central Committee resolution launched a "struggle for cotton self-sufficiency of the USSR." In 1940, the year before the German invasion, the harvest was reportedly 2.24 million tons. By 1960, the wartime slump in production had been overcome and the harvest was said to have nearly doubled, to 4.29 million.

In 1961, the Twenty-Second Party Congress approved an additional sharp increase in production of this 'white gold,' amounting in the case of Uzbekistan to further doubling and more over a 20-year period.[2]

In the 40 years from 1940 to 1980, the Soviet gross cotton harvest rose from 2.24 to 9.10 million tons, a fourfold increase. Most of this was contributed by the three republics of Uzbekistan, Tajikistan and Turkmenistan, which in normal times now account for about seven-eighths of the entire Soviet crop. Part of the increase was due to improved yields, but it also required that land sown to cotton be nearly doubled. This was made possible by massive expansion of the irrigation system.

The cotton drive reached something of a crescendo in the 1970s with a visit to Tashkent by Brezhnev: when Sharaf Rashidov, then Uzbek First Secretary, promised Brezhnev more than five million tons of cotton a year, the Russian leader reportedly told him, "Round it off to six million, Sharafchik!" and Rashidov allegedly replied, "Yes, sir, Leonid Il'ich."[3] The "achievement" of that goal, first reported in 1980, was made possible only by padding production figures. Table 4.1 tells the story for the country as a whole.

TABLE 4.1 Land Sown to Cotton, by Year

Year	Hectares
1940	2,080,000
1960	2,190,000
1970	2,750,000
1980	3,150,000
1985	3,320,000
1986	3,470,000

Source: Derived from *Narodnoe khozyaystvo SSSR za 70 let* (Narkhoz 70), Moscow 1987, p. 224.

Table 4.2 shows the impact on Uzbekistan and other cotton-growing republics.

TABLE 4.2   Cotton Sowings (Million Hectares)

Unit	1940	1971-75*	1976-80*	1981-85*	1985	1986	Increase, 1940-86 (Percent)
USSR	2.071	2.808	3.042	3.248	3.316	3.474	68
SSR:							
Uzbek	.924	1.718	1.823	1.932	1.993	2.053	122
Kazak	.101	.115	.117	.130	.130	.129	28
Azerb.	.188	.204	.231	.296	.295	.303	61
Kirghiz	.064	.074	.073	.046	.028	.029	55
Tajik	.106	.264	.295	.308	.312	.314	196
Turkmen	.151	.438	.504	.534	.560	.650	330

*Average per year for this period.
Source: Narkhoz 70, computed from delivery and yield data on p. 228.

Cotton and Nationalism

The drive to increase cotton production led those responsible to throw caution to the wind. Their recklessness was later to play directly into the hands of those elements in the local societies who sought to stir resentment of Moscow. Some of their actions were discussed at a symposium held in Tashkent in 1987, in the encouragingly open new atmosphere, to air the accumulated problems. This was a key event in development and publicizing of the elites' campaign against the monoculture.

Speakers at the symposium noted that rotation of cotton with other crops, essential to prevent deterioration of the land, had been abandoned. This opened the way to increased wind erosion. In addition, the insect population increased, leading to use of strong pesticides. As insects developed immunity, usage was stepped up, to as much as 55 kilos of chemicals per hectare (49 pounds per acre).[4] In more recent years, attempts were made for gradual re-introduction of rotation to offset this damage,[5] but as one of the speakers observed, the planting of grasses and other alternate crops would have to be accompanied by development of new land for cotton, unless output was to suffer; this would reduce still further the acreage available for badly needed food production in Uzbekistan.

The most dramatic effect of reckless cotton expansion was in its catastrophic impact on the region's water resources. Central Asia's climate, with its long frost-free season and days of sunshine, is ideal for cotton in all respects but one. Cotton plants are thirsty, and rainfall in the region is limited. For a season's growth, cotton needs more than 30 inches of rain, but in Uzbekistan, for example, there is apt to be no rain at all during the actual growing season, and the average annual precipitation in places is as little as four inches and nowhere more than 14 inches. The difference must come from irrigation.[6]

For centuries, the inhabitants of the Central Asian oases have been irrigating the surrounding desert to provide themselves with farm produce. In this now largely Turkic region, the traditional Tajik (Persian) expression *ab-i-hayat*, "life water," is still in current usage as a reminder of the link between water and human existence. Now, Moscow's demands for cotton, and the food needs of the expanding population, have stretched water resources to the limit.

The way for expansion of irrigation had been paved in Stalin's day by construction in 1939-1941 of a number of canals, the largest being the 215-mile-long Great Ferghana Canal through Uzbekistan and Tajikistan, a "people's project" on which 180,000 collective-farmers labored largely by hand.[7] The Uzbek branch of the Great Ferghana, 177 miles long, was completed in only 45 days. After World War II, priority was again given to irrigation. By 1959 the first stage of the new Kara Kum Canal had begun to carry water from the Amu into the desert. It and other projects made possible the continued rapid expansion of irrigated land in the three cotton republics shown in Table 4.3.

In the 21-year span between 1965 and 1986, land under irrigation in the three republics increased by 62 percent, an annual rate of 2.3 percent. In just six years between 1980 and 1986, the total increased by 17 percent, an accelerated annual rate of 2.7 percent. Turkmenistan, a republic with large desert tracts seemingly waiting to be reclaimed, experienced the largest increase in those six years: 131 percent, or 4.1 percent annually.

TABLE 4.3 Land Under Irrigation (Thousand Hectares)

	1965	1970	1980	1985	1986
Uzbek	2,639	2,696	3,476	3,930	4,020
Tajik	468	518	617	653	662
Turkmen	514	643	927	1,107	1,185
TOTAL	3,621	3,857	5,020	5,690	5,867

Source: Narkhoz 70, p. 245 and *Narodnoe khoziaistvo SSSR v 1980 g.*, Moscow 1981, p. 226.

Deterioration of the soil caused by this extensive development and the accompanying neglect of sound conservation practices drastically reduced cotton yields, causing a drop in the overall harvests. In Uzbekistan, the principal producer, the yield fell from a 1976-1980 average of 29.4 to 24.3 centners per hectare in 1986. The gross harvest fell from the 1976-1980 average of 5.4 to 4.9 million tons in 1987, more than 1.5 million below the republic's plan commitment.[8] In Turkmenistan the decline was even steeper, from 23.0 in 1985 to 17.5 in 1986; but the gross harvest, after slumping in 1986, in 1987 returned to 20.1 almost the 1985 level, thanks in part to reclamation of additional land for irrigation.

The Backlash

In subsequent years, cotton yields improved, thanks in part to favorable weather conditions, but also to the fact that, under the pressure for relief put on Moscow by Central Asian interests, plans were scaled down to more reasonable levels. In addition, in 1990 cotton workers benefited from an increase in procurement prices accepted by Moscow under pressure from Uzbekistan's new President Karimov. But by this time, resentment of the monoculture had become a potent political weapon in the hands of the local elites, who were now clamoring for control of much of the cotton harvest, which they hoped to sell directly abroad for hard currency that would flow into the exchequers of Uzbekistan.

Still, the scars caused by the monoculture are far from healing. It has caused enormous damage to climate and the environment, to food production, to drinking-water supplies, and to public health, especially of women and children. One of its most spectacularly disastrous consequences, the rapid drying of the Aral Sea, will be explored in the next chapter.

Even leaving aside such corollary blights produced by the monoculture, its purely economic harm has been enormous. At the height of the cotton expansion, that crop's demand for land, labor and other resources squeezed out food crops, especially the fruits and vegetables for which Central Asia was famous in the past. In the face of rising population needs, the rate of growth for production of these crops flattened, or swung downward.

As part of the drive to expand cotton acreage at all costs, hard-pressed officials even took away the small private plots which peasants had been allowed to farm after collectivization. Deprived of their principal source of food, the peasants resorted to desperate measures to feed their families. A participant in the 1987 Tashkent symposium recalled that centralization and consolidation of acreage under cotton had created fields as large as 100 hectares (247 acres) in some districts. In places, he said, peasants had taken advantage of this to sow illegal crops of scarce vegetables and melons secretly in the center of the field, where they were invisible from the distant edges.[9]

There is more than a little irony in the fact that some of the specific abuses connected with the cotton monoculture, such as depriving the *dehqans* of their private plots or cutting down trees to make more room for cotton plants, were exactly parallel to charges leveled in the indictment which had sent the two Uzbek leaders Faizulla Khojaev and Akmal Ikramov to their executions in 1938.[10] In that earlier day, the prosecutor accused Khojaev and Ikramov of engaging in these practices in order to discredit the Soviet regime. By the 1960s, the practices had become Moscow policy.

Corollary Damage

In Uzbekistan, grain deliveries dropped by a third in the years leading up to 1987.[11] In the words of a Russian journalist writing in that year, "The wrong strategy has caused serious troubles, and to continue not to notice them from the heights of the economic plan administration, to consider Central Asia a subtropical paradise where rich Uzbeks (Tajiks, Turkmens, Kirghiz . . .) eat their rice pilav with melons and get rich on 'white gold' is today simply inhumane. . . ."[12]

As an example of the pinch being felt by the public in Uzbekistan, sources in the republic complained that per-capita consumption of meat there in 1987--when conditions were better than they became later on-- was just 26 percent of the so-called Soviet "medical norm."[13] The corresponding figure for milk was 42 percent. In this land noted in the past for an abundance of fruit, consumption of fruit products was said to be only half the medical norm. Millions reportedly still lived in housing sub-standard even for the Soviet Union. It was claimed that, in 1988, 45 percent of Uzbekistan's population "had an average per capita income from all sources of 75 rubles or less a month, in other words below the official subsistence level of 78 rubles a month."[14] Given that the 1989 census gave Uzbekistan's population as 20 million, this meant that nine million people were living below the line.

Massive unemployment among rural Central Asians is another problem traced to the monoculture. It is charged by critics that since Moscow's only interest is to plunder cotton and other Central Asian raw materials, it has deliberately refused to invest capital in building up the economy of the region other than for primary extracting industry or for centrally-operated plants, which rely largely on imported European labor. Unemployment was repeatedly cited as a factor in the 1989 Ferghana Valley riots. As a result of it, more than two-fifths of the population of Uzbekistan were said in the early perestroika period to be "dependent on others," whether relatives or the state.[15]

In the past, when Moscow still exercised a large measure of control over the media, there had been a tendency to blame unemployment in part on the Central Asians themselves and their cultural conditioning, which allegedly led them to shun work in industry in favor of service jobs (men as barbers and cooks, women as secretaries) and to refuse to leave their overpopulated home villages for factory work in the unfamiliar surroundings of towns and cities.[16] Writers in the Moscow press, infuriated many Uzbeks by insinuating--whether justifiably or not--that, in the countryside, where the majority of natives still reside, males spent much of their time on trading in the "second economy" or on social activities centered around Islam, allegedly leaving it to women and children to meet production quotas on state and collective farms.

While there may have been an element of truth in such statements, the fact that they were made by outsiders perceived as responsible for the overall economic disaster, or by native officials acting on behalf of the center, only increased local resentment. Above all, in indigenous eyes the lack of jobs was due first and foremost to the center's stingy investment policies, which were seen as directly related to the monoculture in that they reflected Moscow's desire to have Uzbekistan remain little more than a gigantic cotton plantation and base for other raw materials to be exploited by the central planners. A former Soviet economist now at Harvard who knows Central Asia from having worked in the region has found, in a detailed study of cotton-related problems, that there was no objective justification for Moscow's refusal to provide investment funds to construct textile factories in the region, close to the source of raw material.[17]

Unbalanced economic growth and environmental damage due to over-cultivation of cotton reached the point where, even if Gorbachev's economic reforms were to succeed in all other parts of the country, the Central Asian republics--already at the bottom rank of USSR living standards--appeared doomed to suffer steadily deteriorating conditions for the rest of this century and beyond. One of the world's fastest-increasing populations had exhausted the resources available for further economic development to match its expanding needs.

The Demographic Dimension

Table 4.4 shows how Uzbekistan's demographic explosion from 1959 through 1989, the year of the last Soviet census, has added to the strain on the Uzbek economy.

There has been some slowing of growth, but it has been predicted that the population of Uzbekistan will reach 26.5 million by 2000, and 32 million by 2010.[18] These estimates are based upon a projected average annual population growth rate of 2.6 percent for the first period, and a lower (based on official hopes that the rate will taper off still more) rate of 1.9 for the second. These figures include the slower-growing Russians and other Europeans who live in the republic. The actual figure for Asian population growth is therefore correspondingly much higher.

If one considers Uzbekistan together with its three neighboring Central Asian republics of Kirghizia, Tajikistan, and Turkmenistan as a cultural and religious bloc, the combined 1989 population was nearly 33 million, with an annual growth rate of 2.57. At this rate, the

The Cotton Monoculture

TABLE 4.4 Population of Uzbekistan in Millions by Year

	Population			Annual Growth Rates	
1959	1970	1979	1989	1959-89	1979-89
8.119	11.799	15.391	19.906	3.03	2.61

Sources: Narkhoz 70; for 1989, Ann Sheehy, "Preliminary Results of the All-Union Census Published," *Report on the USSR*, May 19, 1989, p.3.

population of the four republics would increase by 2000 to more than 43 million, by 2010 to 56 million, while European population growth in the USSR is essentially stagnant. In Uzbekistan, Tajikistan and Turkmenistan, the overall growth rates for all nationalities from 1979 to 1989 were 2.61, 3.01, and 2.86 percent, respectively. In Kirghizia, with a relatively large proportion of Russians the rate was less, 1.97 percent. In general, a population with a sustained annual growth rate of 3.0 percent will double in about 24 years, with a rate of 2.5 percent in about 29 years.

The higher Asian growth places special strains on the resources of the three cotton-growing republics of Uzbekistan, Tajikistan, and Turkmenistan, where European settlers are relatively scarce, particularly in the poorer rural areas. Still, the idea of families with large children, which the Uzbeks call *serfarzandlik*, is deeply engrained in tradition and a source of much ethnic pride.

Thus, on top of the injury to the Uzbeks' morale caused by the economic and environmental consequences of the monoculture, they were further affronted by attempts of spokesmen for the central authorities to deal with these problems by telling them to slow their population growth. This merely added a new irritant to relations between Uzbekistan and Moscow, one that lent itself to political exploitation by nationalist forces at home.

For example, former Uzbek First Secretary Nishanov, whose reputation had already been tarnished in Uzbek eyes by the perception that he was a renegade servant of Moscow's interests, added to his local unpopularity by pressing for lower birth-rates. His warning about having too many babies, which was unprecedented in public discourse in Uzbekistan, was viewed as tantamount to desecration of the inviolable child-bearing tradition of Central Asian Muslims. Speaking of high birth-rates at a plenum of the republican Central Committee in Tashkent in January 1988, the then newly-appointed Nishanov had cautioned:

> This rate of demographic growth is far ahead of the republic's economic and social development. The contrast is ever clearer between the high rate of growth of the population and of labor reserves and the low level of efficiency of public production, between the need for social benefits and realistic possibilities of satisfying them. The number of people who are not self-supporting is two-fifths of the entire population. Why, labor productivity and what the worker produces are lower among us both in industry and agriculture by one-and-a-half to two times the average for the country as a whole. . . .
>
> . . . If this tendency continues, the population's living standard in the foreseeable future will. . . not only not increase, it will decline.[19]

This attempt by Nishanov to broach the issue set in motion what was to become a howl of protest. A few weeks after his speech, a newspaper writer cautiously launched an indirect challenge to Nishanov's proposal. Describing family planning in the Uzbek context as limiting children to "five or six" per family, he suggested that Uzbekistan was not yet ready to achieve even that modest goal. The reasons: the medical sector was not up to the challenge, and "people are not prepared psychologically."[20] This last point was brought home very quickly at a meeting on the subject held soon afterward in Tashkent, where young writers took to the podium with a less cautious approach, resorting to what an official newspaper called, disapprovingly, "hasty appeals to the kindling of national feelings." Their remarks were reported to resound "like thunder in a clear sky."[21] Again emboldened by the newly-developing glasnost, Nishanov's critics argued that the problem was not too many babies but inferior living standards, and that it should be attacked on that basis, not by depriving Central Asians of their traditional large families. (That this was a circular argument, given the reverse link between population and living standards, did not deter the critics.) In suggesting "reasonable family planning," Nishanov was flying in the face of one of the principal ingredients of Uzbek ethnic pride, *serfarzandlik*. Nishanov's departure from Uzbekistan in June 1989 to become Chairman of the Council of Nationalities of the USSR Supreme Soviet--a promotion seen by Uzbek patriots as a reward for his slavish devotion to Moscow and his willingness to sell out the interests of his own people--was greeted with enthusiasm by many of his countrymen. His successor, Karimov, has pointedly refrained from such blunt talk about the demographic problem.

Whatever the true state of affairs, spokesmen for the Uzbek elites, playing to an aroused public, continued to blame the economic crisis not on demography but on Moscow's exploitation. They were able to use the gravity of the economic crisis as a telling weapon against the hegemony of the central administration.

Other remedies suggested by the center to cope with the unemployment problem only increased popular resentment. In addition to much-resented proposals for population control, planners began pressing local enterprises to convert to two- or three-shift operation so that a single workplace could provide multiple employment. Given the inadequacy of service facilities like transportation and catering even during daylight hours, nighttime work was viewed not as a welcome source of additional jobs but as a new form of economic exploitation.

Another unpopular scheme put forth by the central planners was to reduce population pressures by moving surplus Central Asians to labor-short regions like Siberia, where they can earn their keep. Central Asian love of the homeland is clearly borne out by census data; despite all of the dislocations of the Soviet period, and the region's socioeconomic and environmental problems, very few natives have moved to other parts of the Soviet Union. When proposed some years ago, a mandatory relocation scheme met with massive popular resistance, even from native officials loyal to Moscow they realized its explosive potential). In recent years, the scheme has acquired a still more sinister coloration in Uzbek eyes with a suggestion, published in the vernacular press, that recent ethnic violence--notably the 1989 Ferghana riots whose principal victims were Meskhetian Turkic settlers deported from their homeland by Stalin--was in fact fomented by Moscow agents plotting to frighten the Meskhetians into moving into labor-short areas of the Russian republic.[22] In any case, the Karimov administration in Uzbekistan has been soft-pedaling this scheme, like other unpopular ones originating in Moscow.

The Monoculture as Political Weapon

Part of the Uzbeks' complaint against the monoculture has been that it vitiated the region's economic independence, forcing it to rely on trade with other areas. Local economists point to the irony of shipping their republic's cotton to European Russia, then buying it back in the form of textiles. There is also outrage that in recent years, Moscow has been selling Central Asian cotton abroad--to countries like France and Germany—and keeping the hard-currency proceeds for its own purposes.

The monoculture also has been condemned for its dependence on large-scale operation of state and collective farms, where regimentation of labor, often under harsh conditions, reduced the independence of individual rural families. Indeed, until Nishanov's departure from Uzbekistan for Moscow in 1989 and his replacement by Karimov, officials had openly broken solemn promises, made in the spirit of perestroika, to stop using schoolchildren to help in the cotton harvest. They continued in some areas to resort to the longstanding practice, anathema to Uzbek parents, of taking pupils out of class, even in the cold months of November and December, and sending them to work in the fields along with other "volunteers" from the cities.

In sum, the cotton monoculture, intended originally to serve the interests of the center, provided the Uzbek elites with a potent political and psychological weapon for use against that very center. As Moscow's power in Central Asia declined, there were few inhibitions on public vilification of the monoculture and those behind it. Typical of the complaints voiced by Central Asians over Moscow's insatiable demands for more and more cotton was an outburst by the Uzbek poet Muhammad Ali, who lamented that "the worst thing is that the cotton monoculture has become an ethical and cultural monoculture," making cotton dominate every aspect of life. He charged that even after the evils of excessive emphasis on cotton had been recognized, cotton was still king: although the 1988 plan called for seeding acreage with one-third grasses, to permit limited (and still inadequate) crop-rotation, the actual figure was only 14 to 15 percent. He insisted that the one way to restore the disappearing Aral Sea was "liquidation" of the monoculture, and that this must be done in the next Five Year Plan. The poet saw 1988's modest reduction in the cotton quota as only a "first step." He dismissed the idea--stressed in traditional propaganda--that "cotton is the pride of the Uzbek people" as "false patriotism."[23]

The Cotton Monoculture

By late 1990, Uzbek President (and Party First Secretary) Karimov was telling an audience of his countrymen that the republic's desperate economic situation was the result of "many years of central economic policy that had made Uzbekistan into a raw-materials base," and that this exploitation had been further compounded by Moscow's requisition of Uzbek cotton "at unjustly low prices."[24]

Notes

1. On this issue, see Annette Bohr, "Self-Immolation Among Central Asian Women," *Radio Liberty Research (RLR)* 126/88, March 20, 1988.

2. *Uzbekskaya SSR*, Tashkent (Gosudarstvennoe izdatel'stvo Uzbekskoy SSR) 1963, p. 221.

3. *Pravda*, July 17, 1988. This article consisted of interviews with former Uzbek Party officials in prison in Moscow on charges of corruption.

4. In 1988 it was reported that in five of the thirteen oblasts of Usbekistan, one kilogram of mineral fertilizer was being used for every 1.2 to 1.5 kilos of cotton raised, almost a one-to-one ratio (see *Pravda Vostoka*, March 13, 1988). Use of chemicals in Uzbek agriculture has been said to be ten times higher than the Soviet or American average.

5. *Pravda Vostoka*, March 13, 1988.

6. This discussion is based on *Uzbekskaya SSR*, p. 215.

7. *Uzbekskaya SSR*, p. 212.

8. *Sovet Ozbekistani*, January 31, 1988, and *Pravda Vostoka*, March 13, 1988.

9. *Sharq yulduzi*, October 1987, pp. 5 *ff*.

10. See People's Commissariat of Justice of the USSR, *Report of Court Proceedings in the Case of the Anti-Soviet "Bloc of Rights and Trotskyites Heard Before the Collegium of the Supreme Court of the USSR, Moscow, March 2-13, 1938*, Moscow 1938, p. 232 (in English).

11. *Narodnoe khozyaystvo SSSR v 1970 g. (Narkhoz 70)*, pp. 219, 233, 240.

12. "Sud'ba Arala" (The Fate of the Aral), *Literaturnaya gazeta*, November 18, 1987.

13. Ibid.

14. See Ann Sheehy, "Social and Economic Background to Recent Events in the Fergana Valley," Radio Liberty *Report on the USSR*, June 23, 1989.

15. Rafik N. Nishanov, Report to Ninth Uzbek Plenum, *Pravda Vostoka*, January 31, 1988.

16. See *Obshchestvennye nauki v Uzbekistane*, No. 11, 1986, p. 9 on the Uzbeks' alleged affinity for being barbers, etc. The economist R. Ubaydullaeva revealed in 1987 in an article on unemployment (*Kommunist Uzbekistana*, No.

10, 1987, pp. 24-29) that only about half of working Uzbeks were employed in regular agricultural and industrial jobs (p. 25).

17. Boris Rumer, "Central Asian Cotton: The Picture Now," *Central Asian Survey*, Vol. 6, No. 4, 1987, p. 87.

18. *Sovet Ozbekistani*, June 17, 1989.

19. Sources: *Narkhoz 70*; for 1989, Ann Sheehy, "Preliminary Results of the All-Union Census Published," *Report on the USSR*, May 19, 1989, p. 3.

20. *Ozbekistan adabiyati va san"ati (OAS)*, March 4, 1988, p. 7.

21. *Pravda Vostoka*, March 3, 1988.

22. This accusation was the subject of a full page in *OAS* for October 5, 1990, which implicated officials acting on behalf of Moscow and charged that the actual unrest was instigated by non-Uzbeks wearing Uzbek national dress.

23. Muhammad Ali (Akhmedov), "Avladlar nasibasi," *OAS*, August 26, 1988.

24. *Pravda Vostoka*, November 29, 1990.

5

Rape of the Environment

In Uzbekistan, people who had known for years of their republic's environmental problems had little opportunity until the mid-1980s to raise the issue publicly, given censorship of the media and the charges of subversion that were sure to follow an incautious utterance. With glasnost and the wave of disclosures that followed Chernobyl, persons with environmental concerns began to be more vocal.

The April 26, 1986 explosion of a nuclear reactor at Chernobyl in the Ukraine focused prolonged world attention for the first time on the Soviet environmental crisis. In the aftermath of Chernobyl it became obvious that those who controlled the Soviet economic machine had neglected safety norms and other humanitarian considerations in a ruthless effort to ratchet their inefficient system up to a higher level of performance. From all corners of the country, the Soviet communications media began to report new stories of environmental disasters.

Thanks to many trouble-spots, of which Chernobyl was only the most dramatic and visible, the world now knows that in pre-perestroika days environmental abuse was endemic in the command economies of the Soviet Union and Eastern Europe, where there was no separation of political and economic powers. In the words of one Polish environmentalist, it was "like a hare that was entrusted with taking care of a head of cabbage."[1]

The Central Asian republics had their unfortunate share in this ecological catastrophe. The cotton monoculture and its drain on water and land resources, accompanied by pollution from pesticides, herbicides and chemical fertilizers, played a leading role. At the same time, the problem was exacerbated the effluvium from industrial plants sited in the region by fiat of planners in far-off Moscow. These factories used up local raw materials but shipped their output to other parts of the Soviet Union, generally employing non-indigenous labor for all but the most menial jobs. The wastes from these alien presences fouled the atmosphere and poisoned land and water. Industrial pollution was one of the underlying causes of the 1989 ethnic riots in the Ferghana Valley.

Inevitably, Uzbek environmental complaints took on an ethnic coloration. Although depredations to the environment had taken place with the tacit acquiescence of Uzbek officials, it was clear to average Uzbeks that the real culprits were the central planners in that very Russian city of Moscow. Looking back, Uzbeks recalled that even in the early days of Russian rule, before the Soviet period, most irrigation projects had been failures, "causing enormous harm to the population"; at times, the failures created large tracts of swampland and spread fever.[2] When it became known in 1989 that, on top of everything else, Central Asian territory was being used by the center as a dump for toxic wastes, some of them nuclear, transported in from other parts of the Soviet Union, local media stressed Russia proper as a point of origin. Such circumstances were grist for the political mill of Uzbek nationalists in their struggle to garner public support against the center's hegemony.

Cotton as Chief Culprit

In Uzbekistan, the cotton monoculture was demonstrably the greatest cause of environmental ills. A principal factor was its drain on regional water resources.

Uzbekistan and Central Asia's other cotton-growing republics depend for water on two major rivers, the Amu-Darya and Syr-Darya ("*darya*," from the Persian for river, is used in the local Turkic languages as well as in Tajik).[3] Both rivers rise in mountains to the east and flow westward through desert and oases toward the Aral Sea, a large body of water on the boundary between Uzbekistan and Kazakhstan and near Uzbekistan's border with Turkmenistan. Between them, the two rivers attain an average annual flow of 78 cubic-kilometers.[4] That is about 13 percent of the Mississippi's flow, or roughly equivalent to that of the Nile at Aswan.

By the late 1980s, practically *all* of this combined water resource was being diverted to irrigation. The mouth of the Syr was reported by then to be completely dry, and only a paltry three to four cubic-kilometers per year[5] was reaching the mouth of the Amu, less than 10 percent of its flow, at the point where it emptied into the Aral. Worse, a Karakalpak delegate to the Soviet Congress complained in June 1989 that so far that year the Amu had received "not a single drop" of the eight cubic-kilometers of water that were its "sanitary" minimum.[6]

The dire economic and social consequences of the water shortage have been described by a British economist:

> A failure to obtain access to additional water resources will in all probability, prevent the regeneration of Uzbek agriculture. And that, in the absence of growing subsidies, will make it difficult to ensure continuing increases in the incomes of rural population. This must, inevitably, increase levels of popular dissatisfaction (even if, at the same time, it increases the rate of out-migration and so helps to solve the problem of labour shortage in Siberia and the Central Industrial Provinces).
>
> Thus, it is possible that an impoverished or dislocated "peasantry" will emerge at the same time that reduced growth leads to the frustration of aspirations for mobility into the economic and social elite. In 1982 there were just over a million "specialists" employed in the USSR; they will want to see their offspring attain specialist status too. So will numbers of workers and peasants. Given the size of Uzbek families this betokens a significant continuing demand on the economy to produce high-level jobs in the next two or three decades, a demand that it is unlikely to be able to satisfy. The combination of a frustrated potential elite and an impoverished or dislocated "peasantry" may prove politically and socially explosive.[7]

The 1980s brought a wealth of emerging evidence that the region's appalling water crisis had already had a calamitous impact on the economy and the environment. As is discussed in greater detail below, in the sensitive area of public health the consequences were particularly acute. Yet officials were slow to halt expansion of irrigated land. In Turkmenistan, the expansion actually picked up speed between 1985 and 1986, a rate of 7.1 percent compared with that republic's 21-year rate of 4.1 percent. As late as September 1990, by which time the Uzbek hue and cry about environmental abuse had already struck a disastrous blow to Moscow's political interests, it was revealed that construction had not been halted on a new irrigation canal that was threatening to undermine and destroy the ancient historical monuments of the Uzbek city of Khiva.[8]

Part of the irony of the situation caused by poor planning was implicit in the fact that while areas of Uzbekistan were desperate for water, the once arid city of Ashkhabad, the capital of neighboring Turkmenistan near the 500-mile-long Kara Kum irrigation canal was undergoing flooding. The Kara Kum was carrying water through the desert at the rate of 7,000 cubic-feet per second, enough of it seeping into Ashkhabad from the inefficient and wasteful hydraulic system created by the canal to require 150 pumping stations working night and day to deal with the invasion of polluted underground water.

The Vanishing Aral

The Aral sea is a staggering example of the water crisis. It was once the world's fourth largest inland body of water--larger in area than Lake Michigan. The Aral basin had been producer of 95 percent of all Soviet cotton.[9] With its tributary rivers diverted to irrigation, Soviet scientists predicted in 1987 that at the existing rate of evaporation--40 cubic-kilometers per year--the sea-bed would be essentially dry by the year 2010. Already the drying had created, where once were waves, a new desert tract larger than Massachusetts. The Aral fishing fleet, which in its day produced more than a tenth of the entire Soviet catch and helped save Russian cities from starvation during the famines of the 1920s, was now rusting at its moorings, half-covered with sand and dozens of miles from the nearest water.[10]

The plight of the Aral became known throughout Uzbekistan in January 1987, when an emotional eyewitness article was published in the intellectual weekly *Ozbekistan adabiyati va san"ati* by the writer Ma"ruf Jalil.[11] The article, entitled "The Sea that is Fleeing Its Shores," was accompanied by dramatic photographs of sand dunes surrounding the rusting fishing fleet.

Later that year, basic facts about the Aral were made public record in two consecutive issues of the monthly organ of the Uzbek Academy of Sciences, *Obshchestvennye nauki v Uzbekistane*. One article was by a team of scholars headed by the historian S.K. Kamalov, chairman of the Karakalpak branch of the Uzbek Academy;[12] the second was written by D. S. Yadgarov, chairman of the Council of Ministers of the

Karakalpak Autonomous Soviet Socialist Republic (ASSR).[13] The Karakalpak ASSR, whose approximately one million inhabitants are situated near the fast-receding southern shoreline of the Aral, at the delta of the Amu-Darya, has borne much of the brunt of the disaster together with the neighboring Khorezm Oblast of Uzbekistan and Turkmenistan's Tashauz Oblast.

The Kamalov team referred to the Aral's plight as "an unprecedented fact of anthropogenic impact on nature," one that was "unique, without analogy in its scale," and "the work of man's hand, of his stormy economic activity."[14] The authors calculated that, if the Aral were to dry completely, it would be replaced by 60,000 square-kilometers of desert. They did not hesitate to place the blame on "extensive irrigation of agriculture, onesided reclamation of new lands and farfetched decisions in general, and the mistakes of scholars" who approved the corresponding measures after only superficial study. Two Soviet scholars, both with European names, were singled out for personal censure.

The newly-created desert, with its heavy salt content, was said to differ from the nearby Kyzyl Kum and Kara Kum deserts by virtue of its scant vegetation and vast barren wastes. Sand dunes were advancing southward on the former seabed at the rate of one kilometer a year. Hardest hit by this manmade tragedy was the former Aral littoral, which once had a thriving community of 10,000 fishermen,[15] but the impact extended far beyond the immediate area because of changes in climate and soil conditions.

According to Soviet scientists, the climatic influence of the Aral in its pristine state had been considerable. Its effect on temperature extended 200 or 250 kilometers beyond its perimeter, and on the moisture-content of the air, 350 or 400 kilometers. At its original size, the Aral absorbed solar energy equivalent to seven billion metric tons of conventional fuel annually, moderating the extreme heat of the Central Asian summer. It fed this energy back into the atmosphere in colder weather to produce a warming effect.[16] The shrinking of the sea has raised summer temperatures, increased the dryness of the air, and shortened the frost-free season. This poses a threat to cotton-growing in the entire lower basin of the Amu, which used to account for more than one million metric tons of raw cotton annually, since it was only the presence of the Aral that made it possible to raise cotton at such northerly latitudes. Scientists have predicted that cotton production in the Aral region may in future be completely wiped out by ecological changes occurring there. As if to confirm this forecast, a snowstorm that took place in 1989 unusually late in the year--at the time of the May Day celebrations--damaged one million hectares of cotton plants, forcing nine-tenths of the area to be replanted. In the same year, a crippling drought was attributed to the dwindling of the Aral and its climatic consequences.[17]

Soil erosion from the new desert has affected agriculture far beyond the immediate area. By 1987, more than one billion metric tons of salty dust from the dried eastern portion of the Aral had already been spread by the wind over a belt that ranged up to 400 kilometers long and 40 kilometers wide, damaging previously fertile crop land. More salt and sand were being deposited at the rate of 70 million metric tons a year, destroying soil fertility. Some of this noxious material was traveling over great distances, with toxic salts deposited "1000 km. to the southeast of the sea in the fertile Ferghana Valley, in Georgia on the Black Sea coast, and even along the arctic shore of the Soviet Union."[18]   Also by 1987, the frequency of destructive dust-storms had doubled, from five or six a year to nine or twelve.[19] The result of wind erosion from the Aral was compounded by construction throughout the cotton-growing area of a large system of collecting-basins to hold water for irrigation until needed. When full, these basins destroyed plant life on the bottom; when empty, they allowed the soil, no longer protected by plant growth, to be carried away.[20]

Corollary Problems

Not solely in the Aral district but generally throughout the region, the problem of wind erosion had been exacerbated by the center's policy of deforestation of the land. Speakers at the 1987 Tashkent symposium (see Chapter 4) described the mass felling of trees which had taken place as part of the frenzy to expand cotton production. This had been done to consolidate fields and reduce barriers to mechanization. One speaker, playing on ethnic feelings, noted pointedly that, while forty percent of the Russian Republic was covered by forests, the corresponding figure for Uzbekistan had been reduced to three percent. In Uzbekistan, where trees once occupied fifteen percent of the land in populated areas, they had come to occupy only one percent in the irrigated zone itself. This increased wind erosion and damage to plants, especially by eliminating protection from the *garmsel*, a hot dry wind "that in two to three hours can undo six to seven months of peasants' work."[21] The painful impact on the comfort and health of cotton-workers was brought home by the accusation voiced at the symposium that deforestation had deprived workers of shade for refuge from the burning Central Asian sun, even during rest-periods.[22]

As the enormity of the Aral crisis became known, there were calls from some quarters to evacuate the entire population of the surrounding area, numbering nearly four million.[23] This zone had the Soviet Union's highest infant mortality: more than 100 babies were dying before reaching the age of one year. A special clinic had to be built at Muynak, a city in the area, to treat diseases caused by the ecology.

Directly related to the problem of the Aral was pollution of the Amu, traditionally a source of water for both drinking and irrigation. Moreover, seepage of polluted water from the Amu was now contaminating other sources of fresh water. Representatives of the Karakalpak ASSR, situated at the delta of the Amu, complained that the river's pollution was largely caused by impurities draining from the upstream Surkhan-Dar'ya, Kashka-Dar'ya, and Bukhara oblasts of Uzbekistan, and the Chardzhou oblast of Turkmenia. A large part of the problem came from water used to rinse from the soil of those oblasts the chemical salts deposited by irrigation and fertilization. In the words of Chairman Yadgarov, a vicious circle was resulting:

> So far there are no precise and unmistakable data as to how much we are losing from pollution of the Amu-Darya water. But one thing is clear: because of it, soil conditions are deteriorating, the salt content of the earth is increasing, and the ability of the Amu-Darya water to rinse away soil salts is diminishing; as a result, it is necessary to increase the amounts of water used both for rinsing and for irrigating plants. The end-result is that the area of heavily-salted lands is rapidly expanding; such lands do not yield even half of their potential harvest.[24]

Salinity of the Aral's tributary water made the sea's predicament still worse. By the beginning of 1987, the average salt content of the Aral had risen to twenty-seven grams/liter, compared with ten grams/liter in 1960.[25] Not only had fishing in the Aral been destroyed, but a once-flourishing muskrat-fur industry in the vicinity was crippled by the effects. Bad as the local consequences of salination of the Aral may have been, the fact that the sea was no longer the region's "natural salt collector" was even worse: instead of absorbing salt from the environment, it now spread it, as noted above, over arable land as winds carried deposits from parts of its bottom that were exposed by desiccation.

Yadgarov estimated that his autonomous republic was losing one-third of its crops due to poor water quality. He also held that, if one factored in the number of man-days lost due to illness of workers and their families caused by impure drinking-water, then the overall cost of the losses to his republic "cancels out the economic effect of increased acreage" in those upstream areas that drain their used water into the river. He demanded that upstream acreage under cultivation be reduced in order to cut down on pollution and bring relief to Karakalpakia.[26] In support of a similar argument, the Kamalov team invoked "one of the fundamental principles of socialist economy—the absolute inadmissibility of developing some regions to the detriment of others."[27]

In the face of such alarming disclosures, people in the area, led by prominent Uzbek intellectuals, made "saving the Aral" the object of a campaign. A "Save the Aral" Committee was formed in Tashkent, headed by the well-known Uzbek writer Pirmat Shermuhamedov. Newspapers featured emotional verse by prominent poets, and on-the-spot reports, to dramatize the ongoing catastrophe.[28] Among prominent contributors to a fund in aid of the Aral were the internationally-known Kirghiz writer Chingiz Aitmatov, the cosmonaut V. A. Dzhanibekov, and the geneticist Academician N. P. Dubinin. The public was invited to send money to Account No. 000700778 in the Kuybyshev district branch of the State Bank in Tashkent.[29] In ensuing years, there was a steady drum-beat of publicity for the plight of the Aral, with local celebrities playing the leading role.

Tragic as it was, the Aral issue was made to order as a theme of nationalism in Uzbekistan, Kazakhstan, and Turkmenistan, the three republics most directly affected. It brought home to the masses the disastrous consequences of reckless cotton expansion imposed by Moscow in order to fulfill its plan quotas. Increased infant mortality in the Aral region, colder winters and hotter summers, clouds of salt and sand carried by wind erosion from the dried-up sea-bed: all of these were tangible phenomena that could be traced directly to the central government's plundering and mismanagement of the region's water resources. As a symbol of environmental abuse, the Aral heightened public outrage over what outsiders had done to the Central Asian homeland.

Uzbeks were appalled by accounts like that of an Uzbek writer who visited the formerly seaside town of Muynak, once situated astride a neck of land with fishing boats moored on both sides, and found only desert as far as the eye could see.[30] He described yellowed drinking water that was "fourteen percent salt." The writer cleverly mobilized Lenin in defense of the Aral, quoting from his 1921 appeal to Aral fishermen to contribute their catch to save Russian cities from famine.[31] Lest readers lose sight of the contrast between the fishermen's generosity and Moscow's denial of water from Siberia, he pointed to a six-kilometer dam built in 1982 (before the decision on denial) to create a 3000-hectare artificial lake for fish breeding, now standing unused for lack of water. The main Uzbek cultural newspaper front-paged the poem "Aral" by the venerable Establishment poet Uyghun, who lamented the sea's calamity as a "horror," pictured salt flats as encroaching on the Aral "like a shroud," warned of the affront to nature and the disgrace in the eyes of future generations, and demanded a remedy.[32]

In Central Asian eyes, the Aral crisis was directly damaging to the prestige of Mikhail Gorbachev, for he had presided over the decision to deny the one source of relief on which people had been pinning their hopes for relief from the water crisis. The project to divert water to Central Asia from rivers of Siberia was already well into the planning stage and appeared on its way to execution when, in August 1986, the central government had announced its cancellation.[33] Whatever the justification for the decision[34] to kill the project, which had been hotly opposed by Russian environmentalists, it was deeply shocking to Central Asian sensibilities and viewed as one more example of regional and ethnic discrimination.

Moscow Reacts: Too Little, Too Late

The leadership in Moscow, faced with the uproar in Central Asia created by the Aral's deteriorating situation and its own decision to withhold relief in the form of Siberian water, began to seek palliative courses of action. A commission was appointed to look into the matter, and in September 1988 it was announced that the Politburo, headed by

Gorbachev, had reviewed the commission's findings and taken a decision to ease the problem.

In fact, the Politburo's decision and the findings of the government commission on which it was based[35] left many questions unanswered, and many problems unsolved. Two facts emerged, however: (1) the leadership remained unwilling to seek relief for Central Asian water problems through a radical cutback in cotton production, as had been suggested by spokesmen for regional interests, and (2) the leadership's August 1986 refusal to remedy the problem through diversion of water from Siberian rivers still stood, despite efforts in some quarters to revive the plan.[36]

It was clear that the actions envisaged by the Politburo, even if fully implemented, stopped far short of restoring the Aral to its former size, and would indeed permit additional shrinkage of the sea before its final stabilization at a further reduced level. Some of the phenomena associated with the problem, particularly the shorter growing-season already caused by loss of the Aral's moderating effect on climate, therefore had become irreversible.

Although it fell far short of providing effective remedies, the Politburo announcement did have the important political consequence of giving official recognition, for the first time, to the harm done to the Central Asian economy and ecology by years of insistence on expanding the cotton monoculture. In his statement published in *Pravda*, the chairman of the government commission, Yurii Antonievich Izrael', went so far as to concede the desirability of a "partial" cutback in cotton production in the Aral basin, but apparently only to the extent required to permit crop-rotation (and thus restore the badly depleted yields of present acreage), the need for which had already been acknowledged.[37] Izrael' also called categorically for a ban on expansion of cotton production to new lands.[38] He admitted that a side-effect of cotton-growing was its deprivation of Central Asians of land needed to raise food for a fast-growing population.

As for the Aral itself, the main focus of the decision was on conservation. The decree dashed the hopes of those Central Asian interests who still clung to the idea that Moscow might come to their rescue by bringing in new water from outside the region. Izrael' declared that water for the Sea "can and must" be found in the area under irrigation. He claimed that, in some instances, waste of water for irrigation amounted to 100 percent over plan. (This emphasis on conservation touched a local nerve, for Uzbeks were resentful of charges in the Soviet central media that they were "wasteful" of water.) He reported, apparently on behalf of the commission, that the efficiency of irrigation could be increased by fifteen to twenty-five percent, thus saving an estimated fifteen cubic-kilometers of water annually. An additional six cubic-kilometers yearly could be restored to the sea, he said, by channeling water drained from the irrigated fields. (Such drainage water, it was already known from other sources, was "saline, frequently above three grams per liter, and pesticide- and herbicide-laden.")[39]

The eventual annual water supply to the Aral, including precipitation, that was envisaged by the Politburo decree came to twenty-five to thirty cubic-kilometers. Yet according to a 1987 estimate, forty-five cubic-kilometers a year of additional water were needed to keep the Aral even at its then-existing level.[40] This left a deficit of fifteen to twenty cubic-kilometers, even after the Politburo's measures were implemented, thus dooming the Aral to further shrinkage until--at some unspecified later date--it became so small that its rate of evaporation would no longer exceed inflow. (The sea had already lost sixty-six percent of its original volume.)[41]

Izrael' indicated that other remedial measures were still being investigated, evidently rather unhurriedly. Among these were the Siberian rivers scheme (which Izrael' downgraded as something that would not have provided water directly for the Aral anyway), a plan to transport water from the Caspian Sea, and even the possibility of acting on clouds to increase rainfall.

The commission chairman listed a number of proposed measures which, in essence, provided for treatment of the symptoms of the problem rather than the cause. First priority was to be accorded to providing the region with pure drinking water piped in from outside and to improving health care. As for the ecological consequences, efforts were to be made to introduce vegetation to the former sea-bed in order to reduce wind-erosion. Where these efforts failed, according to Izrael', there would be attempts at "physical and chemical methods of soil-cover."

The net effect of the Politburo measure was to admit to one and all the gravity of the crisis and its causes while stopping short of effective action. Apparently the once-flourishing Aral fishing industry, for example, was now a thing of the past. Perhaps most troublesome for the future was the fact that none of the proposed measures would restore the Aral's moderating effect on climate as it once was, leaving a situation where several years earlier the growing season in the northern delta of the Amu-Darya had already "been reduced an average of ten days, forcing cotton plantations to switch to rice-growing."[42]

In September 1990, a little more than two years after the Politburo decree, the "Save the Aral" Committee convened a meeting in Tashkent to review progress on implementing it. The findings were bleak. The newspaper *Ozbekistan adabiyati va san"ati* reported that whatever hopes had been awakened by the decree were nothing but a "mirage." The most important measures envisaged in the decree had remained on paper. The newspaper quoted Shermuhamedov, the "Save the Aral" Committee's chairman, as saying that the Aral was still headed for oblivion, that it was now farther than ever from its former banks, and that there had been no diminution in diseases caused by salt pollution or in infant and maternal mortality. All of this despite the fact that more than forty organizations were supposedly engaged in the effort to ease the crisis. The net effect was to speed the death of the Aral, while their appropriations were being squandered. As it was, those appropriations were far from adequate: the all-Union Gosplan had provided only five million rubles, whereas speakers at the meeting said that restoration of normal life in the Aral district would require twelve billion rubles, 240 times what had been given. Various speakers placed the main blame for the fiasco on the all-union government in Moscow. Uzbek officials were also taken to task: the deputy minister of the republican ministry responsible for water economy was said to be unable to answer a question about how much water had been supplied to the Aral since the beginning of the year. But the central government was seen as the chief offender. Participants in the meeting adopted a message to Gorbachev calling for a "decisive solution."

The outcome of the meeting seemed to confirm that, by now, even the Aral's most ardent defenders have all but given up on their dream of restoring the sea to its former splendor. Their last best hope is to find a way of forestalling its total disappearance.

The Health Crisis

While the Aral is perhaps the most visible symbol of the devastation caused by the monoculture, the latter's pernicious effects are not localized to the immediate area of the sea but have been felt far more widely, throughout the cotton-growing region and beyond. In terms of human costs, the most excruciating impact is on longevity and health, especially of small children in those large families that are the pride of Central Asian tradition. The primary cause is massive contamination of drinking-water sources.

If stream-flow reduction on a scale unprecedented in irrigation history was the reason for the desiccation of the Aral, a related phenomenon--permeation of the environment with toxic salts--is also directly traceable to irrigated cotton-growing. At the height of the cotton boom, officials ordered unbridled use of chemicals--herbicides, pesticides, fertilizers--without regard to their environmental impact. There was also the problem of salinity which afflicts all irrigation systems. American specialists have described the phenomenon in the U.S. Far West:

> All water used for irrigation carries salts, and the salt content of the water increases as water evaporates, is consumed by the plants, or passes over saline soils. Salts both in the water and the soil create problems for agriculture; they inhibit plant growth and in extreme cases render the land useless for agriculture. Where drainage is adequate, salts can be flushed from the root zones if there is sufficient rainfall or additional irrigation water is applied for this purpose. But this seldom eliminates the salinity problem.[43]

The lack of abundant water for leaching (rinsing) the soil has aggravated the salt problem in Central Asia. But while leaching eliminates some salt concentrations, it can cause others by creating salt deposits where the leaching run-off collects. This is a special problem in Central Asia, where the environment is essentially a closed system without ocean drainage. An Uzbek journalist once described his impressions of the landscape around Bukhara as his plane circled for a landing there. Through the plane's window he saw white patches, and decided there had been a recent snowstorm. Only on the ground did he learn that the white was not snow but salt precipitated by irrigation.[44]

As we have seen, the salinity of the Aral nearly tripled in less than thirty years due to evaporation of its water and the increased pollution of its water source.

Another difficulty caused by run-off from irrigation and leaching is the raising of the water table in places with inadequate drainage. Ironically, this has meant that in Central Asia, a region with an extreme water shortage, some places have too much water, as in the case of flooding in Ashkhabad noted earlier in this chapter. "The desert," as one prominent Soviet writer told colleagues, "has been turned into swamp."[45] This also increased the problem of salinity: "If the water table reaches the root zone of the plants, capillary action carries water close to the soil surface, where it evaporates and leaves a salt residue."[46]

Drainage from irrigation was a major factor in pollution of drinking-water and the related spread of diseases of the stomach, intestines and liver. It was reported in 1987 that more than eleven cubic-kilometers of used irrigation water yearly were being fed into the Amu alone from irrigation drains, equal to about thirty percent of the flow reaching the river's middle course at the town of Darganata. This was said to be a forty-percent increase in a period of only three years. In summer, when irrigation was at its peak and the river's natural flow down due to lack of rainfall, mineral content of the water reached 2.5 to 2.8 grams per liter. This water was considered unfit not only for drinking but even for irrigation, yet plans were under way to drain additional irrigation water into the river.[47]

It was reported that thirty percent of communal water systems and fifty percent of isolated systems (at factories and farms, for example) in Uzbekistan did not meet modern sanitary standards. Moreover, a fifth of the population--and half in rural areas--did not have access to drinking-water systems. They had to rely on wells and open-flowing ditches and canals ("*aryks*" and "*ankhars*"), many of which were contaminated.[48]

Thanks in part to glasnost, it became apparent that the region was in the throes of a major health crisis. One response was a flurry of activity, particularly in summer, designed to alleviate medical problems, particularly those of women and children, stemming from ecological phenomena. Large "brigades" of doctors and other specialists from other parts of the Soviet Union were rushed to Central Asia during July and August, the season when infant mortality is highest due to intestinal diseases. According to one report, in a single year this effort saved the lives of 500 children.[49]

In mid-August of 1987, the USSR Minister of Health, the internationally-known physician Evgenii I. Chazov (who has since left his post), told a meeting of the republican party *aktiv* in Tashkent that the "grave" state of the drinking-water supply was the basic cause of an increase in acute infectious intestinal diseases. He upbraided those present for the poor quality of sanitation and medical care in the republic. Once again, a Moscow representative had blamed Uzbekistan for problems that the Uzbeks themselves were laying at Moscow's door. Indeed, improvement in medical care depended in large part on slow-moving construction of new facilities and installation of modern equipment, but the tight investment policies of the Gorbachev administration did not bode well for early progress, even though priority was being given to certain projects to pipe drinking-water into the Aral region over long distances.

The impact of the contaminated water system was mind-boggling. In one district of Uzbekistan, chemical salts in the milk of nursing mothers were officially reported to be "several times normal." A Karakalpak writer pleaded with the Congress of People's Deputies, "This defies the imagination--mother's milk turned to poison."[50] In Uzbekistan's neighboring Turkmenistan, the rate of reported infant deaths soared by 12 percent from 1985 to 1986.[51] In some Central Asian oblasts, one infant in ten was dying before reaching the age of one year.[52] Still, the indigenous population of the Central Asian republics kept on (and keeps on) growing by about 3 percent a year, enough to double it in less than a generation.

Local media were now pulling few punches in publicizing the health crisis. An Uzbek television program, "We Ache for the Fate of the Aral," described "the menacing deterioration of the epidemiological situation, and the rise in infection with life-threatening diseases among the inhabitants of Karakalpakia, Khorezm, and adjacent oblasts . . ."[53] Another account reported that a 150-bed clinic and medical research institute has been opened in Nukus, the capital of Karakalpakia, its opening linked directly with the desertification of the Aral region.[54] Participants in a round-table discussion organized by the newspaper *Sovet Ozbekistani* referred to the great incidence of hepatitis (*sariq kasalligi*) in Uzbekistan as caused by "disruption of the ecological balance."[55] The same media that not long ago had been praising the Moscow leadership for its enlightened policy and thanking the Russian "elder brother" for his fraternal assistance were now going all out to drive home the disasters wrought by seven decades of Soviet rule.

Nuclear Contamination: From Russia with Love?

On top of Uzbekistan's other environmental ills, in late 1989 fear of nuclear contamination entered the picture with disclosures of an alleged nuclear dump near Tashkent for radioactive wastes produced in other parts of the Soviet Union. The Moscow region was cited as one of the points of origin of this potentially dangerous material, a further environmental irritant to bruised Uzbek ethnic sensitivities.

It was charged that the population of Tashkent and environs was in danger from radioactive and other harmful substances which had been accumulating for years at a dump site near the city. The author of this accusation was Dada Khan Nuriy, an Uzbek writer who specializes in environmental questions.[56] Nuriy offered proof that some of these dangerous materials had been brought to Uzbekistan from other Soviet republics, including the RSFSR. He accused officials of systematically lying to the Uzbek public about the nature and origin of the wastes, on orders from higher up.

Nuriy quoted an Uzbek scientist, Academician Bekjan A. Tashmuhamedov, as affirming, on the basis of scientific calculations, that the "extremely dangerous" materials lying buried at the site "are enough to exterminate every living thing in the entire Tashkent region." The population of Tashkent oblast, which had doubled in the past thirty years, was now more than two million.

Ironically, the dump, known as "Yawchiqqan,"[57] was located in the Bostanlyk district of Tashkent oblast, a scenic area near the Uzbek capital, where for years preservationists have been concentrating last-ditch efforts to prevent disfigurement of the landscape by industrial development. It was next to the village of Haydar Ali, with a population of several thousand, across the river from the suburban city of Chirchik, about thirty kilometers from Tashkent. From Yawchiqqan, Tashkent can be seen "as clearly as the palm of your hand."

The author wrote of toxic powders lying around wet and boiling up into the air from spontaneous combustion, and of huge pools of black waste. He quoted an elderly resident of the village, Toqsanbay-Ata Qalimbetov, on the dump's environmental impact:

"Its smell invades our village. You can't breathe. In summertime you can't get a night's sleep. It's especially hard on young children."

Another inhabitant, Jilqibay Jaldasov, described the scene when it rained:

"Water flowing from the dump turns into poison. If livestock belonging to the kolkhoz or individuals drink it, they will die by the hundreds. Recently three head of cattle died."

Still another inhabitant, Khuydaykul Narbekov, informed the author:

"If you take a look around that place, your eye is struck by thousands of corpses of various kinds of dead birds."

Nuriy went into detail about the attempts by officials to cover up the existence of the Yawchiqqan dump. Possibly because of their opposition, his article was rather vague about the exact nature of the materials buried there and the level of their radioactivity. He did report, however, that Pit #8 at the dump was filling up with toxic refuse, including more than a thousand tons of acid waste with radioactive and highly toxic arsenic compounds evidently transported from the Moscow region. It appeared from his article that Uzbeks were particularly outraged by indications that their republic had been selected as a dumping ground for toxic wastes from the RSFSR and other republics.

If Nuriy's story was sparse in scientific detail, he did a thorough job of documenting the evasiveness and mendacity of officialdom. At first, the public had been assured that the dump wastes came only from Uzbek enterprises, not even from as far away as the neighboring Central Asian republics. Then one official who had insisted on that point reversed himself under persistent questioning, admitting that some of the wastes had come from Kazakhstan but refusing to say anything about other points of origin. Finally, the site's director, F. Saidumarov, also caved in under questioning at a dramatic confrontation with environmentalists, and confessed to the Moscow connection. Here is part of Nuriy's record of the session with Saidumarov:

"What is the total of radioactive materials in the pits at the site?"

93

"I can't tell you anything specific."

"Do you know about the presence in the composition of the materials buried under the earth of many compounds that are extremely dangerous for human life and the environment?"

"Yes, I know. But they are all from here! After all, radioactive wastes have to be buried somewhere! Who else would allow them to be buried on their own territory?"

"You're right, no one would allow them to be buried on his own territory, especially not right on top of a city where millions are living! But you're burying them!"

"They haven't been buried. No wastes have been brought from outside (Uzbekistan)."

"Is that true?"

"Yes, it's true!"

"But we have evidence! And now we can release it to the public. . . Won't you be ashamed afterward? . . ."

This unexpected information placed Saidumarov in an awkward situation and forced him to break his silence, producing the following admission by him:

"As long as we have glasnost, then so be it: the truth is, comrades, that in 1985, on instructions from higher authority, arsenic wastes were brought from the Ministry of Electronics Industry in the Moscow region and buried. . . . I had to obey orders."

Even after this, Nuriy noted, Saidumarov was unwilling to say from "which republics" the instructions had come.

Nuriy condemned years of media cover-up of the dump, and the fact that it had taken him six months to get his own story into print. He was particularly scathing of an earlier story put out by Yu. Kruzhilin, a reporter for Uztag, the Uzbek press agency, of evidently Russian origin, who had allegedly concealed and distorted facts about the site, claiming that it was "far from any human habitation." (Kruzhilin had already blotted his copybook with the Uzbek intelligentsia back in December 1988, when he co-authored a story likening the popular poet and political activist Muhammad Salih to Nazi propaganda chief Josef Goebbels for having complained to a *New York Times* correspondent about Soviet cotton exploitation of Uzbekistan.)

The writer also recalled a July 1988 incident in which the Russian Second Secretary of the Uzbek Communist Party, Vladimir Petrovich Anishchev, was so angered by the success of Uzbek scientists and cultural workers in publicizing the ecological problems of the Bostanlyk district that he called a press-conference and branded the group "liars." When a Russian writer based in Uzbekistan, Evgeniy Berezikov, went to Anishchev's office to remonstrate with him over this disrespectful treatment of his Uzbek colleagues, his fellow-Russian threw him out, heaving a book at his head. Anishchev, whose conduct had made him singularly unpopular in Uzbekistan, was later transferred out of the republic.

In Nuriy's view, "any civilized state" would require by law that hazardous wastes be sealed in containers and, even at great cost, placed in the ocean or some other place where human beings do not set foot, with people who violate the law being severely punished. "As for us," he wrote, "we praise ourselves foolishly for saving on costs." Saying that "nature's cup of patience is full," he urged in the name of future generations that the warnings of prominent scientists be heeded, and concluded with a slogan in capital letters:

"NATURE DOES NOT CONDONE VIOLENCE!"

While there can be little doubt that the raising of environmental issues in Uzbekistan, especially by prominent native intellectuals like Dada Khan Nuriy, was motivated by genuine concern over the issues themselves, it is also certain that the issues were explosive ammunition in the hands of those who were pursuing a political agenda.

Notes

1. Quoted in Fred Singleton (ed.), *Environmental Problems in the Soviet Union and Eastern Europe*, Boulder and London (Lynne Rienner) 1987.

2. V. V. Barthold, *Istoriya kul'turnoy zhizni Turkestana,* Leningrad (USSR Academy of Sciences Press) 1927, pp. 151-55.

3. From ancient times, the Amu and Syr have also been known in the West by their classical names of Oxus and Jaxartes.

4. "Aral yashamaghi kerak" (The Aral Must Live), *Sharq yulduzi,* No. 10, 1987, p. 7.

5. *Literaturnaya gazeta,* November 18, 1987.

6. Tolapbergan Kaipberganov, quoted in *Pravda Vostoka,* June 3, 1989.

7. Alastair McAuley, "Economic Development and Political Nationalism in Uzbekistan," *Central Asian Survey,* Vol. 5, No. 3/4, 1986, p. 179.

8. *Ozbekistan adabiyati va san"ati (OAS),* September 14, 1990. The author of this revelation was Erkin Madrahimov, an official of the writers' organization in Khorezm Oblast, where Khiva is located. Once again, it was an Uzbek creative intellectural who was in the forefront of the attack on central environmental policy.

9. *Pravda,* September 12, 1988.

10. Ma"ruf Jalil, "Qirchaq qachayatgan dengiz" (The Sea That Is Fleeing Its Shore), *OAS,* January 16, 1987.

11. Ibid.

12. S. K. Kamalov, S. K. Kabulov, E. L. Zolotarev, A. A. Rafikov, "Antropogennoe opustynivanie priaral'ia" (Anthropogenic Desertification of the Aral Region), *Obshchestvennye nauki v Uzbekistane (ONU),* No. 4, 1987, pp. 8 *ff.* Unless otherwise indicated, the information presented here is derived from the Kamalov team's report.

13. D. S. Yadgarov, "Voprosy intensifikatsii i ratsional'nogo ispol'zovaniya osnovnykh fondov Karakalpakskoy ASSR" (Problems of Intensification and Rational Exploitation of the Basic Resources of the Karakalpak ASSR), *ONU,* No. 3, 1987, pp. 15 *ff.*

14. Kamalov *et al.,* p. 8.

15. Ibid.

16. *Literaturnaya gazeta,* November 18, 1987.

17. Rafik N. Nishanov, Report to the Thirteenth Plenum of the Uzbek Communist Party, *Pravda Vostoka,* May 20, 1989. Also, "Zasukha" (Drought), *Pravda Vostoka,* June 27, 1989.

18. Philip P. Micklin, "Desiccation of the Aral Sea: A Water Management Disaster in the Soviet Union," *Science,* September 2, 1988, p. 1172 (citing Soviet sources).

19. *Literaturnaya gazeta,* November 18, 1987.

20. *Sharq yulduzi,* October 1987, p. 5.

21. "Aral yashamaghi kerak."

22. Ibid.

23. The estimated combined population of Kzyl Orda Oblast (Kazakhstan), Tashauz Oblast (Turkmenistan), and Khorezm Oblast and the Karakalpak ASSR (Uzbekistan).

24. Yadgarov, p. 16.

25. Soviet sources, cited in Micklin, p. 1170.

26. Ibid., pp. 16-17.

27. Kamalov *et al.*, p. 11.

28. For an example, see "Aral fajiyasi" (The Aral Tragedy), *Sovet Ozbekistani*, July 7, 1987.

29. "Bol' nasha--Aral" (Our Anguish is the Aral), *Pravda Vostoka*, July 5, 1987.

30. Jalil, "*Qirchaq qachayatgan dengiz.*"

31. V. I. Lenin, *Polnoe sobranie sochineniy* (5th ed.), Moscow (*Politizdat*), Vol, 58, pp. 246-48.

32. Uyghun (real name Rahmatulla Ataqoziev, born 1905), "Aral," *OAS*, December 19, 1987.

33. "V Tsentral'nom Komitete KPSS i Sovete Ministrov SSR" (report on session of the CPSU Central Committee and the USSR Council of Ministers), *Pravda*, August 20, 1986.

34. "V Politburo KPSS" (report on Politburo meeting), *Pravda*, September 2, 1988. For other background on the Aral problem, see *Radio Liberty Research* 392/87.

35. The findings were reviewed by the commission's chairman in "Spasenie morya" (Saving the Sea), *Pravda*, September 12, 1988.

36. Micklin, p. 1172.

37. *Pravda*, September 12, 1988. Izrael' is identified as chairman of the USSR State Committee on Hydrometeorology and a corresponding member of the USSR Academy of Sciences.

In the 1987 plan, cotton deliveries in Uzbekistan, the largest producer of that crop, were lowered--with considerable fanfare--from 5.75 to 5.25 million tons, or only 8.7 percent, leaving the reduced figure still greater than the 1981-1985 average of 5.159 tons. See *Pravda Vostoka*, December 18, 1987.

After Islam A. Karimov replaced Rafik N. Nishanov as First Secretary in 1989, there was a further reduction in the crop, but by then it was clear that this would not solve the basic problem of restoring the Aral.

38. G. Voropaev, "Ot ekoisterii--k real'nosti" (From Ecological Hysteria to Reality), *Zvezda Vostoka*, No. 4, 1988, p. 12. As reported there, the commission called only for "limiting growth of irrigated lands."

39. Micklin, p. 1174.

40. *Literaturnaya gazeta*, November 18, 1987.

41. Micklin, p. 1170.

42. Micklin, p. 1173.

43. Kenneth D. Frederick with James C. Hanson, *Water for Western Agriculture*, Washington, D.C. (Resources for the Future), 1982.

44. Jora Sa"dullaev, "Dalalardagi aq daghlar" (White Spots in the Fields), *Sharq yulduzi*, No. 9, 1987, p. 139 .

45. Sergey Zalygin, speech at plenum of USSR Writers' Union quoted in *Literaturnaya gazeta*, March 9, 1988. Zalygin also complained that in Karakalpakia flourishing lands whose cultivation had been developed over thousands of years had been flooded. He linked these phenomena to the claim that "every eight or tenth child is born abnormal."

46. Data from *Narkhoz 70*, p. 245 and *Narodnoe khozyaystvo SSSR v 1980 g.*, Moscow 1981, p. 226.

47. *ONU*, No. 8, 1987, p. 25 and *Sovet Ozbekistani*, August 19, 1987.

48. *Sovet Ozbekistani*, August 29, 1987.

49. Ibid.

50. *Pravda Vostoka*, June 3, 1989.

51. *Narkhoz 70*.

52. An American correspondent, one of the few foreigners to be admitted to the Aral region, reported that in one rayon in the Karakalpak republic, infant mortality in 1988 had reached 111 per thousand (*New York Times*, August 14, 1989).

53. "Bol' nasha—Aral."

54. "Aral dengizi va adamlar salamatligi" (The Aral Sea and Human Health), *Sovet Ozbekistani*, July 7, 1987.

55. "Ekologiya, iqtisad, ma"naviyat" (Ecology, Economics, Mortality), *Sovet Ozbekistani*, July 18, 1987.

56. *OAS*, December 15, 1989.

57. Meaning roughly: 'The Place the Enemy Comes From."

6

Objection to the Russian Presence

One of the most effective issues exploited by the Uzbek elites in their campaign against Moscow was general resentment of the official Russian presence and the alien authority wielded by representatives of the center from Moscow. Here we shall examine three selected aspects of that resentment: (1) the problem of linguistic russification imposed by the center over many decades; (2) the problem of toponymy, specifically the drive to restore native names to places that, in the old colonial tradition, had been renamed to honor tsarist or Soviet persons or institutions; (3) popular resentment of those Russians who were perceived as monopolizing the better jobs in Uzbekistan.

The Clash of Languages

Are we Uzbeks or aren't we?
--from speech by the writer Shukrulla denouncing Uzbekistan's draft law "on languages."[1]

Throughout the Soviet period, Central Asian intellectuals--even those who favored modernization--have seen themselves as the heirs of a great indigenous cultural tradition that stems from the days of such Muslim greats as Avicenna or Babur. Even under the repressive reign of Stalin and his successors, they quietly resisted attempts to brand their intellectual progenitors as reactionary, their minds and creative output inferior to those of such representatives of the Russian "elder brother" as Mikhail Lomonosov or Alexander Pushkin.

A specimen of Central Asian resistance to cultural russification was the 14-volume Uzbek Soviet Encyclopedia, published at the depth of the "stagnation" period presided over by Brezhnev. In the encyclopedia's thousands of pages there was much that reflected Moscow's central ideological control, such as the obligatory use of articles translated from the Russian on such topics as foreign policy or social science. But what gave the encyclopedia, the first ever in the Uzbek language, its special stamp were the many articles dealing with local topics that originated from within the Uzbek cultural establishment. The encyclopedia carried biography after biography of Central Asian cultural figures of the pre-Soviet, pre-Russian period, complete with the Arabic rendering of their names. From the standpoint of Communist orthodoxy, there were striking anomalies, such as the fact that Avicenna received more space than Karl Marx.

In due course, the Kremlin's cultural watchdogs woke up to what the editors of the Uzbek encyclopedia had achieved, and there were vitriolic attacks in the press. The attacks had little effect, however; with Brezhnev's departure from the scene and the eventual accession of Gorbachev, the climate gradually improved for such cultural sallies. There was not immediate smooth sailing, however; after the 1986 Moscow Party Congress, the first at which Gorbachev presided, making Uzbekistan's alleged transgressions a national cause célèbre, ideological conservatives launched a new attack against glorification of the local culture in the republic. One of the principal targets of the attack was a respected Uzbek writer, Pirimqul Qadirov, author of a historical novel portraying Babur in a favorable light, for which he now received public censure.

Issues like the Uzbek encyclopedia or the Qadirov affair were of interest to intellectuals. What the elites needed, as they dug in their heels to counter pressure from Moscow, were issues that would capture the popular imagination and help them mobilize the masses as allies. One of the first issues on which they seized was that of language.

In a multiethnic situation, language is a prime determinant of socioeconomic status. If you speak the dominant language of the society, you are on the inside track to social acceptance and career success. If you do not, you are apt to become a victim of discrimination. In the United States, we see a reflection of this in efforts by minorities to have their languages granted equal status in official use, and in the campaign to counter it, especially in areas of heavy Hispanic settlement, by those who seek to pass laws making English the one and only "official" language. In Canada, the French in the province of Quebec, who were once snubbed by the dominant Anglophones even in their own homeland, have been fighting back in recent years through provincial legislation restricting public use of English. The national government, concerned about the divisive effect of linguistic differences, has been promoting policies of bilingualism and, beyond that, multiculturalism throughout Canada.

In the Soviet Union, first under Stalin and then under his successors Khrushchev and Brezhnev, the nationalities were subjected to unrelenting pressures of russification. Language policy was based on the assumption that the country was headed toward social homogeneity, and that sooner or later everyone would be speaking the same language, Russian. Just as the Russians dominated the society, so was their language at the top of the linguistic pecking-order. Those who did not master Russian were at a disadvantage, particularly in getting access to jobs and higher education, and in dealing with officials. The same disadvantage weighed in other multiethnic situations, such as military service, where recruits who spoke Russian badly, or not at all, were objects of mockery.

In Central Asia, there were no national languages as such until 1924, when the republics of Uzbekistan, Tajikistan, Turkmenistan and Kirghizia were carved out of the former territory of the tsarist province of Turkestan. (Kazakhstan already existed as a separate republic.) Before that time, the natives of Central Asia spoke a variety of different dialects, some Turkic, some Iranian. When the republics were born, commissions set about codifying the dialects of their principal inhabitants into Uzbek, Tajik and other "languages." Since then, years of schooling, of media exposure, and other public uses of the languages have engrained them deeply in the citizens of the republics, although the process is not yet complete.

In Uzbekistan, as in other non-Russian republics, the national language emerged as an effective vehicle for opposition to russification. It also became a potent force in consolidating nationalism.

A barometer of the excited state of Uzbek national sentiment was the public discussion held in the summer of 1989 on a draft of legislation purporting to make Uzbek the "state language" of Uzbekistan.[2] Introduction of the bill was an obvious attempt to defuse nationalist agitation against russification and linguistic discrimination. As in other republics, the opening of debate on the language bill aroused more passions than it cooled, stirring up a hornet's nest of public recrimination. In the Uzbek case, tempers were particularly inflamed by the suspicion that the bill was conceived not to redress grievances but as a cunning means of calming nationalist agitation with high-sounding phrases while offering very little in the way of genuine concessions that might trouble the status quo. This slyly unyielding ploy seemed to have been the parting shot of former Uzbek First Secretary Rafik N. Nishanov, who had gained a reputation as Moscow's stalking horse in the republic.[3]

Uzbeks charged that the bill's publication and the ensuing discussion, which at first the authorities had planned to cut off after only two months, were timed to coincide with the absence on summer vacation of university students, who had been in the forefront of agitation over the language issue.[4] If that was the case, the cleverness of higher authority backfired from the very outset, as Uzbek intellectuals led a chorus of indignant protest over the shortcomings of the bill and the presumed treachery of its authors. A leading writer and magazine editor, Asqad Mukhtar, wrote that "the most important thing is that in reality the draft is straining to defend an unjust bilingualism, I say unjust because we now understand bilingualism to cover only one part of the republic's population and not to apply to Russian-speakers, who feel no need to know a second language." Uzbekistan's Komsomol organ, calling editorially for a total overhaul of the bill, quoted approvingly the prominent poet Erkin Vahidov's disparagement of it as a string of "obsequious phrases resembling a longwinded apology to other languages."[5] A senior associate of the republican institute of Party history stated succinctly that the draft made him think of a circus conjurer with his "now you see it, now you don't."[6]

Such criticisms were accompanied by concrete demands aimed at putting teeth into the wording of this or that paragraph. A group of 25 members of the USSR Writers' Union in Uzbekistan published a letter proposing a revised text that would make use of Uzbek compulsory in public life within one year.[7] The Uzbek Minister of Culture, Olmas Umarbekov, was derided for attempting to justify the status quo.[8] When another republican minister, Sarvar Azimov, holder of the foreign-affairs portfolio, tried to save the day for higher authority by offering a substitute draft that differed from the earlier one mainly in having more sugarcoating, his effort was quickly dismissed by a group of thirteen letter-writers from all walks of life as a mere pretense that "Ali Khoja is not Khoja Ali."[9]

The words of the poet Jamal Kamal summed up the position of many Uzbeks: "Every citizen living in Uzbekistan, regardless of nationality, must know and understand the Uzbek language."[10] Predictably, Russian residents of the republic, who up to now had been able to thrive without knowledge of Uzbek, reacted with mixed anger and alarm. Their fears were heightened by statements like one Uzbek's that, since only 10.8 percent of the republic's population were Russian speakers, equal use of language in fact represented "inequality."[11] In general, the discussion was a dialogue of the deaf, in which each side concentrated on its own positions without addressing the concerns of the opponent, as argument and counter-argument flew past each other in opposite directions, unheeded.

Weeks of public debate brought embarrassing revelations. The poet Vahidov, after analyzing the text of the bill, charged that it had been translated into Uzbek from a Russian original.[12] It developed that in their zeal to protect the status of Russian in Uzbekistan, the framers had, by actual count, mentioned Russian in the text more often (51 times) than Uzbek (47 times), despite the fact that advancement of Uzbek was supposedly the whole point of the bill. Members of the commission appointed to prepare the draft complained that their suggestions had been ignored by higher authority.[13] Thus, what seemed to have been conceived originally as a meaningless sop to Uzbek national feelings had had the effect of arousing those feelings to fever pitch. One immediate consequence of the resultant outcry was a concession by the Uzbek Supreme Soviet to extend discussion of the bill until October 1 from the earlier cutoff in mid-August.

The Roots of Discontent

In the "stagnation period" of Brezhnev and Rashidov, Soviet linguistic policy in Uzbekistan had used the slogan of "bilingualism" as a screen for preferential teaching of Russian as a stepping-stone to the ultimate goal of rapprochement (*sblizhenie*) of nationalities. At the same time, the Uzbek language was quietly allowed to atrophy in public life. By 1989, when the language bill was introduced, this goal was no longer espoused openly, but it was clearly present in the minds of those who masterminded preparation of the bill. Their crafty strategy relied on the fact, well-documented in multiethnic societies of all ideological casts, that the language of the dominant ethnic group, the "language of success," has a tendency to squeeze out other languages as the medium of administration, education, and high-level economic activity, unless barriers are erected to block this natural evolution. Uzbeks had begun expressing interest in the situation in Canada, where the provincial government of French-speaking Quebec responded to the linguistic expansionism of English by essentially banning the use of that language in many areas of public life. In the Soviet Union, natural processes fueled by the superior status of Russians and those who speak their language had placed the non-Russian languages at a disadvantage, as much as any calculated policy of "russification." Thus, defense of the status quo in effect doomed the nationality languages to further attrition.

By 1989, Uzbek activists, encouraged by perestroika, were joining other non-Russian nationalists in pressing for legal mechanisms that would reverse the trend against their languages. If the Uzbeks seemed blind to Russian fears, they were showing themselves to be acutely aware that their language movement was part of a historic process involving other Soviet peoples. Uzbek media referred frequently to the situation in the Baltic republics, or the Caucasus, or Moldavia.

In the case of the Uzbek language bill, an Uzbek economist asserted that "every Uzbek person. . . had awaited the draft legislation with profound emotion, like parents hopefully expecting the birth of their first child." Alas, he added, "a malformed child was born."[14]

"Ukazhite adres!"

Uzbek outrage tinged with ridicule reached a crescendo in the speeches at a special meeting of literary people held in Tashkent on July 12,[15] a few weeks after the draft was published. The poet Muhammad Salih, a leading spokesman for national causes, presided.[16] In his opening remarks, Salih referred to a "comical illogicality" in: ". . . A draft that is published to give the Uzbek language the standing of the state language, and in reality makes the Russian language the state language and gives it legal standing." The speakers overwhelmingly rejected the "bilingualism" of the bill as incompatible with their insistence that in Uzbekistan the dominant language must be Uzbek. They scoffed at the bill's first article providing for Uzbek to be "the state language" of the republic, saying that this was contradicted throughout by the remainder of the text and by the title of the bill itself: "Law of the Uzbek SSR on Languages" (i.e., not just one Uzbek language). Speaker after speaker attacked the premise of the bill that Russian might be used optionally as an alternative to Uzbek.

As the meeting continued, emotions built to an ever higher pitch, with participants vying with each other to relate stories of linguistic grievances: The writer Mirmuhsin (Mirsaidov), a longstanding pillar of the Uzbek literary establishment, told of a case where an employment application written in Uzbek was returned by the personnel department with an admonition to the applicant, "We can't understand this, write in Russian." The poet Vahidov recalled having to help an old Uzbek shepherd gain admittance to the Uzbek Central Committee offices because the receptionist could not understand him. He reminded listeners that if you became ill in Tashkent or your home caught fire there was a good chance that you would not be able to get help by telephoning in Uzbek, and that when a court was deciding someone's fate he had better not try to defend himself in Uzbek. He asserted that, of the "hundreds of thousands of people" who worked in places that serve the public, 80 percent did not know Uzbek.

One of the most telling indictments came from an editor of the Uzbek Pioneer magazine *Gulkhan*, who said that, in answering the hundreds of letters it had received complaining about the language bill, his magazine had made a point of addressing the replies in Uzbek, only to have them all returned by the post office with a notice in Russian, "*Ukazhite adres!*" ("Indicate the address").

In a caustic reference to some Uzbek officials who were now more at home in Russian than in their own language, another speaker observed that "our leaders themselves don't know Uzbek." There were complaints that in Uzbek schools they taught six hours of Russian but in Russian schools only two hours of Uzbek, and that the main Tashkent pedagogical institute in 1989 had 100 places for teachers of Russian but only fifty for teachers of Uzbek, despite the deplorable state of Uzbek teaching.

The proceedings were rounded out by demands that the bill's references to the "old Uzbek" language (written in Arabic script) be strengthened.[17] The draft had called rather vaguely for making "old Uzbek" an optional subject. Instead, one speaker insisted, this vehicle of "one thousand years of the Uzbek people's history" should become compulsory, with students required to take some of their examinations in it, and with its own newspaper, magazine, and publishing-house.[18]

Before the meeting ended, threats were voiced against certain unnamed Uzbeks who were seen as parties to the draft. Members of the commission assigned to prepare the bill asserted defensively that their suggestions had been ignored. One member reported a conversation "in the Central Committee" in which he and his colleagues had been deceived. He said that he had warned "certain comrades" that their failure to understand could lead to "evil, unpleasant consequences." He asked, rather ominously, for the creation of a commission to determine who else had taken part in this "illiterate" draft, who had edited the final text, and "through whose hands it had passed."

The Russian Side

Uzbek intellectuals had even begun to question the vaunted role of Russian as "the medium of international communication." Professor Begali Qasimov suggested that Russian was redundant as far as the Turkic world was concerned, recalling the pre-revolutionary day when the same Turkic newspapers, written in Arabic script, could be understood by readers from Kazan on the Volga to Herat in Afghanistan, and from Izmir in Turkey to Urumchi in China, i.e. before heterogeneous Cyrillic alphabets were imposed on Turkic literature in the Soviet Union. He went on to suggest that modern Uzbek using Arabic script might serve as a similar inter-Turkic medium.[19] A speaker at the July 12 literary meeting pointed to the absurdity of having an Uzbek speak to a Kazakh in Russian, or an Uzbek to a Karakalpak, or a Kirghiz to an Uigur, when their languages are so close to one another (and so far from Russian). Uzbeks, who lately had been demonstrating a growing interest in reaching out to the outside world through the medium of English, may also have been intrigued by a Tashkent newspaper's reprint of a *Komsomolskaya Pravda* dispatch from India making the point that in that country English, a non-native language, serves as a medium of communication between different native groups.[20]

Apparently many Russians in Uzbekistan had already begun to study Uzbek in response to the groundswell of linguistic nationalism in the republic. A speaker at the July 12 literary meeting reported that Russians had been looking for dictionaries and means of independent study. Moreover, they had "begun to regard the Uzbek language and the Uzbek people with respect." He complained, however, that after the appearance of the hateful draft this movement had stopped.

Where Uzbek critics condemned the legislation for being too weak, Russians objected that it went too far. For their part, Russians tended to use arguments against language reform that were utilitarian: "The USSR is a single economic complex," "The Russian language is the vehicle of international communication," "The Russian language is the key to the world treasure of culture," or "Without knowledge of Russian it is difficult to serve in the army."[21] A Russian engineer criticized reform attempts on the basis that the region's overwhelming problem was economic, and that "introduction of Uzbek as the state language can be economically desirable only if Uzbekistan leaves the USSR." He displayed further insensitivity to Uzbek feelings by claiming that the merging of cultures would produce a "higher culture," and that the appalling state of medical care in Uzbekistan was the result of the preference given to Uzbeks in education and hiring.[22] Another Russian wrote that having to issue all public documents in Uzbek would "paralyze" the republic.[23] Typical of the gulf between Russians and Uzbeks was a comment by a Russian in Tashkent who pointed to the extra costs that would be entailed in language reform, adding, "If there's 'extra' money in our republic, let's spend it building swimming pools, saunas and playgrounds."[24] There was a general concern by non-Uzbeks that introducing the Uzbek language criterion would give Uzbeks an unfair advantage in competition for employment.

Some critics of the language reform bill identified themselves as Uzbeks who could no longer function in their native language. For example, four fifth-year law students expressed doubt about their ability to plead a case in Uzbek, or to gain that ability through language study.[25] In general, though, attitudes toward language reform were closely correlated with the person's nationality.

A number of opponents of the bill warned of it as a kind of virus emanating from the Baltic region. In the words of one Russian, "the contrived problem of languages has drifted in from the Baltics," and the "aggressively anti-democratic nature of the bill leaps to the eye."[26] Another argued that the Baltic "model" was unsuitable because "the Central Asian republics (sic) annexed themselves to Russia more than 100 years ago," because Russian was working very well as the state language, and therefore, "why re-invent the wheel?"[27]

The fundamental difference in viewpoint between Russians and Uzbeks living side-by-side in the republic was no doubt exacerbated by the existing vacuum in leadership.[28] It was noteworthy that, in a system where for decades "political indoctrination" had been a primary instrument of rule, there was very little high-level effort to explain the draft language law to either Russians or Uzbeks. There was also a problem of linguistic compartmentalization: if many Uzbeks could read Russian-language publications, very few Russians could read the Uzbek-language sources in which the case for reform was presented most eloquently by its supporters. The Uzbek language bill, with a few modifications, became law in the latter part of 1989. The final text dissatisfied both those Uzbek interests that called for a stricter law that would in effect tell Russians, "Learn our language or get out," and those Russian interests that were threatened by *any* law giving advantages to a language that most Russians were unable to use. On balance, the effect of the law has been to elevate the status of Uzbek in public life. In February of the following year, the republican news agency Uztag reported that documents of the Uzbek party organs were being issued in both Uzbek and Russian (instead of Russian alone). Simultaneous interpretation facilities ordered from a Latvian co-operative had been installed for meetings held in the Central Committee rooms, and Uzbek courses were being organized for party workers. Moreover, letters received by the Central Committee were being answered in Uzbek if written in that language. Further progress was being delayed by a shortage of interpretation facilities and typewriters with Uzbek keyboards. There were 29 district party committees doing business in Uzbek, only a small minority of the total but double the number in the preceding year.[29]

By the time the language law was passed, it was in fact already something of an anticlimax. Even were the government fully disposed and able to do so, it would be difficult to enforce language norms through legislation, as other governments have found. The real change was in the new climate of nationalism engendered by the debate. Courses being taught at institutions of higher education in Uzbekistan were switching from Russian to Uzbek, without waiting for legislation to take effect.[30] That was the reality that, more than any written document, and barring a cataclysm, was the determinant for the future.

The Place-Name Controversy

Even before the debate on the language law, the elites had begun to press their attack in another linguistic area: the non-native names which had been attached to Uzbek cities, towns, villages, streets and other geographic locations throughout the Soviet period. With the more open expression of opinion afforded by glasnost, it became apparent that this colonial practice had long rankled Uzbek identity and national pride. The victory of the elites in this seemingly rather prosaic area actually helped significantly to weaken Moscow's grip on local affairs. There was enormous symbolic value in the fact that major place-names identified with hallowed figures in the Soviet Pantheon--for example, that of Leninabad in neighboring Tajikistan, which in 1991 reverted to its old name of Khojent--fell to the re-nativization movement. The anatomy of the drive against Russian and Soviet toponymy is interesting as a close-up of Uzbek nationalism at work.

The place where individuals live is a prime ingredient of their identity. In their efforts to shape identity for their subjects and to place their own stamp on their possessions, colonial rulers have traditionally manipulated place-names: hence, "Rhodesia" (as the territory now comprising Zimbabwe and Zambia was called), named after the British empire-builder Cecil Rhodes, or "Batavia" (now Djakarta, Indonesia), the capital of the former Dutch East Indies. Toponymic manipulation has been bitterly resented by colonial subjects; as former colonies have won their freedom, they generally have been quick to restore traditional place-names.

The same process has taken place in the Russian and the Soviet Empires. After the Revolution, there was a systematic wave of place-renaming, a part of the campaign to transform the old society. Although under the Soviets toponymic policy was supposedly free of national overtones, it happened that in Central Asia those in control were largely Russians, and they picked names that suited them, like "Frunze," the new name given to the capital of the Kirghiz Soviet Republic, a town formerly called Pishpek. (Mikhail Vasil'evich Frunze was a Russian military commander who helped to subdue Central Asian resistance to the Soviet regime.)

Uzbeks and other Central Asians chafed for decades under the non-native Russian or revolutionary names that were given the towns, or the streets, where they lived. In the more liberal atmosphere of perestroika, there began to be demands to obliterate Russian place names like "Pravda," "Pushkin," and "Krasnogvardeysk" from the map.[31] In what amounted to a deliberate challenge to Moscow's hegemony, Uzbek writers began criticizing the practice of giving Russian and other non-indigenous names to Uzbek locales. Their proposals went considerably closer to the heart of the system than the removal of the names of unpopular deceased leaders like Brezhnev's from public objects.[32]

The Uzbek initiative was not limited to the actions of intellectuals, but had broader grass-roots appeal; for instance, on one occasion letters on the subject appeared in the press, from a village Soviet chairman, an honored artist, a teacher, and a restaurant cook.[33] As a rule, the challenge was impeccably clothed in the language of perestroika, i.e. it was suggested that the unwelcome names were a result of the abuses of the periods of "cult of personality" and "stagnation." But even ideologically acceptable names like "Leninsk" or "Pushkin" came under assault as the work of overzealous toadies who had sought during those periods to protect themselves or their jobs. Thus, there were in Uzbekistan 15 villages named "Kalinin."[34] It was suggested that places bearing such names should at least have a direct connection with the persons being commemorated. Otherwise, the result was said to be "false internationalism."[35]

What is more, this grass-roots campaign to eliminate alien toponyms from the Uzbek scene also reached back into the pre-revolutionary past, to the time "after Central Asia was brought into subjection as a result of the imperialist policy that came from the tsarist conquest. . . ."[36] The article in which this quote appeared reminded readers of an 1898 decree of the Russian Imperial Ministry of Communications which renamed stations on the Tashkent-Samarkand railroad, replacing their traditional native names with Slavic ones like Rostovtsevo, Milyutinskaia, Lomakino, or Chernyaevo. The 1988 Uzbek newspaper printed the verbatim text of a letter published in 1898 by the Tashkent newspaper *Turkestanskie vedomosti* (No. 77) to protest the action, citing reasons why the native names should be preserved and poking fun at the Imperial decree. In an evident jibe at continuing modern Soviet restrictions on expression, the latter-day Uzbek writer described the 1898 letter and its publication in a Russian newspaper as "an example of the free-thinking of that time. . . . " Further, the Uzbek author branded published comments by the tsarist editor disagreeing with the letter as "an attempt to implant in readers a supercilious idea typical of a colonial official."

Many of the names which the Uzbeks sought to eliminate were purely Soviet: "Hundreds and thousands of places have been named, on a mass basis, 'Communism,' 'Socialism,' or after various Party congresses."[37] The point was made, tongue-in-cheek, that these places did not deserve such "great" names in terms of their backward economic level or lack of political activism. "Between naming thousands of places after Lenin and correctly implementing his ideas there is a world of difference." It was recalled that people kept on invoking Lenin's name even while committing crimes (a charge which happened to fit the case of the recently arrested republic first secretary, Inamjan B. Usmankhojaev.)

The practice of using a Russian name where there was a native equivalent was also disputed. "Not long ago the name 'Druzhba' was given one of the towns in the Khorezm oasis. Why 'Druzhba'? If we called that city 'Dostlik' or 'Biradarlik',* would that be nationalism?"*38

The Uzbek author of the above comment also asked why Russian generic words for locations should be used instead of the Uzbek original: thus, why call housing neighborhoods "massiv" or "kvartal" (Russian words) instead of "mahalla" (the Uzbek word for district or neighborhood)?   He observed that some "super-cultured" ("*ota madaniatli*") people thought the name "mahalla" to be "old-fashioned" and "feudal," but that it was not these words that were at fault, but rather what was in the minds of the people who say them.

A particularly biting comment was reserved by the same writer for the Moscow Hotel in Tashkent, which he said was originally supposed to be called the "Asia," but "a careerist and toadying proposal made 'in the people's name' changed it to 'Moscow.' In Moscow and Leningrad are there any hotels named after cities in Uzbekistan?"

The writer printed a long list of traditional Uzbek place names that were no longer used, saying that their restoration was "possible and necessary" (*mumkin va lazim*). He pointed out that in many cases the people had just gone on using the old names anyway.

One way to correct these abuses, this writer suggested, in the case of Tashkent, would be to have on the local toponymic commission, which consisted of 20 to 25 members, "more members of the local nationalities who knew their history and really consulted with the local people." Then, he wrote, "decisions made 'by popular demand' would enter into force on the basis of having studied public opinion." He noted the Georgian practice of having a qualified commission (staffed by linguists and other specialists) pass on names of places and even buildings.

----

* "Dostlik" and "Biradarlik" are the Turkic and Iranian equivalents of the Russian "Druzhba" ("friendship").

111

The Uzbek proposals for toponymic reform were in keeping with the creeping process of "decolonialization," which the German historian Gerhard Simon detected beneath the surface of Soviet society even before perestroika.[39] There were obvious parallels with decolonizing trends in other parts of the world, as when the nation now called Zaire renamed its capital from "Leopoldville" (after a Belgian king) to "Kinshasa." The early Soviet regime, like other revolutionary governments,[40] made wide use of toponymic policy to extirpate the names of "class enemies," to perpetuate those of dead leaders, or for other propaganda purposes. This practice also had roots in Russian tradition (witness St. Petersburg, Tsaritsyn, Ekaterinodar).

Even if the Moscow leadership were sympathetic, however, to the ideological premises of the Uzbek demands, it faced the practical implications--at a critical time in the evolution of nationalities policy--of removing from Uzbekistan and other republics reminders that they were supposed to owe loyalty to a larger political entity-- the USSR. The fact that Gorbachev and the Moscow leadership ultimately had to countenance these demands, which must have been a galling thorn in their sides, was further evidence of the weakening of the center's day-to-day control in republics like Uzbekistan.

Resentment of Russian Settlers

There is perhaps no better barometer of change in the political climate of Uzbekistan than the shift in Russian migration patterns. The traditional influx of Russians to take jobs in administration and industry has slowed to the point where it is more than offset by the flight of Russians from the republic. At the same time, there is continuing resentment of those Russians who remain. It should be noted, however, that Central Asians tend to distinguish between the "good" local Russians, those who consider the region to be their only home and who have learned to co-exist with the native peoples, and the "bad" immigrant Russians, those who are seen as descending on the region to lord it over the natives and siphon off the best jobs. Despite these differences, the overall Russian presence continues to be an irritant to the Uzbeks and other Central Asians--a fact that has been seized on by their elite spokesmen.

Settlers from European Russia have been an irritant in Central Asia ever since the nineteenth century, when large numbers of land-hungry immigrants began to drive the nomadic Kazakhs and Kirghiz from their grazing lands. Following the tsarist conquest with its influx of military and civilian officials, Russian entrepreneurs flocked to the cities eager to make money from cotton and other Central Asian raw materials. The pace of settlement increased in the Soviet period, as Stalin assigned administrators, engineers, and skilled workers from other parts of the country to oversee economic development (or, in the native view, economic exploitation). The foreign Soviet presence became acutely painful in the countryside, as armed force from outside was deployed to impose collectivization, causing massive suffering and loss of life.

Uzbeks are particularly galled by the fact that industry in the Soviet period has been an essentially European preserve. Native participation is largely limited to menial jobs, such as sweeping the factory floor. When Stalin came to power, he soon abandoned Lenin's policy of training native specialists to man the economy. Instead, outsiders--mainly Russians--were dispatched to Uzbekistan and other Central Asian republics to build and staff factories, from the post of director down to the production-line. World War II further increased the outside presence as whole factories and their workers were evacuated to Central Asia from areas near the front, many of them to remain there after the war.

Expressing dissatisfaction with this alien presence was taboo until well after the advent of glasnost. It was only in 1989, after Islam Karimov had replaced the unpopular Rafik Nishanov as head of the Uzbek Communist Party, that the first cautious complaints began to be articulated in public. An early response was restriction on the hiring of imported labor from outside Uzbekistan, through measures adopted by the Uzbek Central Committee and the Tashkent City Committee of the Communist Party. These politically sensitive actions surfaced in an interview with Adyl Yaqubov, secretary of the board of the Uzbek Writers Union, published in the Uzbek cultural weekly *Ozbekistan adabiyati va san"ati*, a leading vehicle of elite nationalism. Yaqubov reported that he had taken part in plenary sessions of those two bodies at which resolutions were adopted calling for limits on hiring of workers "from other regions" for employment at major Uzbek industrial enterprises. Instead of importing labor, he said, Uzbekistan would now concentrate on training to impart skills to workers of the local nationality.

Yaqubov commented that the resolutions "were evidence that the leadership of our republic has been able to assess correctly the serious situations which have arisen in Uzbekistan."[41] At the heart of the problem was the fact that, ever since Stalin's day, many managerial, administrative, and skilled-labor jobs in the Central Asian republics had tended to be earmarked for Russians and other Europeans, while unemployment in the indigenous labor-force had been growing steadily in recent years. (Joblessness was said to have been a major factor in the bloody violence that erupted in June 1989 in Uzbekistan's Fergana Valley, when more than 100 persons were killed and much property was destroyed.)

Yaqubov was evidently referring in his interview to a plenum of the Uzbek Communist Party held in Tashkent on November 24, 1989, at which First Secretary Islam Karimov complained about the failure of enterprises in Uzbekistan to hire local workers, against a background of one million unemployed in the republic, many of them youths. Karimov singled out the steel and non-ferrous industries, which he accused of "systematically" leaving 25,000 jobs vacant, almost half of them in the Tashkent region. Another part of the problem, he said, was that "many enterprises which are subordinate to the Union (i.e. to Moscow), rather than training working cadres locally, resort at times to an easier path, but one that complicates the problem of jobs for the local population-- they recruit ready-trained employees from other regions of the country."[42]

The official communique on the November plenum reported only that it had adopted "a resolution and measures" toward implementation of the CPSU's platform on nationalities, together with the Uzbek Communist Party's own platform for the forthcoming elections, and had reviewed "organizational questions." There was no mention of the resolution barring in-migration announced by Yaqubov in the Uzbek press, perhaps so as not to arouse the feelings of Uzbekistan's Russian minority,[43] but it was clear that, for the first time since the tsarist conquest, the wind was now blowing strongly against further Russian settlement in Uzbekistan.

Yaqubov's comments echoed a much more pointed interview given by Gulchehra Nurullaeva, a well-known Uzbek poetess and then Party member (who later resigned her membership). Nurullaeva called flatly for an end to in-migration of Russians and other non-indigenous workers.[44] She described a ban on this as essential to the well-being of Uzbek workers.

114

In the course of her interview, Nurullaeva spoke candidly about anti-Russian feeling in the republic, which she traced to various causes. First, she said, the Russians had never troubled to learn the Uzbek language, and therefore could not understand the people, mistaking Uzbek kindness for subservience. Secondly, there were historical reasons for enmity, from the "atrocities" (*jalladliklar*) committed by Russians in the last century to Central Asia's relegation in this century to being both a dumping-ground for Russian criminals and a haven for Russian privilege-seekers. Finally, there was the tendency to blame Russians for all of the ills of the Uzbek people, which Nurullaeva personally deplored, saying that the Russians too had suffered from the system. Still, she was categorical about ending in-migration.

The advent of Russians and other European nationalities to Uzbekistan, although it had been dwindling in recent years, was clearly still a major social and political irritant. Although in the intercensal period 1979-1989 there was a net out-migration from the republic of more than half a million persons, this still included a small annual component of in-migration, said to be in the neighborhood of 20 thousand a year.[45] What rankled the Uzbeks was not the size of this influx but its level, the fact that the new arrivals occupied highly-rated jobs that were off-limits to the locals.

Notes

1.   *Ozbekistan adabiyati va san "ati (OAS)*, July 21, 1989.
2.   *Pravda Vostoka*, June 18, 1989.
3.   The decision to publish a language bill was taken May 18 (See *Pravda Vostoka* of May 19). Nishanov was elevated to chairmanship of the USSR Supreme Soviet's Council of Nationalities on June 6, but the appointment of his successor in Uzbekistan was not announced until June 23. The draft was published June 18. Nishanov had served for many years outside Uzbekistan, including ambassadorships to Sri Lanka and Jordan, and there were complaints that he could not even speak Uzbek correctly.
4.   *OAS*, July 14, 1989.
5.   *Yash Leninchi*, Tashkent, August 2, 1989.
6.   *Oqituvchilar gazetasi*, Tashkent, August 19, 1989.
7.   *Yash Leninchi*, August 9, 1989.
8.   *Yash Leninchi*, August 10, 1989. Umarbekov was also the butt of criticism, although not by name, at the July 12 literary meeting in Tashkent.
9.   *Yash Leninchi*, August 4, 1989. Both of these ministers seemingly had rather checkered careers. Umarbekov had been accused of using his earlier

position as deputy minister to palm off his plays on theaters (*Sovetskaya Kul'tura*, August 26, 1986). Azimov was fired as head of the Uzbek Writers' Union allegedly for diverting funds to personal use (*Pravda Vostoka*, November 22, 1985).

10. *OAS*, July 21, 1989.

11. Ibid.

12. *OAS*, July 7, 1989.

13. *OAS*, July 21, 1989.

14. *Oqituvchilar gazetasi*, August 16, 1989. Cited from *Yash Leninchi* (date not given).

15. The speeches cited here are taken from a full-page summary printed in *OAS*, July 21, 1989.

16. In fall 1988, Salih gave an interview to the *New York Times* in which he was outspoken about the damage done to his homeland by Moscow's imposition of plans to expand cotton-growing. This led to an article in the local press by two journalists (one of them Russian) who called him a "Goebbels." It was a sign of the times that he was allowed to publish a rebuttal in the same newspapers, and does not appear to have sustained serious political consequences. (See *New York Times*, November 6, 1988; *Pravda Vostoka* and *Sovet Ozbekistani*, both December 15, 1988 and January 7, 1989.)

17. See Erika Dailey, "Update on Alphabet Legislation," *Radio Liberty Report on the USSR*, No. 32, 1989, p. 29.

18. *OAS*, July 21, 1989.

19. *OAS*, July 14, 1989.

20. *Pravda Vostoka*, August 16, 1989.

21. As summarized by a Central Asian writer who proceeded to refute them, in *Pravda Vostoka*, July 16, 1989.

22. *Pravda Vostoka*, July 12, 1989.

23. *Pravda Vostoka*, July 29, 1989.

24. Ibid.

25. *Pravda Vostoka*, July 6, 1989.

26. *Pravda Vostoka*, July 25, 1989.

27. *Pravda Vostoka*, July 21, 1989.

28. See Critchlow, "Uzbekistan: The Paralysis of Political Power," *Report on the USSR*, July 28, 1989, p. 32.

29. *Pravda Vostoka*, February 8, 1989.

30. *Pravda Vostoka*, July 16, 1989.

31. These three names are cited in Ravshan Haidarov, "Hatira huquqi" (The Right to Remember), *Yash Leninchi*, September 6, 1988.

32. *TASS*, October 25, 1988.

33. *Sovet Ozbekistani*, November 29, 1988.

34. M. Savurov, A. Sheviakov, "Oz Nami bilan Atasak" (Let's Call Things By Their Own Names), *Sovet Ozbekistani*, September 24, 1988.

35. Hajimurad Rasulov, "Degrez mahallasi qaerda?" (Where is the Degrez [Boilermaker] Neighborhood?), *OAS*, November 11, 1988.

36. I. Ghafurov, "Toqsan yil ilgari" (Ninety Years Ago), *OAS*, November 18, 1988.

37. Ibid.

38. Ibid.

39. Gerhard Simon, *Nationalismus und Nationalitätenpolitik in der Sowjetunion*, Baden-Baden (Nomosverlag) 1986. *Now available in English as* Nationalism and Policy toward the Nationalities in the Soviet Union, *Boulder (Westview Press) 1991.*

40. After the French Revolution, 1400 Paris streets were renamed. See Robert Darnton, "What Was Revolutionary About the French Revolution?", *New York Review of Books*, January 19, 1989.

41. *OAS*, December 8, 1989 (interview with A. Yakubov).

42. *Pravda Vostoka*, November 25, 1989.

43. Ibid.

44. *Mushtum*, No. 20, 1989, pp. 10-11 (interview with Gulchehra Nurullaeva).

45. On migration balance, see Ann Sheehy, "1989 Census Data on Internal Migration in the USSR," *Report on the USSR*, November 10, 1989, p. 7.

7

Undoing the Russian Version of History

Generations of Uzbeks had been brought up on a Russocentric Stalinist version of history, which portrayed the non-Russian nationalities as backward peoples who had received support and enlightenment from the Russian "elder brother." For decades, the Uzbeks chafed under this rewriting of their history, which had been continued with little modification under Stalin's successors Khrushchev and Brezhnev. They felt themselves demeaned by their portrayal in official Soviet historiography as primitives dependent for their culture on others whom they regarded as the real primitives. They were made particularly resentful of this by their own perception of their nation as the heir of a high Asian civilization which had spawned intellectual greats long before Moscow was even a rude forest settlement. They also remembered that in Lenin's heyday things had been different, that historians like M. V. Pokrovskiy, later purged by Stalin, had described the subjects of the Russian Empire as victims of colonial oppression.[1] But in Stalin's day, Soviet ideologists moved away from the early Marxist idea of the Russian Empire as a "prison of the peoples." Instead, a wholesale rewriting of history, which persisted well beyond Stalin's death, made "friendship" between the Russian state and the non-Russian peoples retroactive to the pre-revolutionary period.[2] Non-Russian historians were compelled to portray the annexation of their homelands by the tsars in a positive light.

As long as Stalinism held sway, those who challenged the official historiography were apt to be labeled "nationalists," which was tantamount to a criminal charge. Patriotic Uzbek scholars had to limit themselves for the most part to such oblique devices as promoting the *miras,* or national cultural heritage, but always without questioning the supposed superiority of Russian civilization.

Yet even before perestroika, some Uzbek historians had made cautious attempts to redress the historical balance more directly. In the early Brezhnev period, apparently with momentum gained from the relative liberalization of the Khrushchev era, a new four-volume history of Uzbekistan sponsored by the Uzbek Academy of Sciences pronounced the 1898 Andizhan uprising, despite its religious and other supposedly undesirable facets, a "national liberation movement."[3] Such efforts brought down the wrath not only of Moscow's ideologists but also of those opportunists in the Uzbek academic and cultural establishment who had made their reputations as supporters of the Stalinist line. They were disquieting as well to the many who had tacitly accepted the line for no other reason than to survive and now felt threatened by the search for scapegoats. As recently as October 1986, a plenum of the Uzbek Party Central Committee, which was devoted to ideological questions, sharply rapped Uzbek intellectuals for nationalism and "idealizing the (Uzbek) past" through glorification of such "despotic" historical figures as Timur (Tamerlane) and Babur.

Despite such reverses, it ultimately became possible with glasnost to undo the Stalinist rewriting of Uzbek national history and to take a more objective view of relations with Russia. The forces of change won out over defenders of the status quo, if only because many Uzbeks, regardless of their past ties, recognized that their nation's well-being depended on frank confrontation with the past. This chapter retraces, through three selected topics, some of the stages of the struggle to re-examine and re-evaluate that confrontation.

The Anti-Russian Rebellion of 1898

One of the first tangible results of glasnost in Uzbek historiography came in early 1987, in the form of an article by two Tashkent historians attacking the rewriting--during the Stalin and post-Stalin eras--of Uzbek history so as to play down popular resentment of tsarist rule in Central Asia. The impact of their article was to rebuff the influence of Russian nationalism on Soviet historiographical treatment of the non-Russian peoples. They took as their primary topic the historical treatment of the 1898 anti-tsarist uprising in the Ferghana Valley, which was to be the scene of another bloody riot against authority in 1989, ninety-one years later.

Briefly, the Ferghana uprising began on May 17, 1898 in the Andizhan *uezd* village of Mingtepe and quickly spread to Andizhan city, by which time its participants had grown to 2000 in number.[4] At three o'clock in the morning of the next day, the crowd attacked a Russian Army barracks, killing twenty-two and wounding twenty-four soldiers. The untrained rebels were eventually overwhelmed, but not before unrest had triggered troubles in other towns of the Ferghana Valley, including Kokand, Namangan, and Osh. The leader of the uprising, Madali, a Sufi *ishan* nicknamed "Dukchi" ("Spindlemaker"), and five of his comrades were hanged publicly in Andizhan. There were 226 death sentences, and 777 prison sentences. The French historians Bennigsen and Lemercier-Quelquejay have attributed the events to the influence of Wahhabism, a Muslim fundamentalist reform movement.[5]

A principal target of the two historians was the Stalinist toady Mavlan Vahabov (Vakhabov), who had long been dominant in the Uzbek ideological and academic establishment. Vahabov fought back in a later article, but was effectively discredited. The measure of his defeat was signified by the fact that one of his critics, Erkin Yusupov, subsequently went on to play an influential role in the politics of the republic.

In the name of "anti-colonialism" and "national liberation," the historians Yusupov and B. V. Lunin, writing in a publication of the Uzbek Academy of Sciences, now issued a sharp challenge to the Soviet version of history that glossed over past antagonisms between Russians and other nationalities of the tsarist Empire. The authors condemned those who, in keeping with the prevailing ideology, had dismissed the 1898 uprising as a manifestation of religious fanaticism aimed at restoring feudalism.[6] While conceding that the uprising took place "under the green banner of Islam," they charged that those who cited this as proof of its "reactionary nature" were divorced from the reality of those years. They directed much of their fire at the venerable apologist Vahabov, who for a time under Stalin had been a secretary of the Uzbek Party Central Committee. According to Yusupov and Lunin, Vahabov had taken the October 1986 plenum as a signal to renew his attack on the Andizhan uprising.

Yusupov and Lunin objected to the strong language that Vahabov had used in an article[7] published two months after the October 1986 plenum to take advantage of the reactionary atmosphere it had created. Vahabov had written then that:

Certain scholars have behaved like newly-proclaimed kinglets and beys, like "appanage princes" of a certain kind, endowed with the absolute right to pronounce on this or that historical event. . . . At their insistent behest, and against historical facts, the questionable venture of the thoroughgoing obscurantist Madali Ishan in Andizhan in 1898, using the reactionary slogan of "*gazavat*" (holy war) against all Russians, has been announced as the culmination of the popular and anti-colonial movement of the toilers of Turkestan *kray*.[8]

In rebuttal to the substance of Vahabov's thesis, Yusupov and Lunin argued--in cautious deference to the residual sway of of Stalinist survivals--that the anti-Russian content of the uprising was beside the point, that what really mattered was its "social" context. They quoted an eyewitness to the Andizhan events, Prince Mansyrev, as seeing the underlying cause in bribetaking, requisitions, the Russian administration's view of the local population as "a lower race incapable of thought or feeling," and other causes of popular dissatisfaction. "But what a witness to events almost 90 years ago was able to see," they added in a pointed swipe at Vahabov, "some of the researchers of our days are incapable of seeing."

The two authors also cited a version of the events published in 1947, before history had been definitively rewritten in the name of "friendship of the peoples." In it, the historian M.V. Nechkina listed among causes of the uprising the enslavement of the toiling masses in Ferghana as a "cotton region" (a somewhat incendiary reminder even in the early glasnost period), the lowering of their standard of living, the ruinous hegemony of Russian capitalists and local bey-feudal elements, and other socioeconomic factors.[9] Yusupov and Lunin asked a rhetorical question: "Would it have been possible for the harsh colonial regime established here by tsarism . . . not to have engendered in those masses feelings of discontent, protest and anger?"

As for the uprising's religious content, a statement by Engels was cited: "If class warfare . . . has a religious coating, that in no way changes the matter and is easily explained by the conditions of the time." In general, said Vahabov's critics, manifestations of the national-liberation movement should not be dismissed merely because they failed to fit classical forms: "with respect to the specific conditions of Central Asia, this would mean (in keeping with the popular saying) throwing the baby out with the bath water . . . ."

And as for Vahabov himself, "he should not with a single stroke of the pen hand down sentence, figuratively speaking, without right of appeal, on all other historians, his scientific colleagues, who have allowed themselves to express a different view of the 1898 uprising . . ." With apparent irony, the authors recalled in this connection that even Stalin had held that national movements should be approached analytically, in terms of concrete conditions, and they chided Vahabov--with tongue in cheek--for failing to heed this precept.

This indictment of Vahabov had implications well beyond the immediate subject. Vahabov's broadside at the October plenum had placed in jeopardy a range of positions and themes espoused by Uzbek intellectuals who had been attempting to depict the Central Asian past as distinct from--and by implication better than--that of the Russians. Thus, the dispute was central to the whole question of ideological evolution and national autonomy in Uzbekistan and other republics.

The audacity of Yusupov and Lunin in attacking Vahabov, a longtime director (after 1970) of the Uzbek CP's Higher Party School, extended far beyond their immediate target. A prominent Central Asian exponent of the negative view of the Andizhan uprising was Babajan G. Gafurov who, as First Secretary of the Tajik Communist Party (1946-1956) and then until his death in 1977 as director of the Institute of Eastern Studies of the USSR Academy of Sciences, had been a pillar of the Soviet regime's policy in Central Asia.[10] Gafurov was the most prominent Central Asian advocate of the "friendship of the peoples" school of history; thus, not only Vahabov, but all those who had been aligned with Gafurov's views were placed in jeopardy by the Yusupov-Lunin article.

The Yusupov-Lunin publication was significant because of its timing as the earliest full-fledged public victory of historiographical reformers over those who had russified Uzbek history. Much remained to be done, however.

Soviet Suppression of Central Asia's Early Independence

Uzbekistan's declarations of economic and political "sovereignty" in 1990 gave new impetus to the campaign to make history more objective. Still pending resolution, however, were delicate issues in the historiography of the Soviet period which had obvious bearing not only on ongoing relations with Moscow but also on the legitimacy of the traditional power structure in Uzbekistan. By 1990, political evolution had reached the point where native intellectuals could take a new and more jaundiced look at the very underpinnings of Soviet rule.

A pivotal event in the establishment of the Soviet regime, the overthrow in February 1918 of the autonomous Muslim government of Central Asia (the *Qoqan muhtariyati*), whose seat was in the Ferghana Valley city of Kokand, was now being subjected to a searching reappraisal. In a republic where ideology still counted for something, even though no longer dominated by Marxism-Leninism, this revision of history was an important key to official attitudes toward the center.

The political framework for a review of historical treatment of the Kokand government was reflected in high-level declarations like the one made in late November 1990 by Uzbek President Karimov, in which he saw the future of the Soviet Union as one of confederation, an "association of independent states."[11] Karimov and other Uzbek officials were also stressing that delegation of authority by the republics to the center must be entirely voluntary. They were, in effect, attacking the legitimacy of central Soviet rule as it had existed in Central Asia for more than seven decades. They were also affirming Uzbekistan's right to independence; overthrow of Muslim autonomy in Kokand had paved the way for loss of that right.

The story of the independent Muslim government that emerged in the city of Kokand in November 1917 to provide self-rule for the Turkestan territory is full of complexities and contradictions. Briefly, the Kokand government claimed to hold sway over an area largely coterminous with today's republics of Uzbekistan, Tajikistan, Kirghizia, and Turkmenistan (and with parts of Kazakhstan). Its parent body was the Fourth Extraordinary Territorial Muslim Conference, convened in Kokand in the wake of the collapse of the Provisional Government, which was centered in Petrograd. Its brutal overthrow in 1917 by Soviet forces helped to galvanize anti-Soviet resistance in Central Asia. The ethnic character of this action was implicit in the fact that the troops of the Tashkent Soviet in the forefront of the attack on Kokand were largely Russian. Before the action was over, the military commander of the Tashkent forces, Perfil'ev, had ordered artillery to be deployed against the old city of Kokand, causing heavy damage to persons and property, and the invading forces had run amok among the civilian population. Contemporary accounts, even by writers sympathetic to the Bolshevik cause, admit that there were senseless looting and slaughter that "reached monstrous proportions."[12] Although the storming of Kokand was supposedly aimed at relieving a beleaguered pro-Soviet garrison in the citadel of the old city, plundering of the natives extended to outlying villages. According to one Western account:

> The Bolshevik forces easily broke the resistance of the small Muslim detachment defending Kokand, and the city was put to the sack. After three days of massacre and pillage, the utterly ruined city was set on fire. The exact number of Muslims massacred is not known, but it seems to have been very great. A Russian observer, B. Olimsky, reported a few days after its capture: "Kokand is now a dead city." Richard Pipes observes that the population of Kokand, numbering 120,000 before the revolution, had fallen to 69,300 in 1926.[13]

As noted in the first chapter, one consequence of the Kokand action was to swell the ranks of the "Basmachis," the anti-Soviet partisans, who were joined by many new recruits from among Muslims disillusioned with this act of the new regime.

Subsequently, Soviet propagandists attempted to gloss over the atrocities by depicting the Muslim government in Kokand as reactionary and chauvinistic, and by ignoring the excesses of the conquerors. An article that appeared in Brezhnev's last years in the tightly-censored Uzbek Soviet Encyclopedia was typical of the official line still current at that time. This entirely negative treatment referred pejoratively to the Kokand "muhtariyat" as a "bourgeois-nationalist 'government.'" The article charged its leaders with such various sins as seeking to end Soviet rule in Turkestan; wanting to restore the old Kokand khanate, which had been put out of existence by tsarist administrators back in 1876 (the khanate was referred to elsewhere in the Encyclopedia as "feudal," with a "backward socioeconomic order"); trying to detach Turkestan from Soviet Russia; and trying to unite Muslims into a single state headed by Turkey. The autonomous Kokand government was also taxed with having made common cause with White forces against the new "workers and peasants" regime. The Encyclopedia was vague about the demise of the autonomy movement, saying only that it was put down by Red Guards acting in concert with "Red Muslim partisans," local miners, and Kokand workers, and that some of its leaders were arrested. There was no mention of civilian losses or the brutality of the largely non-Muslim invaders.[14]

By contrast, materials published in Uzbekistan in 1990 and afterward took a much more sympathetic view of the Kokand government. A writer named Khasanov devoted an article to the government in the Tashkent literary monthly *Zvezda Vostoka*, with the suggestive title, "An Alternative." He noted that the Muslim Congress that formed the Kokand government "has for many decades been pasted with the label of a band of nationalists and reactionary clergy," and he insisted that this description could only have been the result of dishonesty. In the writer's words:

> After all, a whole row of democratically oriented representatives of the national intelligentsia uttered ideas during the congress which would never have occurred to narrow-minded nationalists. In particular, the well-known Uzbek reformer M. Behbudi, in a speech about the competence of the congress bore down hard on the fact that "the decisions of the congress will be all the more authoritative in that representatives of the European population of Turkestan are present." Behbudi proposed forming the presidium of the congress so that it would include representatives of various non-Muslim groups-- Russians, Jews *et al.*[15]

Khasanov, who reported that he had used archives previously inaccessible to Soviet researchers, disclosed that one-third of the seats at the congress were earmarked for the European component of the territorial population, which at the time made up only about seven percent of the total number of inhabitants of Turkestan.[16]

As for the actual overthrow of the Kokand government, Khasanov questioned whether the use of artillery was justified "from the military or the moral point of view." He concluded that it was not, if only because many of those who suffered had nothing to do with the political forces in Kokand. He cited indignant contemporary comments by the native press and a memorandum prepared for the Ferghana military commander concluding that "the actions of the authorities were purely colonialist and unconsciously fostered development of an active nationalist movement."[17]

The new preoccupation of Central Asians with the issue of the Kokand Muslim government and its suppression by the Tashkent Soviet was evident from the frequency of mentions which had begun to appear in local press, especially in the Uzbek intellectual weekly *Ozbekistan adabiyati va san"ati.* In September 1990, the weekly carried a scholarly roundtable in which one of the participants asserted that widespread support of the Kokand Muslim government by Central Asian intellectuals of the day showed that they had accepted it as "the most correct path." The speaker referred to verse composed in its honor by the Uzbek poet Hamza, generally regarded even in the Stalin period as a pillar of fellow-traveling orthodoxy.[18] The following month, October 1990, another writer in the same newspaper, recalling the independent Muslim government established there, declared that "Kokand was one of the centers where the national spirit was kept pure under seventy years of politics."[19] Also in that month, a corresponding member of the Uzbek Academy of Sciences published an article in which he contrasted the Kokand government and its majority of native members with the Turkestan Territory's Soviet Council of People's Commissars, formed earlier the same month "without a single representative of a local nationality."[20]

By the time these articles appeared, the practical problems associated with Uzbekistan's new "sovereign" existence had begun to bring home a more realistic appreciation of the need to co-operate with the center and with other Soviet republics. At the same time, the old myths of allegiance to a benign Russian "elder brother" had been irreparably shattered by revelations like those about the true nature of the region's first and only progressive Muslim government and its cold-blooded extermination more than seven decades ago by Russian-dominated forces acting in the name of Moscow.

The Russian Conquest Revisited

Central to the question of the Russian presence in Central Asia, in both the tsarist and Soviet periods, was the Russian conquest with which it had begun in the nineteenth century. As such, the conquest was a delicate political topic that historians had long evaded. It was only in the latter part of 1990 that a serious attempt was made by an Uzbek

127

writer to come to grips with it, in the form of an outspoken article in the Uzbek literary monthly *Sharq Yulduzi*.[21]   The author was a well-known Uzbek historian, Hamid Z. Ziyaev, who had been in the forefront of those seeking to expose fictions invented by Soviet historians under Stalin and his successors to justify tsarist colonial policy in Central Asia.

In reviewing the conquest, Professor Ziyaev used archival sources, apparently some of them previously unpublished. This was how he summed up the impact of colonial policy on the Central Asian territory:

> In setting up its colonialist policy over the rich and endless spaces of Central Asia and Kazakhstan, the tsarist government harshly exploited the broad mass of toilers and ruthlessly plundered natural resources. It constantly hindered the development of national languages and culture. A great and wealthy territory was converted to Russia's raw-materials base and market for finished goods. That is why V. I. Lenin called Turkestan "the purest example of colonialism."[22]

Professor Ziyaev, who was sixty-eight years of age at the time of writing and had already authored numerous historical works, was in December 1987 the principal protagonist in a bitter confrontation with native Stalinist historians who had made their reputations in earlier days through slavish defense of Russian colonial rule.   The confrontation came at a meeting held in Tashkent for the immediate purpose of re-evaluating the historiography of the 1898 Andizhan uprising, and to adjudicate the conflict between the old Stalinist Vahabov and his critics Yusupov and Lunin. In fact, the discussion had ideological implications that far transcended the topic at hand, since it called into question the entire Stalinist and neo-Stalinist school of historiography.   In his speech to the meeting, Ziyaev succeeded in demolishing the arguments of Vahabov, who made a desperate last-ditch defense of the Stalin-era thesis that the uprising of Central Asian Muslims had been "reactionary and anti-popular."[23]

Cruelty and Cupidity

Now turning his attention to the Russian military conquest in his latest article, Ziyaev prefaced it with a summary of Russia's centuries of southeastward expansion through Siberia and Kazakhstan "under the banner" of trade and border security.[24] He traced Russia's designs on the region back to the time of Peter the Great, recalling that in 1717 a well-armed force of 1,500 soldiers commanded by Prince A. Bekovich-Cherkasskiy had set out to attack Khiva but had been destroyed by the army of the khanate. By the middle of the last century, tsarist armies were positioned to threaten in strength the three Central Asian khanates of Bukhara, Khiva and Kokand.

Professor Ziyaev stressed the cruelty and cupidity of the invaders and the desperate intensity of native resistance to them. He recalled the Muslim defense of the town of Turkistan (in present-day Kazakhstan) in June 1864, which cost hundreds of native lives and was broken only when the Russians threatened to cannonade a Muslim holy place, the tomb of the twelfth-century Sufi philosopher Ahmad Yasawii (whose work, incidentally, is again today evoking attention from Central Asian admirers looking for new sources of inspiration). When a Muslim clergyman of Tashkent, Salih Bek Akhun, defiantly rejected a demand by the Russian military commander, General (then Colonel) Chernyaev, to sign a mendacious statement (see below) saying that the invaders had been received without resistance and with open arms, he and seven of his followers were clapped into prison cells and then exiled to Siberia.[25] When Samarkand became a focus of rebellion against the occupation, Russian General K. P. Kaufman ordered the city's bazaar and shops burned, the execution of 19 participants, and the lifelong exile to Siberia of 19 others. (Russian casualties were 275 killed and wounded.) When an uprising swept the Ferghana Valley, General Skobelev personally had houses leveled to the ground and thousands of people "exterminated." In Andizhan alone, the scene of the later 1898 uprising, 20,000 persons were "bestially" liquidated. After the conquest of the Bukhara and Khiva khanates, they were ordered--despite the killing and wounding of thousands of their inhabitants--to pay the costs of the war, assessed, respectively, at 500,000 and 2,500,000 rubles. Ziyaev quoted the tsarist Finance Minister as having gloatingly observed that Central Asia was "the most valuable jewel in the Russian crown."

Determined Resistance

As an example of Central Asian defiance of the invaders, Ziyaev cited the answer given to a Russian surrender demand by the defenders of the fortress of Aq Machit (today, Kzyl Orda in Kazakhstan): "As long as we still have a bit of powder and a brickbat in the street, we'll fight until our weapons are completely useless."[26] Aq Machit, he wrote, had been subdued only after 22 days of siege and fighting, when the tsarist attackers finally succeeded in demolishing it. No more than 74 of the defenders remained alive; the tsarist army lost 25 killed and 46 wounded. In later years, Muslim forces made desperate efforts to retake the fortress but were repulsed with heavy losses.

In Tashkent, Salih Bek Akhun's reply to Colonel Chernyaev's coercion of the city elders to obtain a statement that they had welcomed the invasion was a further instance of defiance in the face of superior force. The reply, whose truculent stress on the indomitable spirit of the defenders so angered Chernyaev, was quoted by Ziyaev as follows:

> ... The city of Tashkent was without water and food from the middle of Dhu al-Hijjah to the twelfth of Safar (Muslim months), or for forty-two days. When Mulla Alim Qul, the commander, was killed, it remained without a military leader. Those in Bukhara, Khorezm and Ferghana did not give assistance. (But) the people of Tashkent stood up for their homelands and their religion and kept fighting even after, on Tuesday mid-evening, Russian soldiers, with victory in the offing, entered through the street gate and over the wall of the fortress. From then until Thursday, two nights and days later, they kept up the battle. Only after many buildings, shops and homes were burned down, after hand-to-hand fighting without food and water, was a truce finally concluded.[27]

Stalinist Rewriting of History

This picture of determined Central Asian resistance to the Russian advance was in marked contrast to the Stalinist version of "voluntary" annexation, which prevailed in Soviet historiography long after Stalin's death. In a work published in 1969, the American historian Lowell Tillett wrote:

> With the advent of Soviet patriotism, it became axiomatic that Russian acquisitions of land were, regardless of the circumstances, historically progressive acts. In time the manner of acquisition itself has been re-examined and reinterpreted. In a large number of cases

territories are said to have been acquired *voluntarily* (emphasis added), through the wishes of their leaders, and even of their peoples. Even when the use of force is admitted, it has been softened by a great variety of euphemisms and justified by extenuating circumstances, involving the defense of the local people, the growth of the Russian state, and the economic and cultural betterment of the population.[28]

This Russocentric interpretation cited by Tillett, which prevailed in Stalin's later years, is greatly at odds with the writings of Soviet historians of the earlier post-revolutionary period and even well into Stalin's reign, who still saw Russian colonialism as a great evil and did not hesitate to document popular resistance to it; Tillett pointed out that "as late as 1949" a Soviet textbook noted that "the peoples of Central Asia offered prolonged resistance, and subordination to Russian rule was nowhere voluntary."[29] However, before Stalin left the scene the official view of Russian expansionism as a boon welcomed by its non-Russian victims had become obligatory. By the late Khrushchev period, the de-Stalinization campaign made possible some attempts to restore a measure of historical verity whose momentum carried over into the early Brezhnev period: thus, the four-volume Uzbek history published in 1968 referred to "the predatory aims of tsarism" and gave quotes from contemporary native and Russian accounts of hard fighting by the defenders. In Brezhnev's later years, however, Stalinist historians in Central Asia, like Vahabov, regained much of their leverage, and it was only well into the perestroika period that the tide began to turn once more.

The Tsarist Antecedents

Soviet rewriting of Russian colonial history had its tsarist precursors. Even at the time of the conquest, Ziyaev charged, Russian officials like Chernyaev deliberately downplayed the fierceness of the defenders' resistance in order to soothe opinion at home and abroad. In the case of Tashkent, the statement extracted by Chernyaev from the city elders to make it appear that they had welcomed the Russians was distributed in the form of handbills by the Russian ambassador in Constantinople.[30]

Ziyaev described another device used to make it appear that Central Asia had been pacified: a ceremonial visit to St. Petersburg in the spring of 1867 by a group of native collaborators who were received with "high pomp" by the Tsar and shown around the city's points of interest. At that point, Central Asia was actually so far from peaceful acceptance of Russian rule that not long after the beginning of the visit, Ziyaev recalled, there was a pitched battle in Yangikurghan (between Jizzakh [Dzhizak] and Samarkand) involving a force of 45,000 Bukharan troops and volunteers. This was followed by an attack on Samarkand, then part of the Bukharan Emirate.

Some Central Asian Villains

Not all of the villains of the conquest as portrayed by Ziyaev were Russians. In his view, it was not the lack of determination of the ordinary Central Asians which resulted in their defeat, but the incompetence and lack of preparedness of the khans who ruled over them. In this indictment, the shining exception was the Kokand military leader and de facto ruler, Alim Qul, who was killed leading the defense of Tashkent. Ziyaev was unsparing in his condemnation of the Emir of Bukhara, Muzaffar Khan, who was concerned mainly for his own skin; who took advantage of the Russian presence to attack a fellow Muslim ruler; who ordered the execution of the messenger who brought him the unwelcome news that the Russians were attacking Samarkand; and who was goaded into resisting the attack only because he was threatened by an uprising of his own people if he did not.

According to Ziyaev, the distraught Emir turned to his entourage of beks for advice on how to deal with the Russians. One of his military commanders, Usman Bek, assured him: "The people of the khanate demand continuation of the war; at the same time, they would rather fight to the last drop of blood than pay tribute to the infidels." This opinion was unanimously endorsed by participants in the meeting with the Emir, and an army of 15,000 horsemen, 6,000 infantrymen, and 14 cannon prepared to do battle with the Russians. Ziyaev quoted the manifesto which the Emir had been emboldened to issue to the troops:

Faithful Muslim subjects! . . . We are the descendants of Timur (Tamerlane), we shall show how to recapture our land. Muslims! I hope that you will show the infidels how valiantly the Muslim people fight for our religion and our land. The people are expecting victory from you—let them say after the battle that you defended religion and the homeland, and rid our land of the infidels. . . .

This manifesto was read to the troops amid the sound of cannonfire. However, heavy losses led to the defeat of the defenders. According to Ziyaev, news of the defeat so enraged the people of Bukhara that the Emir fled toward the Kizil Kum desert.

The Emir of Bukhara was not the only ruler portrayed by Ziyaev as experiencing popular wrath at his failure to defend his land against the Russians. The Khan of Kokand, Khudayar, avoided action against the invaders in the hope that they would keep him on the throne as his protectors. He did in fact receive an imperial decoration, but in the face of popular indignation was finally overthrown in 1876 and, loading his wealth onto forty carriages, fled to Tashkent. There the Russian Governor-General, Kaufman, repaid his loyalty by confiscating his possessions and exiling him to Orenburg.

The Muslim Masses as Heroes of the Struggle

In Ziyaev's view, it is "natural" for the upper classes of any country to commit treason in the face of foreign aggression. In his rendering of the conquest of Central Asia, it was the common people who were the heroes. Far from being cowardly and demoralized during the more than twenty years (1853-1876) of the Russian advance, they fought bravely against hopeless odds. Ziyaev wrote:

Thousands of ordinary people, armed with axes and sticks, fought valiantly despite being surrounded from all sides by several times more powerful and better armed tsarist armies. They stood steadfast before a hail of bullets raining from the soldiers' cannons and rifles.

Incidentally, this Uzbek historian's judgment is shared by a Western scholar, Edward Allworth:

In open encounters when the Central Asians stood against the concentrated firepower, particularly the grapeshot, of Russian units, the local forces absorbed terrible casualties, losses which the extended Russian offensive columns could not have withstood, and it is therefore misleading to picture, as observers sometimes had, a

133

cowardly Muslim rabble fleeing before heroic Russian exploits. Courage, when it showed itself on a large scale, was characteristic of Central Asians against frightening odds . . . ."[31]

Notes

1. For a book-length discussion of Stalinist historiographical treatment of the non-Russian nationalities, see Lowell Tillett, *The Great Friendship*, Chapel Hill (University of North Carolina Press) 1969.

2. For an account of twists in Soviet historiography on the Andizhan uprising, see the chapter "Classifying the Central Asian Revolts," in Tillett, *Great Friendship*, pp. 171 *ff*. Revision of Central Asian history, while initiated in Stalin's lifetime, exhibited its worst excesses after his death.

3. *Istoriya Uzbekskoy SSR* (in four volumes), Tashkent 1968, Vol. II, Chap. 3.

4. For a relatively objective Uzbek version, see "Andizhan qozghalani" (The Andizhan Uprising), *Ozbek Sovet Entsiklopediyasi*, Tashkent 1971, Vol. I, p. 367. The Encyclopedia was one of the targets of Vahabov's December 1986 tirades (see below).

5. Alexandre Bennigsen and Chantal Lemercier-Quelquejay, *Islam in the Soviet Union* (New York 1967), p. 32.

6. E. Yu. Yusupov and B. V. Lunin, "Andizhanskoe vosstanie 1898 g. v sovetskoy istoricheskoy literature" (The Andizhan Uprising of 1898 in Soviet Historical Literature), *Obshchestvennye nauki v Uzbekistane (ONU)*, No. 1, 1987. Erkin Yusupov, a 58-year-old Tashkent native and Vice-President of the Uzbek Academy of Sciences, had been a full member of that body since 1979. Lunin, from his name a Russian, was identified as doctor of historical sciences and head of the Historiography Department of the Academy's Institute of History.

7. For a discussion of the October plenum and Vahabov's article, in which the Andizhan uprising was only one of many topics, see *Radio Liberty Research (RLR)* 11/87, December 23, 1987.

8. *Pravda Vostoka*, December 4, 1986. As noted in *RLR* 11/87, Vahabov used this article to condemn a wide range of positions adopted by Uzbek writers in praising the national heritage.

9. *Istoriya narodov Uzbekistana*, Tashkent 1947, Vol. II, pp. 362-70.

10. Yusupov and Lunin, "Andizhanskoe vosstanie," recall in a footnote that as late as 1949 Gafurov had held a relatively positive view of the Andizhan affair but had subsequently changed it, presumably under Party pressure.

11. Reported by TASS, November 23, 1990.

12. G. Safarov, *Kolonial'naya revolyutsiya*, Moscow (Gosizdat) 1921, p. 80.

13. Benningsen and Lermercier-Quelquejay, *Islam in the Soviet Union*, p. 85.

14. See "Qoqan muhtariyati" (The Kokand Autonomy), *Ozbekistan Sovet Entsiklopediyasi*, Vol. 14, pp. 298-99, also "Qoqan khanligi" (The Khanate of Kokand), Ibid., pp. 300-302.

15. M. Khasanov, "Al'ternativa" (An Alternative), *Zvezda Vostoka*, No. 7, 1990, p. 107. Mahmud Khoja Behbudi was a well-known reformer associated with the jadid movement.

16. Ibid., p. 108.

17. Ibid., p. 117.

18. *Ozbekistan adabiyati va san"ati (OAS)*, September 28, 1990.

19. *OAS*, October 5, 1990.

20. *OAS*, October 19, 1990.

21. *Sharq Yulduzi*, No. 8, 1990, pp. 184-90.

22. Although many Uzbek intellectuals continue to view the world largely through the prism of their Marxist educations, quotations of Lenin, like this one, were by now appearing in their media chiefly to buttress arguments against the policies of the center, in an effort evidently calculated to let the Moscow rulers be hoist with their own ideological petard.

23. *ONU*, No. 5, 1988. It was the measure of Ziyaev's victory over Vahabov that his report to the meeting was published in the next issue of this same publication. When Ziyaev's 1990 article on the Russian conquest appeared, the 81-year-old Vahabov was still active in public life, although now apparently without institutional affiliation: he was co-author of a reply to a reader's letter in *Kommunist Uzbekistana*, No. 7, 1990. The Uzbek Communist Party's Higher Party School, of which he was once director, was renamed "Institute of Politology"--a sign of the changed ideological climate in Uzbekistan. Vahabov died in the first part of 1991.

24. Ziyaev did not bother with the argument, used until recently by Soviet historians, that the Russian advance was motivated in part by a British threat from the south.

25. Not all clergymen were on the Muslim side. When tsarist troops broke through a city gate to enter Tashkent, the assault was led by a Russian Orthodox priest holding high his cross and shouting,"*Ura!*" The priest was later awarded a medal for valor. See Edward Allworth, *Central Asia: 120 Years of Russian Rule*, Durham (Duke University Press) 1989, p. 1, citing *Turkestankiy kray: sbornik materialov dlya istorii ego zavoevaniya*, Tashkent (Izdanie Shtaba Turkestanskago Voennago Okruga) 1914.

26. Ziyaev gives as his source for this quote *Turkestanskiy sbornik*, Vol. 58, p. 22. This is presumably the work referred to in the previous footnote.

27. Ziyaev gives as his source a manuscript in the archives of the Uzbek Academy of Sciences Oriental Institute.

28. Tillett, *Great Friendship*, p. 331.

29. Ibid., p. 333.

30. *Istoriya uzbekskoy SSR* (in four vols.). Ziyaev was a member of the editorial board of the series.

31. Allworth, *The Modern Uzbeks*, p. 16.

8

Resistance to Authority

The years following Mikhail Gorbachev's virtual declaration of war on the Uzbek elites at the Twenty-Seventh Congress of the Communist Party of the Soviet Union in February 1986 witnessed a progressive hardening of Uzbekistan's resistance to central authority. As we have seen in the preceding three chapters, the broad opportunities offered by glasnost made it possible for the Uzbeks to assess the consequences of the Soviet "experiment" in their homeland with unprecedented public candor. The result, articulation of bitter grievances against Moscow's economic and environmental policies and against the Russian presence itself, was an important factor in mobilizing a collective determination to press for greater autonomy.

In the beginning, resistance was quiet, as the elites avoided direct confrontation with a political power that still seemed all but invincible. Stealth was the order of the day. Later, defiance became more open.

At the same time, as challenges to federal authority evoked no response from the center, or only a feeble one, it became evident that those in Moscow--faced with a Pandora's box of crisis situations throughout the entire country--no longer had the ability, or the will, to display the ruthlessness toward Uzbekistan that had characterized most of the Soviet period.

In this chapter, four subjects have been selected to illustrate milestones in the changing power relationship and political climate of the critical years 1986-1989. The first deals with the early period immediately following the Moscow Congress, the period of indirect resistance.

Thwarting the Purge

When criticism of Uzbekistan at the Moscow Party Congress in February 1986 was followed by threats to replace indigenous Uzbeks with other nationalities in the republic's Party and government apparatus, seasoned observers of Soviet politics assumed that devastating changes would not be long in coming. Even before the Congress, Russians had assumed certain key posts traditionally held by Uzbeks.[1] At the Congress itself, there was Gorbachev's speech singling out Uzbekistan for special criticism, and Ligachev's menacing call for "interrepublican exchange of cadres." In June 1987, the Central Committee in Moscow had issued a decree condemning the Tashkent oblast Party organization, inter alia, for keeping non-Uzbeks out of the Party ranks; the decree became the obligatory text for Party meetings throughout Uzbekistan.[2] Armed with the decree, non-Uzbeks tried to stir up anti-Uzbek feeling by invoking its argument that, given the multinational composition of Uzbekistan, the Uzbek nationality was greatly overrepresented in key positions. Cadre policy became the dominant topic on the Party agenda, always with ethnic overtones, accompanied by resurrection of the hoary Stalinist slogan, "Cadres decide everything." It seemed that Moscow and its supporters were aiming to purge the Uzbek apparatus through a radical ethnic transformation, one that would irreparably weaken the Uzbeks' grip on their own affairs, while strengthening central control.

Contrary to expectation, these plans of the center came to very little. In determining the outcome, events of the three years following the Moscow Congress were crucial. At the end of this period, in 1989, a minute examination of staffing patterns in Uzbekistan showed that the native elites had succeeded, while avoiding frontal conflict, in hamstringing Moscow's personnel policies in their republic. By then, it appeared that the Kremlin had all but abandoned its aggressive personnel policy. Soviet power was still able to target specific jobs or persons, as in the case of former Uzbek First Secretary Inamjan Usmankhojaev, who was dismissed in January 1988 (to be replaced by a fellow Uzbek) and arrested later in the same year, and others who were singled out as individuals and purged. At the same time, the Moscow leadership did not succeed in carrying through wide-ranging ethnic change within the composition of Uzbek Party organs: in the face of determined resistance by the Uzbek elite, the political, social, and economic costs were evidently perceived as too high. This reaffirmed the limitations of Soviet power in confrontation not merely with Uzbekistan, a "backward" area where overt national dissidence was relatively muted, but with the non-Russian republics in general.

Despite the threatening tenor of the rhetoric of Gorbachev and other top Soviet officials at the 1986 Party Congress and after, Uzbek representation in the Party and government apparatus was largely undiminished three years later:

- Uzbeks and other Central Asians[3] continued to maintain a large plurality of first-secretary and chairman posts at all recorded levels of the Party and government apparatus.

- The longstanding pattern of ethnic balancing, with Slavs placed in second-secretary and deputy chairman posts when Central Asians hold the top jobs, or vice versa in the minority of cases where Slavs were at the top, remained largely in force at republican, oblast, and raikom levels.[4] (Even after 1989, as Uzbek power continued to grow, vestiges of this pattern were still discernible, with the difference that Slavic incumbents were more apt to be persons with longstanding residence in the republic and regarded by the Uzbeks as "respectful" of the local culture, instead of apparatchiki sent in by Moscow to guard its interests. The modified pattern seemed to be a way of promoting stability by allowing "friendly" Russians and others of European ethnic origin to participate in political life, and perhaps also of mollifying those in Moscow who were alarmed by overt challenges to central power.)

- In what appeared to be a concession to the federal structure, some important high-level posts occupied by Slavs, such as the chairmanship of the republican KGB, and certain posts in the Central Committee apparatus, were still staffed by Moscow-appointed apparatchiki. If nothing else, this showed Uzbek recognition that Moscow was still to be dealt with cautiously. (As we have seen, Slavic occupancy of strategic positions in Uzbekistan did not always guarantee loyalty to Moscow; the "cotton affair" demonstrated the possibility that outsiders could be co-opted to local interests.)

Similarly, the Slavic presence in law enforcement was strengthened in 1988 by appointment of a Russian in place of a Central Asian to chairmanship of the Committee of People's Control. The republican Prosecutor's Office, which had been a Central Asian position until charges of widespread corruption surfaced at the fateful June 1984 plenum of the Uzbek Central Committee, remained in Russian hands at the top. At the same time, Central Asians retained the ministries of internal affairs and justice, the chairmanship of the Supreme Court, and the Central Committee Commission on People's Control. The shift in favor of Russian incumbents in high-level law-enforcement positions seemed to be a concession to the Kremlin's preoccupation with "crime and corruption" in Uzbekistan. At the same time, the ouster of MVD General Didorenko, discussed in the next section, demonstrated that the center's representatives could no longer trammel Uzbek interests with impunity.

- In 1989, Central Asian incumbents maintained a slight majority (seven seats to six for Slavs) on the Uzbek Party's Central Committee Buro. This was largely a phenomenon of transitional importance, since power was already shifting from the Party to the government, as symbolized by Party First Secretary Karimov's designation in 1990 to be President of Uzbekistan (following the pattern set by Gorbachev in Moscow, but with distinctly Uzbek content). Thus, the staffing of the Uzbek Presidential Council appointed that same year by Karimov in his new status was overwhelmingly Uzbek.[5]

- Of five Central Committee "commissions" created in December 1988 in keeping with the Gorbachev reforms, a majority of three (ideology, legal questions, social and economic development) had Central Asians designated as chairmen, while only two were headed by Slavs (organizational-party work, agroindustrial complex). Rank-and-file members of the commissions were overwhelmingly Central Asian.[6] In the Central Committee secretariat, whose importance had supposedly now been diminished under the reforms, there had been an even 3:3 distribution of appointments between Central Asians and Slavs.

- Central Asians continued by far to outnumber Slavs in the Council of Ministers, both as ministers and chairmen of state committees, although Slavs retained certain key political and economic portfolios. It was noteworthy as an example of resistance to cadre change that, in spite of Moscow's continuing sharp criticism of Uzbekistan for lagging economically, both its all-important agroindustrial complex and its state planning function were entrusted to Uzbeks who had been associated with the Rashidov administration at the height of the "cotton affair." Indeed, the Chairman of the State Committee charged with the agroindustrial complex, Ismail Kh. Jorabekov, had served for years during that period as Minister of Land Reclamation and Water Economy, i.e. at precisely the time when reckless development of irrigation was wreaking incalculable harm on the Uzbek economy and ecology. In the politically sensitive area of the ecology, the State Committee for Environmental Protection was headed in 1989 by an Uzbek, Timur A. Alimov, who had also been a prominent officeholder under Rashidov, when Uzbekistan suffered its worst ecological damage.

- In 1985, shortly before the Party Congress, Moscow had wielded its power to appoint a Russian, Boris F. Satin, to replace an Uzbek as first secretary of the Tashkent City Party Organization. At the time, this had seemed to portend a revolution in cadres policy, evidence that Moscow could have its own way in Uzbekistan. With the hindsight of later years, the Satin appointment seemed to have been an almost isolated instance; moreover, when Satin was eventually removed, the position was restored to Uzbek incumbency.

- At the level of the oblast Party organizations, Slavic representation among the first secretaries was reduced in 1988 from two to one through an administrative-territorial consolidation which eliminated two of thirteen oblasts. This may have been an unintended effect of the reorganization, but it left only the first secretaryship of Syrdar'ya oblast in Slavic hands. In the ten remaining oblasts, the Slav second secretary was very much a lone figure, since the other secretaries were Central Asians (except in Tashkent oblast with its substantial

141

European population, where one of three rank-and-file secretaries was a Slav).

- Perhaps the best evidence that day-to-day control of the machinery remained in Central Asian hands was at the lower but vital level of first secretaryships of district (rayon) Party organizations, which traditionally oversaw the primary Party organizations, presided over admissions to and expulsions from the Party, and functioned "as the basic record offices of the Party."[7] In particular, since the raykoms managed the nomenklatura lists for primary Party organizations at enterprises and institutions, they had more immediate access to the levers of economic and social activity than did higher-ranking bodies with greater nominal authority. Of 71 rural and urban raikoms whose present or recent first secretaries could be identified, 61 (86 percent) were identifiable as Central Asians, 9 (13 percent) as Slavs, and one as an Armenian. For 45 of these 71 posts, approximately two-thirds, it was possible to trace the nationality of pre-1986 incumbents.[8] In only five cases had the nationality of the incumbent changed, four from Central Asian to Slav, and one from Slav to Central Asian, a net gain of only three incumbencies for the Slavs. Thus, while Uzbeks accounted for only slightly more than two-thirds of the Republic's population, they still held--in this sampling of more than a third of total raions--nearly nine-tenths of raikom first secretaryships.[9]

In sum, after announcing its intention to shake up the Uzbek Party and government apparatus on a broad scale, Moscow had failed to do so. The concerted attack on Uzbek cadres launched even before the 1986 Party Congress, which reached its apogee in 1987 with the Central Committee decree nominally devoted to the Tashkent obkom but in effect targeting republican Party organizations throughout Central Asia, had little permanent impact on the ethnicity of the apparatus in Uzbekistan. Most important, while the Kremlin had maintained its dwindling strategic bridgehead at the policy level and at lower watchdog levels, the actual business of governing was still overwhelmingly in Uzbek hands.

Given the considerable growth of Uzbek power vis-à-vis Moscow since 1989, this dissection of the anatomy of Uzbek resistance in the three years preceding is now largely of historical interest. It is worthy of consideration even today, however, for what it tells about the cohesiveness and determination--above all, the nationalism--of the Uzbek elites.

By the watershed year of 1989, Moscow had withdrawn from the offensive, to judge from the diminished emphasis on cadres in official public discussion in Uzbekistan. Some of the causes of this retreat were no doubt external to Uzbekistan: it happened to coincide with the eclipse of Ligachev as Central Committee secretary responsible for cadres, and with the Kremlin's preoccupation with other problems, and crises in other national republics, as perestroika seemed to lose momentum.

At the same time, the root cause was clearly internal: the intransigence of the Uzbek elites as reflected in numerous complaints by spokesmen for Moscow's interests. In a few instances, this intransigence was blatant, as when a deposed city official organized a march of war veterans to protest his dismissal.[10] More typically, it was manifested through circumvention of directives on personnel policy: without the co-operation of the Uzbek elites, Moscow and its proconsuls in the republic simply lacked the means of engineering broad-ranging personnel change. It was the Uzbeks who had their fingers on such levers of personnel power as the cadre "reserve" lists, from which candidates for nomenklatura appointments were selected; before Moscow eventually abandoned its cadre campaign, there were frequent accusations that local interests were manipulating these lists. There were instances of quiet sabotage, as when "compromised" Uzbek officials were stealthily transferred to other posts, or when outsiders brought into the republic were undercut in the performance of their tasks. In all of this, there was an underlying constant: Moscow's inability to overcome its dependency on the local elites, on an uneasy relationship that had persisted ever since the Russian conquest of the last century, necessitated by the inability of Russians to bridge the linguistic and cultural gap which separated them from Central Asians. In the second half of the twentieth century, demographic trends, the relative decrease in size of the Russian core in Uzbekistan, had further intensified that dependency.

When Moscow finally retreated from its scheme to purge the Uzbek apparatus, it left the native elites with a new sense of confidence in their own power.

The Case of MVD General Didorenko

A further test of the changing power relationship between Moscow and Tashkent was not long in coming. Uzbeks had an opportunity to voice their discontent with one of the trappings of Moscow's imperial rule, the longstanding practice of appointing outsiders as officials to administer the republic. The opportunity arose when, in February 1989, a storm of controversy with ethnic overtones was stirred by Uzbekistan's Moscow-appointed First Deputy Minister of Internal Affairs (MVD), General Eduard Alekseevich Didorenko, who had already made himself a target of Uzbek resentment. Now, Didorenko further incensed Uzbeks by claiming in an interview with a Tashkent newspaper that all of the new informal groups that had come to life in the republic in response to "democratization" were in fact "camouflaged criminals." In the interview, he succeeded in offending both Uzbeks and local Europeans, the former with epithets like "pathological nationalist" and the latter by implying that they were tainted with inefficiency and corruption. In response, his critics--who included the republic's main Russian-language newspaper--accused him of "chauvinism," sowing ethnic discord, violations of "socialist legality," and being inept at the job of law enforcement.[11] He was rebuked for adopting a position that was "harmful"--still a dire word in the Soviet lexicon.

Ever since the tsarist occupation of the last century, authority in Central Asia had been wielded by officials sent to govern by the center, first from imperial St. Petersburg, later from Soviet Moscow. It may be recalled that not until 1929, twelve years after the Revolution, was an Uzbek, Akmal Ikramov, named as first secretary to head the Uzbek Communist Party; before that it had been led by Russians. After Ikramov's accession, the power of the native first secretaries was hamstrung by a network of officials assigned to the republic by Moscow, from the proconsular Russian "second" secretary (who traditionally had more power than the Uzbek "first") on down. Moscow also ruled through its tight control of the security organs, the KGB (as it is known in its most recent incarnation) and the MVD (ministry of internal affairs). Thus, General Didorenko was a symbol of alien authority.

Interestingly, the Didorenko case was a reminder that tensions between the center and the national republics were not limited to purely ethnic divisions. Russians long resident in Uzbekistan were angered by the fact that Didorenko had included them as well as the

Uzbeks in his scathing indictment of the republic. Didorenko's interview with the Tashkent newspaper, and the reaction to it, were also interesting because of new light on sociopolitical divisions in the power structure of Central Asia:

- The *priezzhye*: Non-indigenous officials who had been deployed in recent years to Central Asia from posts outside the region, as part of Moscow's campaign to eliminate "corruption" and other "negative phenomena." Judging from Didorenko's complaints, this group, of which he was a prominent member, were frustrated by local resistance to their efforts and by the strangeness and impenetrability of Uzbek society to them as outsiders.

- The *mestnye*: Local Europeans who were born in Central Asia or had resided there for many years. This group had more of a long-term stake in the future of the region, and tended to be relatively more sympathetic to the indigenous nationalities and their ways. As their response to the Didorenko interview showed, they were apt to join the Uzbeks in resenting the "*priezzhye*" and to feel discriminated against by Moscow, while at the same time forced to depend on Soviet power to protect their status and security among the Asian population.

- "Loyal" indigenous Central Asians: Those who had become publicly identified with support for the Soviet system, even though they might on occasion criticize individual Moscow policies. Having cast in their lot with the system, they were at odds with the more nationalistic and independence-minded elements of their own societies. At the same time, Didorenko's comments showed their vulnerability to ethnic prejudice on the part of the *priezzhye*.

- National "extremists" among the indigenous population: Perhaps the only point on which Didorenko and his critics in the Uzbek elite agreed was that there was widespread activity by "extremists," although Didorenko's claim that these were tightly linked with the "informal groups" was heatedly challenged. The actions of the "extremists" allegedly ranged from dissemination of leaflets viewed as subversive to death

145

threats against those who co-operated with the system, whether Europeans or natives. (It should be noted that in Soviet usage the term "extremist" had become a handy label for conservatives to discredit opposition elements spawned in the new climate of perestroika.)

- "Corrupt" officials: Those who took bribes, engaged in padding economic reports, or pursued other activities regarded as illegal by the system. Members of this group, it seemed, operated from a variety of motives, of which personal gain was not the only one: there were cases on record when their "illegalities" were motivated by a desire to circumvent the dysfunctionalism of official institutions on behalf of the public good.
- *Vory v zakone*: These were professional gangsters whose primary goals were criminal, and for whom political activity was said to be only a screen for their real purpose. Didorenko had declared that Uzbekistan had become a center of organized crime for the whole Soviet Union. He alleged that this group had been successful in infiltrating and manipulating the "informals." Even before his interview, there had been allegations that professional criminals were preying on or becoming allied with corrupt officials as well, using blackmail or other means.

Finally, there was a large seventh group, that of the politically inert, not only among the "masses" but also among those members of the professional strata who were functionally apolitical. For the leadership, there was the continuous threat that a crisis might activate members of this neutral group, politicizing it in an anti-Soviet direction, as had happened in other regions of the USSR.

Inasmuch as Didorenko's interview had appeared in the *Tashkentskaya Pravda*, a newspaper not exported outside the country, it did not become available for scrutiny in the West, but from excerpts and comments about it printed by the republican newspaper *Pravda Vostoka* it was clear that the General did not mince his words.[12] Among other things, he was quoted as having told his interviewer that in Uzbekistan "there is a far-reaching shadow headquarters (*shtab*) of opponents of perestroika" which was allegedly suborning informal groups for its sinister purposes. In turn, the informals were reportedly said by Didorenko to be exploiting "the extremely sensitive national question." His critics quoted him as having charged further:

> Every informal grouping wants to get under its banners not only the maximum number of sympathizers but also to recruit anti-social elements who are already set in their views and who possess broad links among various strata of society. In consideration of these ties . . . the informals are camouflaged criminals.

The Didorenko interview was evidently a ploy that backfired, staged jointly by the General and *Tashkentskaya Pravda* in an attempt to discredit certain elements in Uzbekistan. It was timed to coincide with the opening day of an important regional conference sponsored by Moscow, and thus to attract the attention of participants from that city and other Central Asian republics.[13] However, Pravda Vostoka's swift rebuttal to the interview was endorsed by the presidium of the conference. According to *Pravda Vostoka*, there was an energetic anti-Didorenko response from "commonsensical" members of the public, whose letters it promised to continue publishing.

General Didorenko, who had a previous history of attacking the local society in the newspaper,[14] seems to have outdone himself on the latest occasion. If *Pravda Vostoka* was to be believed, he had singled out the respected Vice-President of the Uzbek Academy of Sciences, Erkin Yusupov, as being ringleader of a "witch-hunt" at the Academy, presumably against those identified with the Stalin and Brezhnev eras. (Yusupov, mentioned in the last chapter for his role as a historian, was a moderate spokesman for national causes, such as opposition to compulsory family planning, and a conspicuous public advocate of perestroika.)[15] Didorenko had also branded the popular Uzbek writer Isfandiar (who generally wrote in Russian) as a "mafioso" and nationalist. Unfortunately for the General's credibility, *Pravda Vostoka* achieved a *coup de théâtre* by revealing that on the very day that his interview was published by *Tashkentskaya Pravda* the same newspaper had carried an article about a television program by Isfandiar based on a selfless Russian's campaign to vindicate an Uzbek unjustly brought up on criminal charges by the internal-affairs administration (UVD) in Fergana Oblast, i.e. by Didorenko's own people.

Local Europeans were upset by Didorenko's unflattering comparisons between the *priezzhye*--the General has been in

Uzbekistan for only three years--and the *mestnye*: he was accused of a "we" and "they" dichotomy. In the area of law enforcement, he apparently had implied that the *mestnye* were unqualified and corrupt. *Pravda Vostoka* published a letter from a man with a Russian name writing on behalf of a lawyers' collective to complain that Didorenko had made "the crudest political mistake" in dividing militia, judicial and prosecutorial staffs into "honest" new arrivals and "dishonest" locals.[16]

Also revealing of current political tensions in Uzbekistan, and the uneasy position of those who professed loyalty to Moscow, was the injured reaction of Uzbeks and local Europeans who were particularly stung by Didorenko's suggestion that the activities of Uzbek "extremists" in the informal groups were directed only at getting rid of "European new arrivals." *Pravda Vostoka* reminded Didorenko that *"mestnye"* and natives had also been targets of the extremists, that the dividing line was not based on residence or nationality but "class." It cited the case of an indigenous European, a journalist born fifty years earlier in Tashkent, who had received a letter telling him: "Better get out of here, and out of Central Asia as well. If you don't, you'll be dead." There had also been a threatening telephone call to an Uzbek member of *Pravda Vostoka's* own staff: "How can you come out against the truth that Uzbeks are slaves of cotton? You'll argue yourself to death! (*dosporish'sya!*)."

Rather than content themselves with rebutting his statements, Didorenko's critics went over to the offensive. The General was portrayed as a violator of "socialist legality" on the one hand, and incompetent to deal with organized crime on the other. Thus, the spokesman for the lawyers' collective disclosed that, during Didorenko's three-year term in office, 445 defendants had been acquitted by the courts, at a cost to the state of 800 thousand rubles in damages. The spokesman said that lawyers could cite "more than a single case" of trammeling of rights by Didorenko's men. All in all, the *Pravda Vostoka* writers said, Didorenko's complaints were engendered by a "nostalgia" for the past when verdicts were rendered by the police and not the courts, by his desire to set the clock back to 1937. As for his allegations about people in Uzbekistan, they challenged him to take the information to court, if indeed he had any. They pointed also to the fact that, under Didorenko's stewardship, crime had increased during the past year in the republic.[17] In particular, they turned against him his claims that "on the territory of Uzbekistan ten inter-regional congresses of professional criminals have been detected, with the participation of 'top-ranking' criminals," or that "The informals are camouflaged criminals with pretensions to the role of champions." If this was really true, they asked, then why didn't Didorenko do something about it? Another letter-writer (also with a Russian name) accused the General of exaggerating the crime issue in Uzbekistan in order to enhance his own position, so as to appear as a champion on horseback.

The lawyer group also reopened the issue of the Uzbek Supreme Court, which had been accused the previous fall of being excessively lenient toward major malefactors in the republic. Subsequently, the Court's long-time chairman, S. I. Yigitaliev, was dismissed for shortcomings, although later vindicated to some extent, as we shall in the next section.[18] In the interview, Didorenko had taken the charges against the Court a step further, stating that it had become a "hornet's nest" of unworthy people. Now the lawyers charged in return that such "insults" to the Court reflected a "longing for the model of justice when questions of guilt or innocence were decided by MVD personnel, and the Court 'did not get underfoot.'" They said that Didorenko feared the new independence of the Court, and that he was guilty of no less than "blackmail."

Later in 1989, General Didorenko was reassigned to a post in the Ukraine. In Moscow, his supporters claimed that he had been unjustly hounded from his post for calling attention to the problems of Uzbekistan. In Uzbekistan long after his departure, his name was to appear again and again in the media as a symbol of unjust alien rule.

An Uzbek Justice Assails Violations of Legality

One year after the furor over MVD General Didorenko's interview in *Tashkentskaya Pravda*, the Uzbek elites' political counteroffensive against Moscow was rolling in high gear. A milestone was an interview in an influential Uzbek-language newspaper with the dismissed chairman of the Uzbek Supreme Court chairman, Sadiqjan Yigitaliev.[19] Yigitaliev told the tale of a four-year reign of terror in Uzbekistan, featuring prosecutorial persecution, judicial malfeasance and ethnic feuding. He charged that "more than a few" people were still being unjustly imprisoned in connection with the "cotton affair."

Among those cited by Yigitaliev as Moscow players in the drama were the Communist Party Central Committee and the USSR Supreme Court. The chief villains, according to his testimony, were law-enforcement officials formerly assigned to the republic on orders from Moscow. In addition to the now notorious Didorenko, he singled out the investigative team of Tel'man Gdlyan and Nikolay Ivanov, whom Yigitaliev dismissed as an "investigative Mafia,"[20] the former republican prosecutor, Aleksey Buturlin, Buturlin's former deputy, Oleg Gaydanov, and a head of the ministry's cadre apparatus, A. P. Teplov, as persons who systematically tried to tamper with the scales of justice by incarcerating innocent people in Uzbekistan and pressuring the lower courts to convict them.

Yigitaliev charged that in his time as Supreme Court Chairman (from January 1985 to January 1989) the leadership positions in Uzbekistan were occupied by "protectors of the enemies of progress." He named a "troika" of three Russians who, he maintained, actually controlled the government of Uzbekistan. These were: Vladimir P. Anishchev, the Party Second Secretary; Valentin P. Ogarok, the First Deputy Chairman of the republican Council of Ministers; and Anatoliy P. Romanovskiy, Deputy Chairman of the Presidium of the republican Supreme Soviet. Yigitaliev also cast doubt on the role of the Chairman of the USSR Supreme Soviet's Council of Nationalities, the Uzbek Rafik N. Nishanov, who later, in early 1988, became First Secretary of the Uzbek Communist Party until his elevation to higher office in Moscow in mid-1989, and on that of the republic's still serving prosecutor, Dmitriy A. Usatov.

In his interview, Yigitaliev described the role of the Uzbek Supreme Court during his four years as its chairman in clearing those who had been wrongfully accused. He reported that the number of major "cotton" cases appealed to the Supreme Court in that period exceeded 800, and that more than 500 innocent defendants were completely exculpated. In addition, thousands of cases were sent back to the prosecutor with a demand for additional investigation. Yigitaliev said that his defense of justice had put him on a collision course with Gdlyan and other Moscow representatives in the republic. At the beginning of 1988, when Nishanov was still republican First Secretary, Yigitaliev was dismissed from his post as Chairman, for "shortcomings."[21]

According to Yigitaliev, he became aware of Gdlyan's "criminal work methods" in 1985, the first year of his tenure as Supreme Court

Chairman. (Gdlyan had been assigned to Uzbekistan back in 1983.)
The Uzbek Supreme Court issued a special decree (*ajrim*) on Gdlyan and
Ivanov and sent it to the USSR Prosecutor's Office in Moscow, as a result
of which the two were said to have been punished, but without
publicity. Yigitaliev characterized Gdlyan as "an evil man in his
views and practical activities," who had "the whole republic
beginning to tremble." During 1985, Yigitaliev said, he wrote twice to
Moscow, to the Central Committee, to express the Supreme Court's view
of the situation in Uzbekistan. At one point, he visited the Central
Committee and said he was promised support in defending the
independence of the Uzbek judiciary. (He did not give the name of his
interlocutor.)

At the end of 1985, Yigitaliev's position in the republic was
weakened by the dismissal as Second Secretary of Timofey N. Osetrov,
who had been in office since the infamous Sharaf Rashidov's day as
First Secretary. Osetrov, who reportedly favored leniency for
defendants in "cotton" cases, was later arrested, only to be cleared of
wrongdoing. He was replaced by Anishchev. In December 1985,
Yigitaliev reported, he had his first serious conflict with Prosecutor
Buturlin, who had been assigned to Uzbekistan in July 1984 to replace
the longtime Uzbek incumbent of the job, Naman Borikhojaev.[22] He
described Buturlin rather curiously as "a highly qualified jurist and a
decent man" but one who suffered from prejudice against Uzbeks. The
occasion for their contretemps was a plenum of the Supreme Court, held
to discuss the need for remedial investigation of criminal cases, which,
according to Yigitaliev, Buturlin refused to attend, in violation of his
duty as Prosecutor.

Apparently in part as a result of Yigitaliev's *démarches*, an
"influential" commission came from Moscow toward the beginning of
1986 to study the handling of the cotton cases by prosecutors and
judiciary. In response to the recommendations of the commission, there
were "important" changes in the handling of the cases, "thousands of
people were absolved of criminal responsibility," and others "had
their sentences lightened."

One year later, in December 1986, Yigitaliev reported, he had a
more serious confrontation with Buturlin, who was supposedly furious
because the Supreme Court had vacated a verdict against a defendant
in Tashkent. Buturlin telephoned Yigitaliev, threatening to have him
punished by the Central Committee. Yigitaliev said that he had
reported this incident both to the Central Committee and the

Chairman of the USSR Supreme Court, Vladimir I. Terebilov (who was later to be accused by the Gdlyan faction of illicit ties with the Uzbeks). The result was that several months later Terebilov's first deputy, S. I. Gusev, who was in Uzbekistan for a meeting, had a long talk with Buturlin and Second Secretary Anishchev, following which Yigitaliev and Buturlin were seemingly reconciled.

Yigitaliev said in the interview that law-enforcement officials in the prosecutor's office and the ministry of internal affairs had held him personally responsible for preventing them from having their way. At one point, he was called on the carpet by Nishanov and Anishchev for his intervention in the case of Man-Gim Khvan (Hwan), a Korean kolkhoz chairman who had long been one of the economic heroes of Uzbekistan.[23] The conflict seemed to come to a head in the latter half of 1988. In summer of that year, an anonymous letter against Yigitaliev was circulated, which Anishchev reportedly took seriously despite the stated policy of ignoring such missives.

In September 1988, Yigitaliev sent a recommendation (*taqdimnama*) to the republican Central Committee and Supreme Soviet Presidium complaining about illegal actions by the investigative organs. Not only was his message ignored, but two of his adversaries, Buturlin and Gaydanov, were given medals (for which Yigitaliev blamed their "colleagues" Anishchev and Romanovskiy). In October, Gaydanov gave a newspaper interview in which he warned readers not to interfere with Gdlyan's activities. Then, in November, the work of the Supreme Court was placed on the agenda of the Supreme Soviet, with Yigitaliev making a report. The session adopted a resolution sharply critical of the court system in Uzbekistan for such "lapses" as judicial errors which had allowed criminals to go free.[24] (In his interview, Yigitaliev admitted that the Supreme Court had had problems, but noted that this was in part due to the fact that its caseload had doubled in the period 1985-1988.) Finally, Yigitaliev's dismissal was announced in the press on January 4, 1989.

Publication in early 1990, only a little more than a year after Yigitaliev's dismissal, of a highly favorable interview with him was an indicator of the radical change in Uzbekistan's political climate during that relatively short period. All of those whom he named as adversaries had apparently been shifted to jobs outside the republic. Of the top-level "troika" blamed by Yigitaliev for covering up misdeeds, none was still in office: Second Secretary Anishchev and First Deputy Prime Minister Ogarok were out by summer of 1989, and

Romanovskiy had been replaced in November. Significantly, in view of the policy of bringing in outsiders enunciated by Ligachev at the 1986 Party Congress, all three were replaced by Russians who came from other posts *within* the republic. The new leadership headed by First Secretary (and now President) Islam A. Karimov, while professing loyalty to the Soviet federation, was proving to be much more outspoken than its predecessors in pressing for true sovereignty and redress of Uzbek grievances against the center. No grievance was more sensitive than the widespread feeling among Uzbeks that corruption and the "cotton affair" had been used by Moscow as a pretext to persecute them on ethnic grounds.

It is tempting to speculate about what light the Yigitaliev case could shed on the politics of the Moscow leadership, given the intimate involvement of the controversial Tel'man Gdlyan and the indirect participation of Gorbachev and Ligachev. There was little evidence, however, to correlate the alignment of forces in Tashkent with Moscow issues. Unfortunately, Yigitaliev did not disclose who it was in the Central Committee who had encouraged him to stand up for the Uzbek court system. Moreover, the Gdlyan affair produced shifting alliances: Yigitaliev described being present at a meeting of the Medvedev Commission in Moscow (named to look into the charges against Gdlyan and Ivanov) at which former prosecutor Buturlin, Gdlyan's erstwhile ally in Uzbekistan, had an angry confrontation with the latter. The issues at stake in Tashkent were primarily Uzbek: national sovereignty and the integrity of the Uzbek court system. In particular, it would be unwarranted to assume, in the absence of other evidence, that Gdlyan's great unpopularity in Uzbekistan had predisposed the Uzbeks to make common cause with Ligachev or any of his other targets.

The three issues described above mark the gradual growth of intransigence in the face of Moscow's authority. A fourth, the recruit murder scandal, was to provide Uzbekistan with a new opportunity to challenge the center.

Notes

1. See Ann Sheehy, "Slav Elected First Secretary of Tashkent City Party Committee," in *Radio Liberty Research* (*RLR*) 333/85, October 3, 1985, and the same author, "Slav Presence Increased in Uzbek Party Buro and Secretariat," *RLR* 94/86, February 24, 1986.

2. *Pravda Vostoka*, June 18, 1987.

3. Since the analysis that follows was based on name recognition, which can elicit only general cultural origin, not specific nationality, the broader categories of "Central Asians" (or "Muslims") and "Slavs" were used. In Uzbekistan, naturally, "Central Asians" are preponderantly Uzbeks.

4. In 1988, there was an intriguing harbinger of the way in which the "democratization" being advocated by Gorbachev could further weaken Moscow's control over the ethnic composition of Party bodies in Uzbekistan: In Pakhtachi rayon, where the first secretary was a Central Asian, a secret ballot led to replacement of the Russian second secretary by another Central Asian, thus flouting the principle of ethnic pairing. See *Sovet Ozbekistani*, November 11, 1988, p. 2.

5. *Pravda Vostoka*, October 2, 1990.

6. *Pravda Vostoka*, December 8, 1990.

7. See Merle Fainsod, *How Russia Is Ruled*, Cambridge (Harvard University Press) 1956, p. 194.

8. To facilitate the analysis, computerized data-bases were created. The data-base for past incumbents was derived from the 1976 and 1981 directories of deputies to the Uzbek Supreme Soviet.

9. No claim is made that this is a "scientific" sample.

10. *Pravda Vostoka*, July 15, 1987.

11. *Pravda Vostoka*, February 25 and March 16, 1989. The interview appeared in the February 23 issue of the oblast newspaper *Tashkentskaya Pravda*.

12. The polarization of these two newspapers was significant. The first was the organ of Tashkent Oblast, the bastion of Russian settlement in Central Asia, whose party organization was then headed by a Russian. *Pravda Vostoka*, on the other hand, was the organ of the republic as a whole, where Uzbek leverage was growing. *Pravda Vostoka* took the lesser organ to task not only for publishing Didorenko's remarks, but for printing his "dirt" in full, which it called a violation of the 1988 Party Conference's resolution on glasnost.

13. See James Critchlow, "Regionalism Revisited: A Panacea for Nationality Problems?" *Radio Liberty Report on the USSR*, April 21, 1990, pp. 21-23.

14. Critchlow, "The Growth of Organized Crime in Uzbekistan," *Report on the USSR*, February 17, 1989, pp. 16-17.

15. For example, see *Yash Leninchi*, January 1, 1989.

16. *Pravda Vostoka*, March 16, 1989.

17. Critchlow, "Growth of Organized Crime."

18. *Sovet Ozbekistani*, January 4, 1989.

19. *OAS*, February 23, 1990, interview with Sadiqjan Yigitaliev.

20. Gdlyan and Ivanov had been assigned to Uzbekistan from the office of the USSR Prosecutor's Office in Moscow early in the investigation of the

"cotton affair." Their apparent success in apprehending corrupt officials had earned them nationwide fame, and resulted in 1989 in their election to the Congress of People's Deputies. By then, however, charges had begun to surface that Gdlyan and Ivanov had used illegal methods, reminiscent of the worst excesses of the Stalinist purges of the 1930s, to extract confessions. They were eventually expelled from the Party, although the Supreme Soviet declined to strip them of their immunity as deputies.

21. *Sovet Ozbekistani*, January 4, 1989.

22. Borikhojaev (Burikhodzhaev) had been in office since 1972. See Ann Sheehy, "Major Anti-Corruption Drive in Uzbekistan," *RLR* 324/84, August 30, 1984, p. 10.

23. See Khvan's biography in *Ozbek Sovet Entsiklopediyasi*, Tashkent 1978, Vol. 12, p. 299.

24. *Pravda Vostoka*, November 21, 1988.

9

The Recruit "Murder" Scandal

The furor that arose beginning in 1989 around allegations that Uzbek military recruits were being systematically murdered or otherwise abused while serving in the Soviet Army was a further milestone in defining the new climate of relations with Moscow. What marked the difference, compared with the way earlier national grievances had been treated, was the tone of firm denunciation in the Uzbek media in the face of menacing noises from the central military establishment. In the course of the ensuing brouhaha, the Soviet Minister of Defense was goaded into writing a defensive letter to an Uzbek newspaper, a letter which earned him the newspaper's editorial scorn, and President Karimov responded to public pressure, evidently with Moscow's co-operation, by issuing a decree restricting military service for recruits from Uzbekistan.

From the Baltic to Central Asia, no more emotional issue of nationalism arose in the perestroika period than that of mistreatment of non-Russian recruits in the multiethnic Soviet Army. The issue spoke deeply to the happiness of the family, which was compelled to offer its sons for military service, and to the ethnic pride of the nation from which they came. It fanned resentment of those, mostly Russians, who dominated the officer corps and were held responsible, if not actively culpable, for hazing and other activities that humiliated the recruits and sometimes led to their deaths. The political potential of this problem for nationalist causes was self-evident.

Suspicion that army recruits, especially those from the Ferghana Valley, were being murdered while serving in other parts of the Soviet Union lengthened the list of Uzbek ethnic grievances. The perpetrators were allegedly military personnel of other nationalities seeking revenge for the June 1989 ethnic riots in the region. Uzbekistan thus joined those Soviet national republics whose sons were being said to have become victims of ethnic violence in performing their military obligations.[1] In the Uzbek case, sensitivity was heightened by the explosive volatility of recent public disturbances. The Uzbeks' hostility to Moscow had been fed by a widespread feeling that they had been unjustly stigmatized as a nation by Soviet officials and the central media, beginning with the misdeeds of corrupt officials (some of them Russian) who were charged in the "cotton affair." Uzbek writers and speakers--from President Karimov on down--accused the Moscow media of deliberately fanning an "anti-Uzbek" campaign.[2]

In this delicate matter, public pressure on local officials weighed as never before in Uzbek politics--a further sign of a new power configuration in the republic. The military murder issue was reportedly on the agenda of a seven-hour session of the informal group *Birlik* held in Tashkent in September 1989.[3] At the end of that month it erupted in the press through an emotional full-page article in the weekly *Ozbekistan adabiyati va san"ati* (OAS), the official vernacular mouthpiece of the Uzbek intelligentsia.[4]   The newspaper's correspondent, Karim Bahriev,[5] charged that mistreatment of Uzbek recruits was a direct result of the anti-Uzbek tone of Moscow publications like *Nash sovremennik* and *Ogonek* (from which he cited passages to buttress his point). Growing anger over the reported killings of Uzbek recruits was the subject of a demonstration held on October 1, 1989 in Tashkent by *Birlik*.[6]

The Death of Sharafiddin Abdusalamov

Bahriev personally investigated the death of one young man, Sharafiddin Abdusalamov, whose father had written to the newspaper because he and the mother disbelieved their son's reported suicide. He visited the parents on their remote state farm, accompanied by local officials. After the group had been seated in a building of the village Soviet and recited the *fatiha* (the opening words of the Koran), the journalist was shown cheerful letters written by Sharafiddin in the weeks before his death, in which there were only a few jarring notes: "There are lots of Russians. We eat things fried in pork fat." (Pork is, of course, taboo for Muslims.) Sharafiddin also reported without comment that when he did well as a marksman his squad leader congratulated him by saying "*Molodets, basmach!*" (*Basmach*, more correctly *basmachi*, which generally means "bandit," has been variously applied to Muslim "counter-revolutionaries" of the early Soviet period and the Afghan mujahedin.)

Whether or not the doubts of Sharafiddin's parents about his "suicide" were founded, the circumstances of his body's return home were enough to inflame the sensitivities of a community steeped in Muslim tradition. The father described how his two younger brothers, Sharafiddin's uncles, had gone to an undisclosed location to claim their nephew's remains, only to find them laid out unceremoniously along with four other bodies on a cement floor, all without coffins. The bodies were neither embalmed nor refrigerated, and one of them was already bloated beyond recognition. Fearing that Sharafiddin's corpse would undergo the same fate in the days that it would take to transport it to their state farm, sixty kilometers from the road between Tashkent and Samarkand, the uncles managed to negotiate for an airplane by paying money to someone. One of the uncles described his efforts to obtain a coffin in which to transport the body:

> When I offered money (to get a coffin), it was turned down. "Bring vodka," he said, "and I'll knock one together." Vodka was rationed. We bought a coupon from a lieutenant for 70 rubles, and brought him some vodka.

The father went into further gruesome detail about the condition of his son's body when it finally reached home. He lamented the callousness of officialdom, noting that when a sheep died on the state farm the event was treated with greater ceremony than was the death of his son: "Is a man worth less to the state than a sheep?"

To round out the story of Sharafiddin Abdusalamov, Bahriev described the conditions in which his family was living:

> If Uzbekfilm wanted to do a film about the seventeenth century, they could just go there without having to spend money on a set. The thought of natural gas or sewage drainage is like dreaming of snow in summertime. . . . Society has forgotten these faraway crannies and inaccessible villages. But it hasn't forgotten to take their sons for military service. I thought to myself about how relations between the state and the individual are denoted, about what the state gives us and what we give to the state.

Musurman Qul Aka gave his son Sharafiddin.

Serving in the Soviet Military: "A Great Illness"

As background to the scandals reported by Bahriev, it should be noted that among Central Asians, who have clung to their homeland with remarkable tenacity despite all kinds of pressures to migrate to other regions of the Soviet Union, the subject of military service away from home has long been a delicate one. Before the Revolution, native Central Asians were classed by the Russian Empire as *inorodtsy*,[7] and exempted. When in 1916, however, the imperial government decreed that Central Asians would be conscripted to serve at the front as labor troops, the response was a massive uprising in which 2,325 Russian civilians in the region were killed, and 1,384 missing. After the uprising was put down, 347 of the insurgents were sentenced to death and a number of others to prison terms. The condemned were spared when the February Revolution of 1917 intervened.[8]

During World War II, Central Asians were among those who fought with distinction against the Nazis. Judging from indigenous literature and other sources, morale among Central Asian troops was fairly high. It was helped by organization of units with a high proportion of indigenous personnel, such as the "Panfilov" Division formed in Alma Ata in 1941, in which a number of Uzbek and other Central Asian officers held senior posts.[9] At the same time, the German command was able to form a "Turkestani Legion" from Central Asian prisoners-of-war, who took part in limited military engagements against the Red Army, and in police actions.

The idea of national units was inconsistent with Soviet doctrines of social integration, and was abandoned after World War II. Especially in the 1980s, during the Afghan war, there were widespread reports, both from defectors and in the Soviet press, of morale problems caused by the hard life of army recruits, and particularly by the common practice of brutal hazing by career soldiers, a phenomenon that was exacerbated by ethnic tensions. In addition to the traditional "grandfather system" under which regular personnel tyrannized the recruits, there was also ethnic hazing (referred to in the Bahriev article as *mahalliylik*, or "localism"). Given the fact that many Central Asian recruits spoke little or no Russian, the Soviet Army was a textbook example of the classical theory that conflict is inherent in multiethnic situations where the rate of "social mobilization," in this case intense, exceeds the rate of assimilation, in this case negligible.[10] The problem threatened to become still more acute in years to come, as demographic factors increased the proportion among army recruits of Central Asian youths with inadequate Russian.[11]

Bahriev reported that after visiting Sharafiddin's parents he had made a point of talking to military veterans of all ages, from whom he gained the impression that the problem of military service had "become a great illness." For years, he said, what went on in the military has been a "state secret" behind which injustices had been hidden--perhaps a hint at why he had not provided more details of killings in his article. However, he wrote, the living conditions of the "soldier lads," their food and housing, were not a state secret, and should be talked about. Bahriev's indignation at the mistreatment of Uzbek youth in the military spilled over in his article into invective against militarism and conscription, in which he argued for smaller, purely professional armed forces. Bahriev's article launched an ongoing debate.

General Zakharov Counter-Attacks, Flanked by *Pravda*

The Uzbek article and initial *Birlik* demonstration were followed in a week's time by a Russian-language newspaper's interview with Major-General A. Zakharov, chief of the political administration of the Turkestan military district, who largely dismissed the allegations as "rumors being spread by circles trying to instigate national hatred."[12] On October 17, two days after a second *Birlik* demonstration, *Pravda* entered the controversy with a correspondent's report from Uzbekistan that was essentially a counter-attack, taking a slap at *Birlik* and charging not only that the "rumors" were false but that Uzbek youths conscripted into the armed forces were causing problems because of their low educational level, poor knowledge of Russian, and "narrow horizons."[13] (Talk of the "low educational level" of Uzbek recruits, a regular theme of the Russian-language press, was particularly annoying to Uzbeks, who had been claiming--ever since glasnost first made it possible to do so--that a prime cause of educational deficiency was the longstanding practice of drafting children from school to work in the cotton-fields in order to fulfill the state plan.)

The Zakharov and *Pravda* rebuttals were hardly sufficient to calm local feelings, given the degree of detail which was being cited by the Uzbeks as evidence, and the emotional pitch of the debate. Lists were circulating from hand to hand in Uzbekistan with names of soldiers and the supposedly suspicious circumstances of their deaths.[14] In the article mentioned above, the journalist Bahriev had written that the number of those who "return dead from military service," whom he referred to as *shahids*,[15] had been growing in recent months. He complained that the authorities were systematically concealing the causes of death. In the Sharafiddin Abdusalamov case, the escorting soldiers had told parents of the deceased that they had been ordered by their officers not to reveal how their comrade had died. One of them, a sympathetic Kazakh, took an Uzbek relative aside and told him fearfully, "I'll write you after I'm discharged and go home." A leading figure in the Uzbek literary establishment claimed that in one case of an alleged "suicide" the soldier's body was found to have multiple bullet-holes in the back.[16]

Often, Bahriev had reported, the dead were shipped back in iron coffins which had been welded shut to prevent their being opened. In cases where, despite these precautions, it had been ascertained that death was due to such causes as hanging or electrocution, the authorities were accused of inventing false versions of suicide. Where suicide was implausible, as when the man has been clubbed to death, or shot, the authorities had supposedly manufactured other stories.

Since, according to the journalist, there was no hope of getting reliable data on soldiers' deaths from the Ministry of Defense, he had conducted his own limited survey by making inquiries at Uzbek village soviets; he listed some names of recently deceased soldiers, some of whom had died only days before their scheduled discharge.

If Bahriev's story was somewhat lacking in direct proof that the deaths of Uzbek youths had resulted from ethnic vendetta, General Zakharov's attempt to rebut the accusations raised as many questions as it answered. The general used the baffling argument that the incidence of deaths among recruits from Uzbekistan had been the same during the first nine months of 1989 as it was in the equivalent period of 1988, seemingly overlooking the fact that during all of 1988 Uzbeks were fighting in Afghanistan. Indeed, one of Bahriev's main arguments had been that soldiers should not be dying in peacetime.

Zakharov's other arguments also seemed rather lame in this emotional context. For example, he noted that a survey of recruits had elicited the information that 80 percent of those who attended trade schools (PTUs) were also subjected to hazing--a somewhat different situation from the isolated life of recruits in a multinational military encampment. He cited cases where officers had been punished for mistreatment of recuits. In conclusion, he praised the bravery of Uzbek soldiers in Afghanistan.

The truculent tone of the Pravda article, written by a correspondent named V. Artemenko, also seemed unlikely to soothe Uzbek feelings. The correspondent referred to an investigation of the allegations conducted by two newspapers in Ferghana oblast, *Ferganskaya Pravda* and *Kommuna*. He reported the conclusion of the newspapers that "malicious people are trying to give (the occurrences) their own spin and sow panic among young people and their parents, challenging without foundation the findings of military medical institutions, prosecutors, courts and other state institutions." Moreover, the correspondent wrote, the newspapers' investigation had uncovered "quite a different situation," involving the incidence of disciplinary infractions among young recruits from Ferghana oblast. He adduced one case where a private with the Central Asian name of Ghaipov (Goipov) claimed to have been mistreated as an excuse to come home. To support his contention that all was well with Uzbek recruits, Artemenko quoted an official named Boychenko, the oblast military commissar.

The Uzbeks Fire Back

Bahriev bided his time before replying to the salvos from General Zakharov and *Pravda*. When he did, it was in the form of a bombshell: a full page in the same newspaper but illustrated this time by a grim photomontage of Uzbek soldiers' mutilated bodies, each accompanied by an earlier photograph of the subject showing him in the full bloom of youth. Included in the montage was the facsimile of a death certificate. In the text were letters from heartbroken relatives of recruits who had died violently (and other letters condemning the author for defaming the "glorious" Soviet Army).[17] In a later issue, the newspaper reported that it had received hundreds of letters from parents of soldiers. It also printed a letter from one of the authors of letters published by Bahriev, who had called the latter's expose a "slander." The letterwriter complained that he had been getting anonymous threatening letters, one of them warning, "If you like violence in the Soviet Army you'll have to answer for it." He added that he now realized that he had expressed himself badly in his original letter and wished to apologize to all of his fellow countrymen.

By May 1990, Bahriev's second article and the related general resistance to the spring call-up of recruits had reached the point where concessions were announced. The Uzbek Council of Ministers, caught between popular agitation by *"Birlik"* on the one hand and the need to placate Moscow on the other, adopted a decree promising that the number of Uzbek recruits assigned to the infamous construction battalions (*stroybaty*), although there would be a corresponding increase in recruits drafted into regular line units. It was in the *stroybaty*, which were said to be commanded in many cases by officers who had been removed from regular line units because of alcoholism and other problems, that the worst excesses took place. The decree also provided that, beginning with the fall 1990 draft, recruits from Uzbekistan assigned to *stroybaty* would not have to serve outside the Turkestan Military District, i.e. outside Central Asia.[18] Provisions were also made to have local representatives make regular visits to Uzbek recruits in the units where they were serving.

Even these limited concessions, which fell far short of demands in other republics that all army service be suspended, failed to calm the populace. Moreover, although the decree must have been endorsed by Moscow before being promulgated, the military were failing to honor it completely, continuing to draft some youths from Uzbekistan for service in *stroybaty* outside Central Asia.

In October of the same year, there was a new scandal after the Party first secretary in Andizhan Oblast, which had been the scene of disturbances, became so incensed about deaths within his territory that he wrote directly to Marshall Yazov, the USSR Defense Minister, to complain. The first secretary, whose name was Begijan Rahmanov, pointed out that only seven youths from Andizhan Oblast had perished in Afghanistan, whereas eight had been killed in the army in peacetime. "Can you imagine," he asked Yazov, "your own grandson coming home in a lead coffin? . . . What's going on in the army? Can't order and discipline be established? The army doesn't need lots of soldiers, it needs to have its quality improved. You, respected General, are bringing the army to defeat without even a war. Therefore, I think you should resign."[19]

The newspaper *Ozbekistan adabiyati va san"ati* published Yazov's reply under the derisive headline, "The Philosophy of Generals, or the Smell of Resignation." Its writer mocked Yazov's suggestion that the recruits' poor understanding of Russian and inferior technical training were factors in their deaths. If that were the case, he asked, why hadn't the problem existed decades earlier? He hinted that Yazov's resignation would be a good idea.[20]

The scandal of the recruits' deaths, perhaps more than any other Uzbek grievance, was grist for the mill of the Uzbek elites, now spearheaded by militant informal groups like *Birlik*. There were indications that the Karimov and other Uzbek government leaders were unhappy with the furor which it created, if only because it was an irritant in their own negotiations with Moscow on economic issues; but Uzbekistan had now reached the point where popular political pressures could no longer be ignored. Thus, the deaths of Uzbek recruits helped to move Uzbekistan a step closer to genuine sovereignty.

Notes

1. See Suzanne Crow, "Soviet Conscripts Fall Victim to Ethnic Violence," Radio Liberty *Report on the USSR*, October 13, 1989, p. 8; Stephen Foye, "Baltic Nationalism and the Soviet Military," *Report on the USSR*, June 30, 1989, p. 22.

2. See, for example, speech by Uzbek First Secretary Islam A. Karimov at the September 1989 CPSU plenum on nationalities, *Pravda Vostoka*, September 23, 1989.

3. Personal communication from a participant. The meeting was reported in *Ozbekistan adabiyati va san"ati* (*OAS*) of September 22, but without reference to the discussion of soldiers' deaths.

4. *OAS*, September 29, 1989.

5. Bahriev has also been identified as an Uzbek People's Deputy. See *OAS*, April 6, 1990.

6. Information on this demonstration and the later one on October 15 was telephoned from Tashkent to Radio Liberty's Uzbek service in Munich (private communication).

7. The status of *inorodets* was effectively second-class citizenship. It applied to the Siberian nomads, the Central Asians and the peoples of the North Caucasus, but not to the more advanced--in Russian eyes--Tatars and Azeris. See Andreas Kappeler, "Die zaristische Politik gegenüber den Muslimen des Russischen Reiches" (Tsarist Policy Toward the Muslims of the Russian Empire), in Kappeler *et al.* (eds.), *Die Muslime in der Sowjetunion und in Jugoslawien*, Cologne (Markus Verlag) 1989, p. 124.

8. Turar Ryskulov, "Vosstanie tuzemtsev Turkestana v 1916 g." (The Uprising of Natives of Turkestan in 1916), in Feizula (sic) Khodzhaev *et al.*, *Ocherki revolyutsionnogo dvizheniya v Sredney Azii, sbornik statey*), Moscow

(Izdanie nauchnoi assotsiatsii vostokovedeniya pri Tsik SSSR), 1926, pp. 49 and 83.

9. *Ozbek Sovet Entsiklopediyasi*, Tashkent 1976, Vol. 8, p. 404.

10. See Karl W. Deutsch, *Nationalism and Social Communication*, Cambridge (Massachusetts) 1966, p. 124.

11. See Ann Sheehy, "Russian Share of Soviet Population Down to 50.8 Percent," *Report on the USSR*, October 20, 1989, p. 1.

12. *Pravda Vostoka*, October 7, 1989.

13. *Pravda* , October 17, 1989.

14. *Pravda Vostoka*, October 7, 1989.

15. "*Shahid*," a word of Arabic origin, although sometimes used in secular contexts, traditionally refers to someone who has been martyred for Islam. Its primary definition in the main Uzbek dictionary: "a person who has died on the path of a religion or cult." See *Ozbek tilining izahli lughati*, Moscow 1981, Vol. 2, p. 406.

16. Personal communications.

17. *OAS*, March 9, 1990.

18. *Komsomolets Uzbekistana*, May 17, 1990.

19. *Ozbekistan adabiyati va san"ati*, October 26, 1990, p. 8.

20. Ibid.

10

The Islamic Factor

What distinguishes Uzbekistan and the other Soviet republics with largely Muslim populations from the rest of the USSR is the role of Islam in their history and culture, both past and present. For the true believer, religious doctrine ordains the most minute aspects of daily life. For those who are less religious, Islam is still pervasive in ethnic custom and life-styles: even before perestroika loosened restrictions on religion, it was common to hear of Communist Party officials--professed "atheists" in their public life--who participated actively in religious life-cycle rituals such as weddings, funerals, or circumcisions, and in other observances.

The hold of Islam on Central Asian society, even after decades of official atheism, makes that religion a political factor with formidable potential. In Uzbekistan, beginning in 1989, the leadership abruptly reversed its official hostility toward Islam and switched to the tactic of catering to it through its official representatives. The purpose was clear: by conceding the legitimacy of a religion with roots deep in the society, it sought to enhance its own legitimacy in the eyes of believers. In Moscow, the Soviet leadership was pursuing the same policy *vis-à-vis* the Russian Orthodox church, but this parallel should not obscure the fact that the new emphasis on religion increased the political distance separating Asians and Europeans in the Soviet Union. Thus, an Uzbek party journal criticized the saturation treatment given--in regime media addressed to Central Asian audiences--to the 1988 observance of the millennium of the Christianization of Kievan Rus:

> Did they act correctly in giving wide celebration and press coverage to various meetings devoted to the millennium . . . in a republic where that religion does not have traditional following? Does it follow that Marxist-Leninist science takes different attitudes to different religions?[1]

In no area of Uzbek life has the societal change of recent years been more spectacular than in that of religion. Under Stalin, religion had been largely driven underground, and there it remained, even in the early years of perestroika. At the Twenty-Seventh Party Congress in 1986, Gorbachev lashed out at members of the Uzbek Communist Party for taking part in religious rituals. Subsequently, there were mass expulsions from the Party of such recalcitrant Communists. As recently as 1988, official media were still publishing sharp attacks against Islam and those caught practicing it. Believers were subject to physical harassment. By the following year, 1989, however, religious policy had undergone a dramatic shift. Anti-religious propaganda all but disappeared from the media, and the secular authorities began to give active encouragement to Islamic communitiies through such measures as support for the building and restoration of mosques. Most striking was the new prominence in public life of the Islamic clergy: once persecuted by officialdom, except for a few who were docile members of the state-controlled religious establishment, the Islamic mullahs were suddenly accorded a new status. A case in point was that of the Mufti of Tashkent, Muhammad Sadiq Muhammad Yusuf (Mamayusupov), who became a deputy to the USSR Supreme Soviet and began to appear prominently on television and in the press as an authoritative commentator on social problems, which he intepreted for the general public from the standpoint of Islamic doctrine.

If the new tolerance of Islam was motivated in part by the secular authorities' quest for popular support, the policy was also traceable to a desire to build a backfire against the spreading influence of Islamic fundamentalists and other maverick Muslim tendencies operating outside the official framework. As much as they could in the effervescent atmosphere of perestroika, the secular authorities continued to discourage unofficial Islamic elements from mobilizing for political action. The new policy aimed to enlist new forces in the society to help contain explosive popular resentment of social and economic problems, while channeling their energies through the presumably "loyal" official Islamic establishment. The prominent role of the Tashkent Mufti and other mullahs in helping to quell popular unrest was an illustration of this purpose.

To appreciate the revolutionary nature of this policy change, it is useful to consider some of the stepping-stones which led to it. Extended treatment of the Islamic phenomenon in Central Asia is beyond the scope of this book.[2] The present chapter is limited to sketching some of the developments which preceded the new tolerance. As our baseline, we shall look first at a confrontation between Islam and Communism which took place within the ranks of the party back in the initial days of the Soviet regime, an incident that helped to set the stage for an ongoing struggle.

Islam and Communism: An Early Clash

When Communism came to the Central Asian oases after 1917, it was largely as a foreign import imposed by local Russians by force of arms. The region had been an integral part of the world of Muslim civilization ever since the seventh century when not long after Muhammad's death the Arab armies, bearers of a rapidly expanding Islam, crossed the Amu-Darya from the south and introduced their religion. After the sixteenth century, when European explorers and traders developed water routes to Asia and Africa that eclipsed the caravan routes, the decline of economic prosperity had left the territory in relative isolation. Paradoxically, in the face of this adversity the prestige of its centers of Islamic learning grew within the Muslim world, precisely because their remoteness kept them from exposure to Western influence. "Holy" Bukhara (*Bukhara-i-sherif*), with its mosques and medreses, gained a reputation as one of the most sacred cities of Islam.

The Russian conquest of Central Asia shocked believers, partly because it demonstrated their vulnerability to an infidel power. Russian economic and technological innovation opened the area to social changes which combined to fragment the Islamic community. These developments also opened the region to new influences from outside: one of these was the tide of reform sweeping other Muslim peoples of the Russian Empire and Muslim societies abroad, notably Turkey and Iran. Thus, as noted in the first chapter, Central Asian intellectuals participated in the jadid movement of Muslim reformers who believed that only by modernizing could Muslims hold their own in competition with Russians and other Europeans, and sought to transform the exclusively religious base of Muslim education by introducing secular subjects. It may be recalled that their efforts drew the opposition of the conservative ulema, often with the support of the tsarist colonial authorities, who opposed change for their own reasons

When Revolution came to Central Asia, the jadids had been confronted with the dilemma of choosing to support the new regime, with its atheistic ideology, or joining the "basmachi" resistance led by conservative Muslims, their old enemies. If many of the reformers chose the first course, it was because they believed that in the long run they might advance their cause more from within the system. Many had had their hopes dashed by the brutal action of Soviet forces in destroying the independent Muslim government in Kokand. Chapter 1 noted that many others, seeing in the "basmachi" leadership many of the reactionary elements which they opposed, chose guardedly to collaborate with the new regime, despite its espousal of atheism which was to them repugnant. Their reasons were multifold: the feeling that there was no viable political alternative, given the nature of the resistance movement, and the hope that they would be able to exploit the power of the new system for the ultimate advance of their own nationalistic purposes.

The presence of large numbers of jadid intellectuals in the new Communist hierarchy was an impediment to ideological consolidation. Something of the relatively free-wheeling essence of Central Asian public life in the early 1920s, even in the Communist Party, is revealed by an old document which has lain neglected for more than sixty years in the uncatalogued holdings of the Library of Congress in Washington. The document, a pamphlet by an Uzbek author who was later purged, describes boisterous rejection by Party members of a 1923 effort by the leadership to launch a campaign of "anti-religious agitation." Speakers at Party meetings were interrupted by members' catcalls. The 1923 resistance by the Party rank-and-file forced postponement for five years of the anti-religious drive, until 1928, by which time the consolidation of Stalinist power had tightened discipline and eliminated Party members accused of "bourgeois nationalism" and other sins, many of them former jadids.[3]

In 1923, the Communist Party in the Turkestan Autonomous Soviet Socialist Republic, the territory of the old tsarist Turkestan Government General soon to be divided into Uzbekistan and other smaller republics, had been swollen by a recruitment campaign aimed at increasing the number of members from the Muslim community. Recruitment of Muslims for Party and state posts had been urgently ordered by Moscow in response to a crisis which was threatening the viability of Soviet rule in the region. At the time of the 1917 revolution there had been few native Communists in Central Asia. The Soviet regime had been implanted by Russian and other European workers, whose stronghold was the Tashkent railroad yards. Until 1920, these foreign elements had ridden roughshod over the native population, taking advantage of their isolation from higher authority in Moscow caused by anti-Soviet forces' control of the intervening territory in Siberia. We have seen in an earlier chapter how the autonomous Muslim government in Kokand was attacked by troops from the Tashkent Soviet, with much brutality and loss of life, and how such actions greatly strengthened support for the basmachis.

As soon as communications lines from Moscow were reopened in late 1919, a special Party commission rushed to Tashkent on orders from Lenin, who feared that failure of the regime in Central Asia would jeopardize the appeal of communism throughout the Muslim world.[4] The commission's devastating report about conditions in the region led to far-reaching measures. In 1920, a Congress of the Turkestan Communist Party took note of the need for more Muslims to staff responsible positions.[5]

The dearth of a trained cadre of Muslim communists forced the Party to take what it could find. It made an effort to recruit persons with worker or peasant backgrounds and to give them accelerated education. To meet its immediate needs, however, it had to open the admission gates to the less conservative members of the old Muslim intelligentsia, among whom jadidism was the dominant strain.

While the situation in the Turkestan Communist Party in that period has been known in broad outline from Party documents and other sources, detailed first-hand "insider" accounts are practically non-existent. Mannan Ramiz' pamphlet *From Fantasy to Fact* (*Khayaldan haqiqatga*) is one such inside source. In it, he gives a vivid picture of the continuing influence of Islam even among partymembers.

"If There Is No God, Who Created You?"

Writing in 1928, Ramiz, an Uzbek intellectual who himself professed loyalty to the new Communist regime, recalled incidents that

171

had occurred in the old city of Tashkent (the native quarter) "when in 1923 the matter of our Party's anti-religious agitation among the local people was put up for discussion." He reported that "the following situation was observed among Uzbek communists":

> Some of those who identified themselves as Party members were very upset. The speakers were interrupted, and various questions were asked: "Are you trying to raise the question of anti-religious agitation?" "Is it possible to live without religion?" "If there is no God, who created you?" and similar interesting questions were asked.

Later on, Ramiz related, when a resolution on anti-religious agitation was adopted at a Congress of the Turkestan Communist Party, "still more protests were heard in the Tashkent old city." This was particularly distressing to the leadership, because Tashkent had been considered, as Ramiz noted, to have one of the "most progressive and cultured" Muslim communities.

As a result, according to Ramiz, "it became known that a group of communists had been holding secret evening gatherings and meetings during which all kinds of furtive things were said."
He quoted the participants as saying, for example:

> Communists who damage themselves by saying they are against religion have capitulated to the Russians. Here in the conditions of Turkestan there is no need for a Communism like the Communism in Russia that denies religion. Instead, we must create a Communism that is completely compatible with the Islamic religion.[6]

Ramiz reported that such "mutterings" were widespread, embracing the "majority of Party and non-Party people." He said that there was particular dissension among artisans and office-workers. He added that peasants and tradesmen helped to block approval of the proposal for anti-religious agitation. In general, "there were at that time many persons in the Party with pettybourgeois ideas." Since anti-religious agitation "had to begin with the Communists," the proposal was dropped.

Writing from an obligatory position of Party orthodoxy five years later, in 1928, when discipline had been tightened, Ramiz registered complaints about the "influence of petty *bays*[7] in the majority," saying that "most of the *aktiv* at that time bowed to pressure from that influence and protested together with the non-Party people."

"One Foot in Communism, the Other in Religion"

Ramiz cast doubt, perhaps inadvertently, on the Party's later claims to legitimacy in Central Asia by admitting that in those earlier days the "Bolshevik nucleus" had been in the minority. Looking back from the perspective of 1928, he described the situation in the Turkestan Communist Party five years earlier with these words:

In those days, in the work of building the Party the minority Bolshevik nucleus encountered that kind of opposition whenever it tried to lay a foundation. In trying to raise the Party masses (*amma*) from the swamps of petty bayism, there were powerful struggles.

At that time, things were very different, and in the composition of the *aktiv* there were many persons who were corrupt, incompetent, or hiding behind a mask. They stood with one foot in Communism and the other foot in petty bayism, religion and religious beliefs. They paid lip-service to Communism but had close and friendly ties with the black-group (reactionary) clergy. As we said, at the time the Bolshevik nucleus formed a very small minority in the Party.

Even now it is possible to find such persons, but in those days they were the majority. Their influence was mighty.[8]

Ramiz' pamphlet was written as a guide for Party workers charged with implementing the anti-religious campaign finally launched in 1928. In it, he noted how in five years Party discipline had tamed religious dissent within the ranks, or at least driven it underground:

Today when we raise the matter of anti-religious agitation we compare the memory of those days with present advancement and growth, and we see the great difference and can precisely discern the success of measures to build the Party. Only the blind or those who refuse to look are unable to see it.[9]

173

The pamphlet, which had a print-run of only 3000, was most certainly withdrawn from circulation after Ramiz' arrest at the end of the 1920s on convoluted charges of his involvement in the poisoning of a nationalist who had joined the Soviets. (Other former jadids like Ramiz were being liquidated as "Turkish spies" and "bourgeois nationalists.")[10] Even if copies were to be available today in special archives, its Arabic script would make it incomprehensible to most Uzbek readers.[11] Despite the pamphlet's orthodox stance, its disclosures about Party life in the 1920s, especially the tolerant attitude of Muslim communists of that era toward Islam, are food for thought for today's Central Asian intellectuals in search of new directions.[12]

By the end of the 1920s, most mosques had been closed and their buildings converted for use as anti-religious museums, warehouses or for other public purposes, the property of the *waqfs* (Muslim religious foundations) had likewise been confiscated, the Muslim clergy had been decimated by arrests and executions, and women had been forced to remove their veils (at times triggering violent confrontations). The press and Communist agitators were conducting campaigns to discredit Islam and its believers. Under these conditions, worship was all but driven underground.

During World War II, Stalin's temporary change in course had eased the pressures against Islam, as it had for other religions in an all-out effort to rally people for the war effort. The creation of four Muslim "spiritual directorates" (now commonly called "religious boards"), including the one in Tashkent for "Central Asia and Kazakhstan," headed by a Mufti, was part of this policy.

After the war, when persecution of religion was resumed, these bodies were allowed to continue as a convenient means of channeling religious activity through a controlled mechanism. The regime, while remaining hostile toward religion as such, found in them a useful tool, especially for advancing its foreign-policy interests in Muslim countries. One result was a distrust of "official" Islam by Muslim believers that led to a bifurcation of Muslim religious activity, with many spurning the established religion in favor of an underground variant led by unregistered mullas, the so-called "parallel" Islam.

After Stalin

Although after Stalin's death in 1953 the terror had subsided, his successors maintained a policy of "militant atheism" with continuing harassment of Islamic practitioners. Yet, despite the decades of official sanction, Islam maintained a firm grip. This was brought out with revealing clarity in the 1970s under Brezhnev, when introduction of modern survey-research techniques to study the USSR's Muslim societies documented a startling incidence of continuing belief and practice at all levels. A scholar in Uzbekistan, T. S. Saidbaev, published a book[13] of findings which left little doubt that Islamic observance was still widespread, especially in the case of "life-cycle rituals" like circumcision, marriage, and funerals. The *shariat*, Muslim religious law, was being respected by many in the case of prescribed fasting and feasting, and of taboos on social behavior such as the marriage of Muslim women to non-Muslim men. As an example of Islam's influence at all levels of society, Saidbaev noted that in the USSR the incidence of "religiosity" was considerably greater among Muslims than Christians: for example, it was ten times higher among members of Muslim nationalities with higher education than among their non-Muslim counterparts in the country. Whereas in the Christian religions older people, especially women, were predominant, among Muslims age and sex differences were far less significant.[14]

Islam and Perestroika

In the initial perestroika period, residual fear of Islam remained a preoccupation of officialdom even after many other ideological shibboleths had been abandoned. Gorbachev himself publicly excoriated the religion in his early period in office, especially where Party members were found to be participating in religious observances. In the latter part of 1986, he made a harsh speech during a stopover in Tashkent in which he complained about Party members' taking part in Islamic.[15] (Apparently his references to Islam were so incendiary that the full text of the speech was never published.) One result of Gorbachev's intervention was the expulsion during a six-month period of 53 members from the Uzbek Party for "organizing religious rituals and taking part in them."[16] In 1987, there also were numerous imprisonments of Soviet Muslims for religious activities.[17]

Ironically, it was the youth who were to spearhead a counterattack against persecution of Islam. For those in charge of "atheist indoctrination," it was especially defeating to recognize that young people born and reared under Communism were seemingly no more immune to Islam than their elders. This phenomenon was brought home at a Tashkent student demonstration held in December 1988, while Rafik N. Nishanov--six months later to be elevated to a post in Moscow--was still first secretary of the Uzbek Communist Party.

The spontaneous mass demonstration, at which Tashkent students made Muslim religious gestures and waved what appeared to be the green banner of Islam, caused special concern to the authorities because it underlined the intertwining of Islam and secular cultural issues.[18] The event was originally intended to honor the Uzbek language, and to give students a chance to air their linguistic grievances. Those present signed an appeal calling on the Uzbek Central Committee to make Uzbek the "official language" of the republic, but the speeches went beyond the bounds of linguistic questions.

The students carried posters with the slogans "Let Our Mother Tongue Shine Brightly Again!", "Don't Let Our Language and Cultural Heritage (*Meras*) Be Turned Into a Graveyard!", and "Down With the Ills of the Stagnation Period!" A central poster depicted the peripatetic evolution of Uzbek through its three orthographic phases of Arabic, Latin, and Cyrillic scripts. But some students also waved a green banner, reminiscent of the green flag of Islam, and one of them made the gesture of the *fatiha*, the opening verse of the Koran, which was then repeated by others, as local officials stood by helplessly.

While Islamic ritual at any level was then still frowned on by the authorities, its practice by university students, the next generation of elite, was of particular concern. A newspaper account of the demonstration commented that failure by officials to respond earlier to the students' demands had opened the way for "the young people to follow others who were giving answers."[19]

The December 3 demonstration was followed by other student unrest. On December 24, some 300 students at a dormitory of the Tashkent Geological-Exploration Tekhnikum went on the rampage, allegedly under the influence of alcohol, to protest conditions at the school, and caused injuries and material damage. Ten faculty members had to be admitted to the hospital. Administrators and faculty were subsequently accused of having tried to hide the incident from higher authority. As a result, the first secretary of the Sabir Rahimov rayon (district) Party committee and other officials were reprimanded, and the director of the institution was sacked.[20] The extent to which Islam may have been a factor has not been revealed.

There were soon signs of new religious ferment on other fronts. In early 1989, a demonstration by believers in Tashkent resulted in the overthrow and replacement of the old Mufti, Shamsuddin Khan Babakhanov, a holdover from the Brezhnev period who was accused of womanizing and drinking alcohol. In any case, Babkhanov's time in office had been devoted mainly to ceremonial contacts with foreign Muslim dignitaries and grinding out innocuous *fetwas*, religious decrees, that were well-calculated to please the party ideologists in Moscow, or at least not to trouble them. His "voluntary abdication" ended a family dynasty which had begun under Stalin. There are some indications that it had the acquiescence, if not the direct encouragement, of the Uzbek party leadership.[21] In any case, Mamayusupov as new Mufti was elected shortly thereafter to the Congress of People's Deputies, in a republic where the old patterns of political control by the Party were still notoriously strong. Was this, as has been suggested, part of an effort by nationalist modernizers to purge the registered clergy of charlatans and lackeys, and to transform it into a genuine bastion of progressive Islam? It also happened to coincide with a new attitude in Moscow of greater official liberalism toward religion.

The role of the official clergy in the Muslim regions had become increasingly shrouded in ambiguity. There can be no doubt that it was originally viewed by Stalin and his successors as little more than a cynical device to manipulate Islam, in much the same way that the "national" institutions of the union republics were designed to manipulate ethnic loyalties. Yet in the case of the secular institutions, the history of recent decades, even before perestroika, had shown that the native nominally "Communist" elites who were assigned to staff them often put the interests of their republics ahead of Moscow's. This was revealed with spectacular clarity in the Gorbachev era, as the non-Russian party elites appeared in the forefront of nationalist movements. Was there any reason to think that Islamic clergymen, even those who had had to make compromises, were at heart more faithful to Moscow than the Communist *apparatchiki* who were their fellow countrymen?

Whatever the case, new Mufti Mamayusupov became much more active than his predecessor, especially in secular aspects of public life.

He was elected (together with other Soviet clergymen) to the new USSR Congress of People's Deputies in spring 1989, soon after becoming Mufti. His willingness to assume a political role in his new capacity quickly became apparent when he accompanied a group of Uzbek leaders, headed by First Secretary Nishanov, who were flown hastily from the Congress in June, 1989, to deal with the bloody massacres of the Meshketian Turkic minority in the Ferghana Valley, when more than 100 people were killed and many homes and much other property were destroyed in rioting led by Uzbeks. The Meskhetians were one of the peoples who had been expelled from their homelands in the Caucasus during World War II by Joseph Stalin, on suspicion of harboring pro-German sympathies. Although both the Meskhetians and their attackers were Muslims, it was reported that there was a religious element in the incidents.

The Ferghana tragedy was a watershed in Uzbek politics. It happened to coincide with the conservative and Moscow-leaning Nishanov's departure from the Uzbek scene to take his post in Moscow. His successor, Karimov, proved much more sensitive to local Uzbek concerns, and especially to the underlying roots of social unrest.

Even before the unsettling events in Ferghana, greater tolerance of Islam was evident from a decrease in Uzbek media attacks on religion. In the face of catastrophic economic and social problems, coupled with a loosening of political control, the "anti-religious" campaign had clearly slipped to a lower priority.

By the end of 1988, with glasnost shedding light on the enormity of the region's economic and environmental problems, greater tolerance for Islam was in the wind: Party members were no longer being chastized for participation in Muslim funeral rites. At the same time, there had seemed to be an accompanying change in Mikhail Gorbachev's own attitudes on the subject: when he visited Tashkent again in April 1988 his remarks about religion were affable in tone.[22] Beginning at about the same time, the media began to publish interviews with Muslim religious figures that went beyond the old strictures on religious expression.[23]

Coincidentally with the Ferghana violence, the Uzbek Party journal *Kommunist Uzbekistana* printed an article advocating co-operation between Communism and Islam. The author pointed to Islamic commandments "which correspond to Communist morality," and called for joint action against "alcoholism, drug addiction, prostitution, bribery, fraud, embezzlement and other disgusting ills of our society which would be condemned by any religion." He went an astonishing step further to call for creation of mixed state and religious commissions which would work together on such problems as "morality, freedom of observance of religious denominations, human rights, etc."[24]

The new tolerance of Islam was given an additional seal of official approval in the December 1989 election platform of the Uzbek Communist Party, which read in part:

> The republican Party organization is actively in favor of *freedom of religion and the legal rights of believers* (italics in original), and for co-operation with religious organizations. . . . Believers are entitled to all opportunities for participation in the public political and cultural life of the Republic.[25]

The Wahhabite "Threat"

These new Islamic stirrings in Central Asia sent shockwaves to some quarters in Moscow. Journalists in the capital, perhaps merely looking for a good story in the new climate of capitalistic circulation-building, or perhaps abetted by conservative elements and Russian nationalists allied with Orthodox Church factions, began a campaign to sound the alarm. They were apparently motivated by--or attempting to exploit--fear of further ethnic unrest and traditional Russian distrust of Islam, which had always been heightened by the perceived threat that the Muslim border regions were vulnerable to foreign religious influence. Especially after the Iranian revolution of 1979, there had been fear of Islamic fundamentalists. This fear was fueled in June 1989 by the Ferghana Valley violence.

In the wake of the anti-Meskhetian massacre, and the first death sentences of those convicted of involvement, there were allegations in Moscow that the Wahhabite sect of Islam had been instrumental in fomenting the disturbances. To the extent that Wahhabite activity might have been responsible for the disorders, it suggested a threat from outside to the stability of the region, for the sect has adherents in nearby Afghanistan and India, and a strong political base in Saudi Arabia.

The sect, which originated in the Arabian peninsula and became the religion of the Saudi royal family, is a puritanical offshoot of the Sunni branch of Islam. As a practical political and social movement, it inspired Arab resistance to Ottoman colonial rule and to the official Islamic *ulema,* or clergy, which was a pillar of that rule. Part of its relevance to rural Central Asia today may lie in the Wahhabis' historical experience of founding co-operative farm villages.[26]

According to an article in the Moscow *New Times* devoted to analysis of the Ferghana riots:

> The Wahhabi movement is rapidly gaining strength in the Ferghana Valley and enjoys considerable prestige in different strata of the population--from elite literary circles in Tashkent, to teenagers in technical vocational schools. The latter are especially impressed by the (Wahhabis') contempt of money, their rejection of remuneration for the religious rites they perform, and also by their national fervor that has played its part in creating the general psychological atmosphere in the Ferghana events.[27]

The *New Times* writers went on to say that the Ferghana youths "evinced special enthusiasm not so much for official Islam but for Timur and the kurbashis of the 1920s--Madamin Bek, Kurshimat, Hal Hoja-- who fought under the banner of Islam." (The "kurbashis" of the 1920s were, of course, militant leaders of the "basmachi" rebellion against Soviet rule.)

Wahhabite involvement in the Ferghana unrest was charged even more pointedly by the weekly *Ogonek*, which claimed that the troubles had been preceded in December 1988 by "activization" of the Wahhabite movement in the area.[28] The Wahhabite program was said to include not only purification of Islam but also restriction of women's rights and creation of an Islamic army. (The *Ogonek* article, which painted a lurid picture of pan-Islamic and anti-Russian sentiment among Uzbeks, drew a protest from First Secretary Karimov in his speech at the CPSU plenum on nationalities in September, 1989.)[29]

To the extent that there may have been genuine Wahhabite activity in Central Asia, one can only speculate about the extent to which the war in Afghanistan, and the exposure of Central Asian soldiers and civilian advisors to religious life there, may have been a catalyst in stimulating interest in Wahhabism, which was espoused by some of the mujahedin factions. Soviet sensitivity to Afghanistan in this respect was reflected in the fact that an article on Wahhabism originally published before the Soviet invasion was edited during the war to delete Afghanistan from the list of countries in which Wahhabism is prevalent.[30]

For his part, Mufti Mamayusupov himself played down the allegation of foreign Wahhabite participation, apparently in the belief that Moscow observers were letting their fears run away with them. A Russian interviewer raised with him the question of Wahhabite activity in Central Asia, noting darkly that a Wahhabi was head of the "counter-revolutionary" provisional government of Afghanistan (formed to challenge, and ultimately to replace, the Communist-supported Najibullah regime). The interviewer charged that the man in question was "a front for Saudi Arabia, which in turn is a front for the Americans."[31]

The Mufti was diplomatically cautious in his reply, but disagreed with the questioner. While accepting that Wahhabism had originated in Saudi Arabia, a matter of historical record, he declined to identify present Wahhabi activities in the Soviet Union with Saudi influence. Rather, he said, the younger generation of Soviet Muslims have "their own understanding" of Islam, which differs from that of their parents in a denial of superstition and elaborate rituals, a characteristic of Wahhabism. The Mufti gave his own version of Central Asian "Wahhabism":

> When the old people saw that the young people were acting in a "Wahhabite" way, they began to call them "Wahhabites." At first the young people protested—"why are you calling us that?"—but then they got used to it, and now many are calling themselves "Wahhabites."

The Mufti himself appeared to be more concerend about other outside forces, including the Islamic Revolution in Iran, as "exercising influence on Soviet Muslims." Using the harsh language of an earlier period of Soviet politics, he asserted that "the people must be very vigilant. One must keep a careful eye on the events on our southern borders."

The Mufti's reference to religious differences between younger and older Muslims later received some confirmation from reports of generational violence between believers in Tajikistan, in which "Wahhabism" was apparently an issue.[32] Youths were also in the forefront of the Ferghana riots.

The Mufti as Soviet Journalist

Despite the currents of greater religious tolerance, most Uzbeks must have been unprepared for the sudden appearance early in 1990, in the weekly organ of the Uzbek Writers' Union and Ministry of Culture, of an article--in effect a sermon--signed by the Mufti with both his religious and civil titles.[33] Only two years earlier, the same newspaper had been carrying diatribes against religion.[34]

Not only did the Mufti's sermon deal with a sensitive social topic, the role of the husband in the family, an area where the influence of Islam had always been shunned by Soviet ideologists as "reactionary," but the text was embellished with Muslim rhetorical flourishes whose unaccustomed appearance in a Soviet newspaper must have made readers rub their eyes in disbelief. Thus, references to the Prophet were accompanied by the customarily reverential phrase *Alaykh-es-Salaam* ("May Peace be with Him"), and the Koran was invariably characterized as *Quran karim* ("Koran the Gracious").

If there really were many "militant atheists" in Uzbekistan, as the Party had been insisting for years, they must have felt terribly betrayed by the retreat before the enemy embodied in the Mufti's new prominence. Perhaps sensing their dismay, the Mufti was somewhat apologetic about his appearance in print, saying he believed that no one should object "to my being invited to take pen in hand as a USSR People's Deputy."

That the Mufti was writing as more than just an ordinary People's Deputy quickly became apparent, however. As might be expected, he broke with the time-honored practice in Soviet public discourse of citing Marx, Engels or Lenin as authorities. Instead, he invoked as his sources the Prophet, the Koran, the Hadiths, and Caliph Omar. He expressed satisfaction that "an end had been put to old-fashioned talk that religious ideas or the words of clergymen are sources of evil," and said that "we are happy that perestroika has given the opportunity to think freely." As for his own thoughts, "we do not wish to impose them on anyone in obligatory form." Anyone was free to accept them as he wished, he asserted.

With respect to the family, the Mufti wrote, it was of importance as a microcosm of society. Many of the ills of society stemmed from the ills of the family, such as the rising rate of divorce. Of all the relations between human beings, the most "sacred" was that of marriage. Many problems arose in marriage because the partners are not sure of their proper roles. The Mufti described the institution in patriarchal terms:

> According to Islamic sources, one of the husband's important qualities is as head of the family. We know that every society has a head. A society without a head is not a society. The family is a small society. In it all of the aspects of a society are present in miniature. The leading position of the husband in the life of the family is now sanctioned unanimously by all peoples.

However, the Mufti added, this did not mean that Islam allows the husband to be a tyrant. In the words of one of the Hadiths, "All of you are responsible for the women who are under your hand." In the words of another enunciated by the medieval imam Ahmad ibn Hanbal, "Your food that you give to your wife is also alms for you." But one should not support the family in proscribed (haram) ways, he warned, such as by lying or stealing.

After imparting further practical advice from Islamic sources about the conduct of the husband, even on such detailed matters as giving gifts to the wife, the Mufti concluded with an offer to provide further articles, "if acceptable to the multitude," on Islamic teaching about other family matters, with such proposed titles as "The Woman in Scripture" ("Risaladagi khatin").

The Political Context

The effect of such phenomena as the Mufti's public exposure has been to elevate Islam, or rather one segment of it, to the status of a state religion, a clear violation of both the spirit and letter of the traditional Leninism which long held sway. It was not difficult to discern in this radical policy shift a desperate striving on the part of the Uzbek establishment to bolster the sagging regime with new sources of legitimacy. With the Party and its ideology discredited by the failures and revelations of recent years, espousal of Islam was clearly a bid for support from traditional religious and nationalistic forces in the society.

At the same time, the framers of the new policy were also following the traditional pattern of relying on state Islam as a device to help channel and control dissident Muslim forces. There was an obsession, from Gorbachev on down, with fears of Islamic "fundamentalism" and its reported role in fomenting ethnic violence. All of this had led to calls for a revision of the traditional "Islamophobia" in favor of a more measured and subtle approach.[35]

Additionally, the new policy reflected an attempt to fill the vacuum in society created by the decline of secular authority. A spectacular rise in crime, especially among young people, together with drug addition and other ills had created an atmosphere of near panic.[36] The leadership and the intelligentsia were particularly concerned about mistreatment of women, which had been linked to a dramatic incidence of female suicide.[37] With mounting problems of economic deprivation and unemployment accelerated by population growth, those who were now trying to guide Uzbek society saw in Islam a means of staving off economic and social unrest. The Mufti's sermon described above emphasized social, not spiritual, problems.

Finally, the new policy responded to growing pressures from Uzbek and other Central Asian intellectuals to restore Islam to its rightful place in their history. As a speaker at a Tashkent symposium put it: "If Islam is reactionary, did it not occupy the thoughts of progressive humanitarians of the entire East during more than half a millennium? Did it not influence their creativity and their science?"[38] Such pressures were exacerbated by resentment of the perceived favoritism shown by Moscow authorities toward the Russian Orthodox Church during celebration of the latter's millennium in 1988.

The new Islamic policy thus had some appeal for a disparate coalition of forces, from worried backers of Soviet federalism in Moscow and Leningrad to aggressive Uzbek nationalists in Tashkent and Samarkand. The latter were apt to be disdainful, however, of the limited and cautious role played so far by the Mufti and his clergy. It had been the secular intellectuals, not the clerical establishment, who were speaking out on Uzbek grievances arising from the "cotton monoculture" and other elements of exploitation by Moscow. If the regime had compromised with Islam, the official Islamic clergy had to a considerable extent compromised with the state.

Even so, there were hints of apprehension that the new policy might be creating a *deus ex machina* that could run away with the action. An article in *Kommunist Uzbekistana*, although generally positive about the recent liberalization toward Islam, reminded readers of Lenin's teaching that the proletariat "demands" separation of church and state.[39] And the Uzbek Communist Party's election platform included an assertion that the Party would continue using the methods of propaganda and persuasion to develop an "outlook of scientific materialism" among the workers, and would be outspoken in condemning any activity based on "religious intolerance and fanaticism."[40] It was one thing to deal with a compliant Mufti, quite another to handle Islam at the grass-roots level.

Such appeals to Lenin's teaching were being rapidly made obsolete by changes in the political scene. In the wake of its June 1990 declaration of sovereignty, the Uzbek leadership seemed increasingly ready to abandon, if not authoritarianism, at least the conventional ideology of Communism. "Uzbek history and tradition" were becoming the ideological standards. This opened the door as never before to an Islamic resurgence, but of which brand of Islam?

This situation poses a dilemma for the indigenous intelligentsia, whose leadership role may be pivotal. Its members are in many respects the intellectual and spiritual heirs of the Muslim reformers of old, the jadids who were so influential in the regional Communist party in the early 1920s. They have demonstrated a lively interest in rehabilitating the jadids' once-suppressed writings. They see in Muslim fundamentalism vestiges of the same reactionary Islam which was, until the advent of Communism, the jadids' chief adversary. On the other hand, the modern and pragmatic orientation of the official religious establishment represented by the Mufti offers to educated Central Asians a more congenial avenue for religious strivings than the traditional Islam of the grass roots, which continues to celebrate mysticism and superstition. Yet the Mufti and his small band of official clergy are essentially creatures of the state, discredited in the public eye by past identification with support of unpopular secular policies. The outcome may depend on whether the intelligentsia can enter into direct dialogue with the masses and establish a new Islamic *modus vivendi* to ward off extremism, whether of the Wahhabite, Iranian or other variety.

Notes

1. *Kommunist Uzbekistana*, No. 6, 1989, pp. 47-48.
2. Interested readers may wish to consult other works on the subject listed in the bibliography, such as Alexander Bennigsen's *Islam in the Soviet Union* or Michael Rywkin's *Moscow's Muslim Challenge*. There is also my

chapter, "Islam and Nationalism in Central Asia," in Pedro Ramet (*ed.*), *Religion and Nationalism in Soviet and East European Politics* (2nd edition), Durham and London (Duke University Press) 1989, pp. 196-219.

3. G. Safarov, *Kolonial'naya revolyutsiya* Moscow (*Gosizdat*) 1921, p. 138.

4. Richard Pipes, *The Formation of the Soviet Union*, Cambridge (Harvard University Press) 1964, pp. 181-83.

5. Mannan Ramiz (real name Mannan Abdullaev), *From Fact to Fantasy* (*Khayaldan Haqiqatgha*), Samarkand-Tashkent (Uzbekistan State Publishing House) 1928, pp. 31 *ff.* The pamphlet is printed in the Arabic script then in use for the Uzbek language.

6. Ibid.

7. Wealthy people.

8. Ramiz, pp. 36 *ff.*

9. Ibid.

10. For a discussion of this period, see Bennigsen and Lemercier-Quelquejay, *Islam in the Soviet Union*, and Bennigsen and Wimbush, *Muslim National Communism in the Soviet Union*.

11. For precisely this reason, Uzbeks are now trying to learn to read old literature in Arabic script. Uzbek media have been carrying lessons designed to help readers master the script.

12. See, for example, *Ozbekistan adabiyati va san"ati* (*OAS*), May 26, 1989.

13. T. S. Saidbaev, *Islam i obshchestvo*, Moscow (*Nauka*) 1978. For more on Saidbaev's findings and the general state of Islam in the late Brezhnev era, see my chapter in Ramet, *Religion and Nationalism*.

14. Saidbaev, p. 181.

15. *Pravda Vostoka*, November 25, 1986.

16. *Pravda Vostoka*, August 12, 1987.

17. See Critchlow in Ramet, *Religion and Nationalism*, pp. 196-197.

18. *Yash Leninchi*, January 13, 1989.

19. Ibid.

20. *Sovet Ozbekistani*, December 25, 1988 and December 28, 1988.

21. See Annette Bohr, "Soviet Muslims Demonstrate in Tashkent," Radio Liberty *Report on the USSR*, No. 8, 1989.

22. *Sovet Ozbekistani*, December 11, 1987; for Gorbachev speech, *Pravda Vostoka*, April 10, 1988.

23. John Soper, "Muslim Leaders Interviewed in Soviet Union," *RLR* 265/88, June 15, 1988.

24. N. Usmanov, "Useful Points of Collaboration," *Kommunist Uzbekistana*, June 1989, pp. 47-48.

25. *Pravda Vostoka*, December 7, 1989.

26. For background on the Wahhabite movement, see Fazlur Rahman, "Revival and Reform in Islam," *The Cambridge History of Islam*, Cambridge (Cambridge University Press) 1970, especially Vol. II, p. 637-639. For a pre-

perestroika Soviet commentary on Wahhabism, see L. Klimovich, *Islam*, Moscow (*Nauka*) 1965, pp. 198-204.

27. *New Times*, Moscow, No. 37, 1989, p. 32.

28. *Ogonek*, Moscow, No. 29, 1989, p. 29.

29. *Pravda Vostoka*, September 23, 1989.

30. The article first appeared in 1972 in *Ozbek Sovet Entsiklopediyasi*, Vol. 3, pp. 6-7. It was reprinted, without the reference to Afghanistan, in *Islam-spravochnik*, Tashkent (*Ozbek Sovet Entsiklopediyasi Bash Redaktsiyasi*) 1987. The reference to Afghanistan was the sole deletion in the reprinted version.

31. *Literaturnaya gazeta*, September 13, 1989.

32. *Tajikistani Soveti*, October 13, 1989, as cited in *Radio Liberty Daily Report* for October 27.

33. Mufti Muhammad Sadiq Muhammad Yusuf, "The Husband in the Family," *OAS*, January 5, 1990.

34. See for example, a book review in the issue of January 22, 1988 (p. 5), which referred to religion as "one of the means of cultural poisoning of the proletariat and all working-people."

35. See Paul Goble, "Islamic 'Explosion' Possible in Central Asia," *Report on the USSR*, February 16, 1990, p. 22.

36. *Pravda Vostoka*, January 28, 1990, p. 3.

37. See Annette Bohr, "Self-Immolation among Central Asian Women," *RLR* 126/88.

38. *OAS*, December 22, 1989.

39. T. Osipova and T. Iskanderov, "Konstitutsionnye garantii svobody sovesti" (Constitutional Guarantees of Freedom of Religion), *Kommunist Uzbekistana*, November 1989, p. 64.

40. *Pravda Vostoka*, December 7, 1989.

PART THREE

Problems of Sovereignty

11

Uzbekistan in Transition

The November 1990 Treaty Draft: A Watershed

In November 1990, a draft "union treaty" aimed at defining future relationships between the center and the republics was published in Moscow with Gorbachev as its chief advocate. This event forced the leadership in Uzbekistan to cross a Rubicon: President Karimov announced that--given Uzbekistan's declaration of sovereignty--he had no choice but to take a position against the proposed draft. The reason given: its inconsistency with his republic's newly sovereign status. In doing so he distanced Uzbekistan farther than ever from the Moscow orbit.

Ironically, Karimov did not oppose a union treaty in principle. Given evident assurances by Gorbachev that its sovereignty would be respected, Uzbekistan was one of the nine republics that met with him at a dacha outside Moscow on April 23, 1991, and agreed to such a document. However his willingness to accept a treaty stemmed not from reasons of sentimental loyalty to the USSR but because he looked to Moscow to rescue his republic from its desperate economic situation, which he blamed outspokenly on "many years of central economic policy that made Uzbekistan into a raw-materials base" while "what was produced here received unjustly low prices."[1] Back in October 1990, he had cautiously warned deputies to the Uzbek Supreme Soviet that, "The time will come for political and economic independence, but right now it's more important to feed people." He had stressed that Uzbekistan's problems could "be solved only in the framework of a federation."[2]

Although the November 1990 treaty proposal quickly became a dead issue in the face of determined resistance from the republics, Uzbekistan's reaction to it is worth studying because of what it revealed about the new politics of that republic. The proposal forced Karimov into opposition to Moscow. He could not fail to be aware that Gorbachev's latest move was stirring up a hornet's nest in Uzbekistan. There was open scoffing at the idea that Moscow might help Uzbekistan. As one skeptic put it:

> We seem to be leaving it to the Union to even out the level of development . . . but what is the Union today? It is republics each of which has adopted, ourselves included, its declaration of independence. Are they about to give us free aid? . . . It's doubtful.[3]

Although Karimov was still harbored hopes that Moscow might be willing to help Uzbekistan out of its economic plight, that no longer deterred him from openly savaging the draft put forth by Gorbachev. In a report to the Uzbek Party Congress, he voiced some strong objections to the draft, saying that it needed serious revision, that in particular it had failed to take into consideration the demand for parity and equal rights for all subjects of the Federation, and that it should uphold the sovereignty of the republics. He categorically denied reports in Soviet central media to the effect that "Uzbekistan is ready to sign the Union treaty today on any terms."[4] He insisted on the point that it should not have been drafted by Moscow in the first place, but by the republics.

Uzbek objections to the initial Gorbachev draft did not rule out future ties with Moscow, but public discussion of the document shed revealing light on the climate of hostility to the center which now prevailed in the republic, and the limitations on any future relationship. The Uzbeks also made it clear that, barring some violent action by Moscow, there could be no return to the old set-up in which the center issued directives to Uzbekistan.

Evidence of how far the spirit of independence had progressed appeared on the day the Uzbek Party Congress opened, when the daily *Pravda Vostoka*, the Russian-language organ of the Uzbek Central Committee and Supreme Soviet, and for many years a loyal mouthpiece for Moscow, came out with an article condemning the treaty draft as "hardly able to be a sound basis for a new Union." There was also a dig at Gorbachev in a statement in the article that the slogan "Strong

Center, Strong Republics," once used in speeches by the Soviet leader, was now a "political anachronism."[5]

Commentaries on the treaty draft--from Karimov's on down-- revealed clearly that the Uzbeks had a completely different understanding of the concept of "union" from what had been in the minds of Gorbachev and other central framers of the "renewed Union" concept. Gorbachev was still viewing the Soviet Union, even though he called it "renewed," essentially as subject to Moscow's hegemony. The Uzbeks, on the other hand, already saw the future "Union" as a confederation of absolutely sovereign republics in which the central organs derived their limited authority, in such areas as foreign policy, only from the consent of the republics themselves. Moreover, they brooked no restrictions on the right of any republic to secede, and maintained that *each* republic must have the right to veto any action of the central organs with which it might disagree.

Following publication of the November 1990 draft, a chorus of protests against the proposal was heard throughout Uzbekistan, some of it in the republic's most conservative newspapers, a sign that the protests were sanctioned by higher authority, almost certainly by Karimov himself. The Presidium of the Uzbek Supreme Soviet met to consider a flood of "comments, proposals and amendments" which had been prepared by the Council of Ministers, various Supreme Soviet committees, regional and municipal Soviets, "labor collectives," scholars, and individual citizens. As negative opinions of varying degrees of stridency began to appear in the press, the concrete substance of Uzbek objections became apparent. There was a recurring complaint that the draft was an attempt to retain the Soviet Union as a "unitary state," something regarded as no longer admissible. Overwhelmingly, commentators endorsed Karimov's view that the text was inconsistent with Uzbekistan's new sovereign status. Establishment critics ranged from the poet and liberal people's deputy Muhammad Salih, a founding member of the oppositional Erk political party, to the party stalwart Rima-jan M. Khudayberganova, who in the local context of Uzbek politics could be considered a pillar of party orthodoxy.[6] Presumably, radicals now outside the establishment, like the leadership of the Birlik informal group, were even more vehement in their objections, but their views were less apt to find expression in the official press.

A further hardening of the Uzbek position occurred when the treaty draft was subjected to stinging criticism at a special meeting of the

Uzbek Writers' Union, convened December 14. One of the speakers, the scholar Z. Ziyamov, asserted that, juridically, the treaty should have been drawn up as an international agreement, for the USSR Constitution declared the union republics to be independent states on their own territory. Unfortunately, he said, the draft was full of logical inconsistencies put there for the purpose of preserving the former totalitarian regime. The well-known writer Jamal Kamal complained that all rights had been given to the center, just as before. And how could a state be described as independent, he asked, if it was deprived of its own customs service and boundaries and defense force? He compared Uzbekistan with Turkey, which he had visited recently: that country, with a population of 60 million, produced only a fifth as much cotton as Uzbekistan, and only a fourth as much silk, but with a population three times the size of Uzbekistan's managed to live ten times as well. The reason was that it was in possession of its own wealth. What had happened to all the talk of expanding the independent rights of the republics? There was no trace of these promises in the draft. "The only right they're giving us," he said, "is to dig in with our hoes and work like slaves!" No one with a sense of honor toward his people would sign such a document, Jamal Kamal declared.

The poet and editor Aman Matjan warned against giving in to pressure to sign and thus tying the hands of future generations. He decried the fact that foreign relations and foreign trade were left in Moscow's hands, insisting that the union republics should have been given the right to open embassies in foreign countries; otherwise, they could not join the United Nations. Professor Achil Taghaev reminded the meeting of a statement which he attributed to Academician Andrey Sakharov that for the Union to be voluntary it was necessary for the republics first to leave it, then for those who so wished to rejoin it afterward--that was what you could call "voluntary." He noted further that the intent of the treaty was to strengthen the Union and increase its prestige, but that the draft "was based on coercion right from the start."

The journalist Barnabek Eshpolatov reminded the meeting that in 1917 the new Soviet state had renounced its foreign debts but not its colonial territories, and said that the present draft also displayed such "fantasies." No one could sign it with his eyes open. Writer and editor Mirmuhsin, for years a pillar of the Uzbek literary establishment, complained that the draft kept the center in control of the factories which were still polluting Uzbekistan. Finally, the participants in the meeting adopted a unanimous resolution calling on the government of Uzbekistan not to sign the draft Union treaty; instead, the Uzbek government was urged to conclude horizontal treaties with other republics, not with the center.[7]

The newspaper of the Uzbek Komsomol, *Yash Leninchi* (meaning "Young Leninist," although the paper had recently announced its intention to change its name to something more "Uzbek"), published an article against the draft treaty which was succinctly titled "The Trap." Its authors averred that the section on the prerogatives of the center made it seem that the patronizing Russian "elder brother" was back. They also expressed the opinion that under the proposed system no non-Russian could be elected Union president for at least 200 years, and that the framers of the document had surely known this. Any republican leadership that signed the draft, they wrote, would betray the fundamental interests and destiny of its people.[8]

One of the most trenchant attacks on the draft occupied a full page of *Soviet Ozbekistani*, the Uzbek-language daily organ of the Uzbek Central Committee and Supreme Soviet, an indication that its author, the writer Abduqahhar Ibrahimov, had the support of the republican leadership. Ibrahimov, who was known for his zeal for nationalist causes,[9] scoffed at the statement in the draft's section on "Fundamental Principles" that "each republic participant in the treaty is a sovereign state and possesses all state power on its territory." If that were the case, he argued in a thinly veiled slap at Gorbachev, the Union would be headed not by a single person but by a rotating roster of the presidents of the constituent states, perhaps for a one-year term. With one-man rule, he insisted, the Union would be not a federation but a unitary state. And what about the provision that Russian would be the state language of the renewed Union? Both under international law and from the standpoint of humanitarian considerations, a federation should have not just one privileged language, he argued, for this destroyed the equality of the members and was damaging to friendship; without friendship, a federation could not be stable and would deteriorate. With Russian as the state language, Ibrahimov maintained, the Union would again become "Russia." Lenin had warned against having a single state language. It would be a good idea, Ibrahimov recommended, to take a look at the Swiss confederation with its three official languages.

Ibrahimov found it strange that, while the draft spelled out the prerogatives of the Union, there was "absolutely not a single word" about the prerogatives of the republics. If the eight-part section of the draft on the Union's prerogatives were put into force, he warned, this would constitute a surrender to the center politically, legally, economically, and in other respects, reducing the republics to the status of administrative oblasts. Moreover, if this section were kept, he predicted that no republic that respected its own sovereignty would sign the treaty. In fact, the republics would have little left to do but to comply wordlessly with the center's directives.

The provision of the draft that the center would be responsible for "carrying out a unified financial, credit and monetary policy based on a common currency" also helped to throw into sharp relief the differences between Uzbekistan and the Gorbachev faction as to what constituted a "sovereign republic." "Is there today anywhere on the face of the earth a single state without its own currency?" Ibrahimov asked in outrage. Even the pre-revolutionary khanates of Bukhara and Khiva, he recalled, those "backward, semi-colonial vassals of tsarist Russia," possessed "their own treasury, mint and--of course--currency." He also scoffed at the idea embodied in the draft that the Union should develop a "common economic strategy," saying that precisely that approach was responsible for the country's present horrible economic plight.

Ibrahimov dismissed in disgust still another point of the draft, the idea that the Union should be responsible for "co-ordination of co-operation between the republics." It would be much better, in his opinion, for the republics to work this out among themselves without the center's intervention. He blamed the idea of central co-ordination on the attitude of people in the center that "nothing can get done without us." He found a logical flaw--one of the draft's "fundamental weaknesses"--in the assumption that the Union was a "separate thing." Instead, he insisted, the Union could be no more than the sum of its parts: "the Union is the republics that compose it." Otherwise, the Union would become the ruler of the republics, who would be its subjects, in an "above and below" relationship. This was clearly inadmissible.

On the sensitive question of representation of Uzbeks in the Union government and administrative organs, where they had been victims of discrimination from the beginning of the Soviet regime, Ibrahimov found that the draft treaty gave no better assurances than were contained in earlier documents like the 1936 Stalin Constitution and the

1977 Brezhnev Constitution, which he blamed for turning the USSR into a unitary state.

A further provision which drew fire from Ibrahimov was the provision that the Council of Federation, which would be composed of presidents (chiefs of state) of the republics, would be "under the leadership of the President of the USSR." Similarly, the republican presidents would be members, by virtue of their office, of the USSR Cabinet of Ministers, which in turn would be subordinate to the USSR President. Such denigration of the office of republican president was further evidence, Ibrahimov found, of a return to the concept of a "unitary state," making it necessary to forget that the presidents were sovereign heads of sovereign states.[10] The articles of the draft dealing with the USSR court system were also accused by Ibrahimov of infringing on republican sovereignty.

Ibrahimov fired a parting shot at Gorbachev, reasserting his own view that "there can be no such thing as a federal president" in a Union of sovereign states.

In a second article, Ibrahimov again took issue with Gorbachev by name, this time criticizing the latter's opposition to secession reaffirmed in a recent speech.[11] This, Ibrahimov pointed out, was a violation of Article 73 of the USSR Constitution providing that "every Union republic has the right to leave the USSR." It would be better, Ibrahimov lectured Gorbachev, not to put it in the form that "we cannot secede" but rather to form such a "free and friendly Union" that people would be honored to live in it.[12]

The August, 1991 coup against Gorbachev may have driven such attitudes underground for a time, but in the long run "hard-line" retrogressions cannot stamp them out.

Problems and Opportunities

These reactions to Gorbachev's original union proposal showed an Uzbek elite intent on pursuing a course of independent statehood. For the first time since tsarist armies had occupied the territory more than a century ago, the core of Central Asia was determined to throw off foreign rule.

Even before the August, 1991 coup in the Soviet Union, the new path of national independence raised questions about Uzbekistan's viability as a nation-state. If the republic persisted in this course, it would now have to face its enormous problems largely on its own.

First, there is the economic crisis: the pressing need to find relief for those nine million citizens--nearly half the population--who in 1990 were below the official income poverty line of 75 rubles a month, and for the other five million, disabled, elderly, or children, who were unable to work and received less than 50 rubles a month in public assistance.[13] The number of unemployed is staggering, at least two million. This problem is compounded by the rapid population growth, which confronts the fledgling country with fifty thousand new mouths to feed every month, and the related demand for additional housing and consumer goods.

Closely connected with the economic crisis is the environmental one. Here the most urgent of many tasks is to stave off the threat to life and health faced by the half of the population that lacks pure drinking water. Despite Uzbekistan's economic predicament, funds will have to be found to develop new sources of water supply and distribute the water to the needy. There is a whole spectrum of other environmental emergencies, of which the dying Aral Sea is only the most spectacular and daunting.

Public unrest over shortages and health problems is aggravated by the heterogeneous nature of Uzbekistan's population. Competition for goods and services tends to set group against group: the bloody 1989 riots against Meskhetian Turks in the Ferghana Valley and the lethal feuding the following year between Uzbeks and Kirghiz in the border area joining their two republics were ample evidence of the potential for explosion. According to the 1989 census, some six million residents of Uzbekistan are not Uzbeks. More than one hundred other nationalities were listed. Minorities include nearly two million Slavs (Russians, Ukrainians, Belorussians), almost a million each of Tajiks and Kazakhs, half a million each of Karakalpaks (residents of their own autonomous republic in the northwest of Uzbekistan) and Volga Tatars, and sizeable numbers of Kirghiz and Turkmens. The rest of the population includes remnants, some large, of non-indigenous nationalities deported to the area under Stalin: Crimean Tatars, Chechens and Ingush, Kabardinians and Balkars, Koreans, Kalmyks, and the ill-starred Meskhetian Turks. The Uzbek census also listed four categories of Jews, mainly Ashkenazim and the indigenous Bukharan Jewish community, totalling about 85 thousand.[14] Can a government that is founded on the new ideology of Uzbek nationalism find ways of integrating these outsider nationalities into the new state, of making it attractive to them?

Even among the Uzbeks themselves there is a problem of divisiveness. As we saw in the first chapter, "Who Are the Uzbeks?", the very concept of nationality is an artificial one that has had only a few decades to consolidate. Clan and tribal allegiances are reportedly still strong. Another factor militating against Uzbek unity is localism, the tendency of Bukharans or Khivans or residents of the Ferghana Valley to attach their primary loyalty to those areas and not to that relatively new creation, the Uzbek state. Before the Russians came in the last century, Central Asia--particularly the area that is now Uzbekistan--was riddled by internecine strife among city-based khanates and nomadic leaders in the countryside. Particularly in a climate where Uzbek "national" institutions were functioning badly, such centrifugal forces were again coming into play.

A further source of potential instability is conflict among the different Central Asian republics. As Moscow's central control weakened, the leaderships of those republics met repeatedly to try to work out new regional arrangements. The "summit" held in June 1990 in Alma-Ata was a landmark in this direction.[15] During the author's visit to Uzbekistan in June 1991, an official close to President Kariov complained to him that there were problems of co-operation with Kazakhstan, the vast republic bordering Uzbekistan, because the Kazakhs were "looking only to the North," i.e. toward Russia. Such efforts have continued, but it is too early to predict success. An ever present threat to good relations among the republics of the Amu-Darya basin (and within them) is that of regulation of water resources. Until the devolution of power under Gorbachev, this function was performed--if imperfectly--by the central organs in Moscow; as Moscow retreated from the scene, a new mechanism had to be found. There was some talk of the republics' merging into a single "Turkestan" nation but whatever the popular appeal of such a proposal--which is an affront to the Iranian Tajiks--it met with little enthusiasm from the elites, who identify their status with the institutions of the individual republic.

Some observers have suggested that Islam can be the integrative force that will promote harmony among Central Asian Muslims at both the regional and local levels. There is little doubt about the pervasive influence of Islam. Yet despite the slogan "All Muslims are brothers," Islam itself in Central Asia is riddled with internal contradictions. Just as throughout the Muslim world religion has often been impotent to regulate conflicts between Muslims (witness the Iran-Iraq war), so in Central Asia has it also been failing to do so. In Central Asia itself, there is now a rivalry between competing muftis in Tashkent and Alma Ata, i.e. between Uzbek and Kazakh Muslims. There is the possibly disruptive influence of Iranian fundamentalism, and of "Wahhabites" in the region, mentioned in the preceding chapter.

Perhaps the most significant split in Central Asian Islam is that which divides the Muslim elites, on the one hand, with their adherence to the intellectual, rational heritage of the turn-of-the-century jadid reformers, and, on the other, the masses for whom Islam is a populist movement with emotional and superstitious overtones, one that might some day rally them against the secular authority of the elites.

All of these divisions and instabilities jeopardize the ability of any Uzbek leadership to maintain unity, even under the best of conditions. With Uzbekistan now faced, as its Prime Minister admitted in March 1990, with growing impoverishment, breakdown of social welfare services, galloping inflation, paralysis of public economic activity, and a soaring level of unemployment, the outlook is alarming.

As we have seen, the Uzbek elites have up to now been the key actor on the political scene, but the elites themselves are far from united. They are not immune to divisions along ideological, clan, geographic and other lines. This was brought home in 1990 when *Birlik*, the main informal group in Uzbekistan, split (despite its name, which means "unity"). Many of its leading members left to form a new political party called *Erk* ("Free"), announcing their intention to try to work for reform within the system, and leaving "Birlik" in the hands of more radical activists.

Will Uzbeks, and the others who inhabit their republic, be capable of working together to cope with crises that could defeat even a more homogeneous nation?

President Karimov and those around him responded to these challenges by promising new opportunities for all. Karimov's speeches were impressively concrete and businesslike. He was careful to try to reach out to all groups in the population. Emphasis was given to private initiative, if still within a framework of state ownership of the major means of production. One of Karimov's early moves was to promise a substantial transfer of land to private utilization (if not, for the time being, to private ownership). He and his supporters were resolutely pushing the "transition to market economy." Karimov predicted optimistically that in Uzbekistan "this will be shorter and less painful than in other regions of the country." In support of this contention, he cited Uzbekistan's long "historical" experience with trade, a reminder of the prosperous days when caravans carrying luxury cargoes passed through the area. As part of his policy, he called for a "rebirth" of native economic customs and traditions, including development of ethnic arts and crafts on a cottage-industry basis.[16]

Another part of Karimov's economic policy was aggressive pursuit of direct trade relations with other countries. To this end, an Uzbek "State Committee for Foreign Trade and Direct Overseas Ties" was created. Implicit in this designation was the aim of breaking the economic stranglehold of the central bureaucracy in Moscow. Also at stake was control of Uzbekistan's resources (including cotton) and the industrial objects on its territory.

Meanwhile, the Uzbeks reported some impressive spadework in prospecting for trade links with other parts of the world. Among non-Muslim countries, there were negotiations with Belgian interests about financing construction of textile factories in Uzbekistan's Kashka Darya Valley, and the South Koreans (eying the large Korean minority resident in Uzbekistan) expressed interest in a variety of trading schemes. There was also nearby China, which has its own Turkic population: it happens that the leading executives of a "Sino-Soviet" joint venture that set up a factory in Tashkent to manufacture thermos bottles for sale in the USSR all have Muslim names. For the foreseeable future, however, Uzbekistan will be dependent on Russia and other Soviet (or ex-Soviet) republics for a large part of its economic relations. In the long run, the Uzbek dream is to become a second Japan or South Korea, a center of light industry (electronics is often cited) whose factories would put masses of unemployed to work, earning hard currency for the new nation. To realize this, there are mammoth hurdles to be surmounted: most of the unemployed are unskilled or possess only agricultural skills, and construction of factories requires funds for investment. A primary goal of Karimov's economic policy was somehow to secure from foreign investors the capital that Moscow always denied to Uzbekistan to develop its own industry. To do this, he must also succeed in convincing them of Uzbekistan's political stability, in the face of socioethnic unrest and continued feuding with Moscow.

Whatever Karimov's success as a leader, he could hardly deal with the magnitude of the environmental crisis without outside help.

One avenue of relief yet to be fully explored, if political conditions permit, is the possible participation of global agencies like UNESCO and the World Health Organization, which have dealt with similar problems in other parts of the world; at the very least, that might help to call attention to the catastrophe of Aral desiccation and pollution of soil, air and water--conditions so widespread that they should be of more than local interest.

One earnest of the Uzbek government's seriousness in confronting its problems is an energetic program of foreign training for key personnel. For example, in the 1990-1991 academic year, six Uzbek specialists spent periods ranging up to the full year at Harvard's Institute of International Development, with access to various departments of the university. They represented different disciplines: economics, law, political science. Those selected for Harvard were well-versed in the Western literature of their disciplines and fluent in English.

Despite some democratization in recent years, the political system of Uzbekistan remained authoritarian, even in Gorbachev's day. The republican Communist Party, headed by President Karimov, was powerful and active, although it no longer professed allegiance to the CPSU in Moscow and had all but forsaken Marxism-Leninism in favor of an ideology based on "Uzbek values." Nominations and elections to the Supreme Soviet remained heavily influenced by the Party.

In all of this, there were a few rays of hope. One of these was the person of Karimov himself, who, whatever his autocratic approach as a leader, appeared to be dedicated to the well-being of his republic and willing to stand up to Moscow to defend it. His ability to win concessions from the center on a range of issues involving cotton cannot have hurt his popularity. His decision to make more land available for private use also addressed a pressing need. Karimov's words and actions suggest a genuine concern for the population, especially for such disadvantaged groups as pensioners, teachers and war veterans. In this, he contrasts sharply with his two immediate predecessors, Usmankhojaev and Nishanov, whose speeches might have been--and possibly were--drafted by the Central Committee in Moscow.

There is also the heartening fact that Uzbekistan, if given the opportunity, has modern public institutions capable of being used in the service of good government. These institutions need to be further cleansed of the "administrative-command" tradition under which they operated for decades: activists like the poet-deputy Muhammad Salih have grumbled about their lack of responsiveness to genuine popular needs. Yet the Uzbek Supreme Soviet, like the one in Moscow, has provided a forum for a variety of conflicting opinions, some of them sharply at variance with official policy. If the Uzbek public becomes more accustomed to participation in the governmental process, shedding the apathy engrained by years of enforced submission to a system founded on terror, the institutions are present that might become infused with a spirit of still greater democracy.

Finally, the elites themselves must be viewed as a major national asset. Their backbone is a class of highly-educated native professionals: administrators, economists, scientists, teachers, writers, and artists. This class considers itself to be the intellectual and spiritual heir of both the dynamic medieval Islamic renaissance in Central Asia and of the later pragmatic jadid reformers. Like those of subjects of other colonial systems, its native values have been overlaid by an education according to the curriculum of the occupying power: in this case, not only Marxism-Leninism but Tolstoy, Dostoyevsky, Chekhov, and--at least in Russian translation--Western writers like Balzac, Dickens, and Hemingway. In recent years, debates and discussions in the vernacular press have reflected all of the elements of this elite heritage: it is not surprising to see an Uzbek writer make a political point by quoting both Montesquieu and the proverbial Eastern wit Khoja Nasriddin. The lively, sophisticated give-and-take of those debates and discussions provides an encouraging sign that the elites, if given a chance by external political forces, are capable of shaking off the torpor and passivity of decades of foreign dictatorial rule and ready to advance toward forging a pluralistic, democratic society.

Notes

1. *Pravda Vostoka*, November 29, 1990.
2. *Pravda Vostoka*, October 31, 1990.
3. *Pravda Vostoka*, November 23, 1990.
4. *Pravda Vostoka*, December 8, 1990.
5. *Pravda Vostoka*, December 7, 1990.
6. Khudayberganova, chairman of the Khorezm Oblast Executive Committee, was previously the First Secretary of that oblast's party organization. In October 1990 she made a speech praising the continuing dominance of the Party in her oblast (See *Pravda Vostoka*, October 12, 1990).

7. *Ozbekistan adabiyati wa san"ati (OAS)*, December 21, 1990.

8. *Yash Leninchi*, December 13, 1990.

9. See J. Critchlow, "Will Soviet Central Asia Become a Greater Uzbekistan?" Radio Liberty *Report on the USSR*, September 14, 1990, p. 17.

10. *Sovet Ozbekistani*, December 14, 1990.

11. At the November 17, 1990, Supreme Soviet session.

12. *OAS*, December 14, 1990.

13. *Pravda Vostoka*, October 31, 1990.

14. *Pravda Vostoka*, June 15, 1990.

15. See Paul Goble, "Central Asians Form Political Bloc," *Report on the USSR*, July 13, 1990, p. 18.

16. *Pravda Vostoka*, November 23, 1991.

Afterword

The Shape of Things to Come

Given the turmoil through which the entire Soviet Union has been passing, it would be folly to try to predict with precision the future course of events in Uzbekistan and its neighboring republics. We can, however, identify with reasonable confidence some of the trends now at work, and try to project them ahead with a view to constructing some alternative hypotheses about what may happen.

First, what is the future of relations between Uzbekistan and the Russian metropolis? Proximity and age-old ties have forged such close linkages that the fate of the one is bound to affect the other for a long time to come. Yet at the same time, we are clearly in a new situation: it seems safe to assume that Moscow's grip on Uzbekistan will never be restored in the old pattern of hegemony, whatever the short-term success of "hard-liners" in attempting to set back the clock.

This book has documented the deep resentment of Soviet (and Russian) rule shared by Uzbeks at all social levels. While one feels sympathy for the individuals involved, there is a certain historical justice in the hostile climate felt by Russian settlers in Uzbekistan that is now causing them to leave in droves. For decades, the Russians in Uzbekistan, even those whose parents or grandparents had been born there, had not bothered to learn the language or build bridges to Uzbek society, secure in the belief that this was part of "Russia." During a visit to Tashkent in June 1991, the author found that city's large Russian population in a virtual state of panic. Feeling neglected by Moscow and in fear of becoming victims of native violences (as some had during the Ferghana riots), the Russians were redoubling efforts to emigrate to Russia proper, even though many had never lived there and still considered Uzbekistan their homeland. Meanwhile, Moscow was too preoccupied with its own crisis to devote much attention to helping Russian minorities in Central Asia, or becoming otherwise involved with the problems of the region. The Russians back home tended to view the Muslim regions of their crumbling country with indifference or downright dislike, seeing their inhabitants, rightly or wrongly, as irritating and demanding beggars, unable to shift for themselves and all too ready to take handouts from the central economy. So staunch a Russian patriot as Alexander Solzhenitsyn has come out publicly in favor of letting Central Asia and the other non-Slavic regions of the Soviet Union go their own ways, so that Russia can concentrate on its own problems. Similar sentiments were voiced by senior Moscow officials in private conversations with foreign visitors. All of this, of course, was grist for the mill of Gorbachev's foes.

Given, then, that Uzbekistan (together with the other Central Asian republics) seems headed toward independence, despite whatever obstacles the center may impose to slow down the process, what are the directions in which it can move? Above all, *who will rule Uzbekistan*?

It is possible to imagine two sets of scenarios: the first involving a stable evolution, the second something resembling revolutionary chaos. The former presupposes a gradual political change in which the institutional structure of government is adapted to meet the needs of a newly independent Uzbekistan. The latter is based on the contingency that might arise if continued failure to remedy the Uzbek public's economic, environmental, and social problems were to trigger a mass upheaval, possibly along the lines of the 1989 Ferghana riots but on a more sweeping scale that would engulf all of Uzbekistan, overturning the existing order. Uzbek President Karimov recognized this contingency in a July 1991 newspaper interview when he admitted that the confidence of the people was not unlimited, that is was painful for him to have to tell the public that "improvement should not be expected in the near future."[1]

The Stable Scenario

Under the first scenario, the native elites would likely continue to be the key actors on the political scene, holding on to the reins of government (possibly with increased participation by the masses). Uzbekistan's governing institutions would change, but gradually, to adapt to the newly independent situation. The elites would have to face the fact that Russians and Uzbeks are linked, whether they like it or not, by certain common interests. Two of these are paramount: (1) mutual security and (2) economic co-operation.

The Uzbek elites must be concerned--when they take time to think about it in the present troubled situation--about the possibility that foreign interests, taking advantage of a land in crisis, might intrude. The Mufti of Tashkent, in an interview quoted in Chapter 10, mentioned fear of the possible spread of Islamic revolution from Iran. If such threats became imminent, the Uzbek elites might well swallow their pride and agree voluntarily (or involuntarily) to the stationing of a Soviet (or Russian) presence on their territory, its position regulated by a status of forces agreement not unlike those concluded by the NATO partners.

The more conservative elites might also see such a military force as capable of helping to restore order in times of trouble, just as forces from outside Uzbekistan have been deployed to cope with crises such as the 1989 Ferghana riots. Although a delicate matter politically, the force might also help to prevent flareups between different Central Asian republics. (In that connection, some members of the Uzbek elite have already begun to hint at extending their republic's hegemony over the entire region, but it is unlikely that such grandiose ideas will receive support from a leadership hard-pressed to cope with Uzbekistan's own problems.[2])

For their part, the Russians have a historic fear of foreign invasions. Up to now, the non-Russian republics around the fringes of the USSR have acted as a *cordon sanitaire* against hostile attack from outside. The collapse of that system of buffers must be deeply troubling for those responsible, in present and in future, for Russia's security. Thus, even in a time of turmoil at home, the rulers of Russia could be disposed to provide a military presence in Uzbekistan and other peripheral republics, especially if requested to do so by the local authorities.

For similar reasons of mutual interest, the two sides would be impelled to undertake a program of economic co-operation. Although the Uzbeks and other Central Asian cotton producers have complained, with much justification, about Moscow's exploitation of them and their resources as its sole suppliers of that crop, the fact remains that the region is not self-sufficient, that it will depend for the foreseeable future on marketing raw materials like cotton. For this, Russia-- assuming that it does not descend into total economic chaos--provides the most accessible market.

Meanwhile, the Uzbeks would be expected to continue reaching out for direct ties with other countries, for diplomatic recognition, export markets, investments, and cultural exchanges. The response that they encounter would be a factor in their internal stability and their future international alignment.

The Revolutionary Scenario

What if Karimov or his successors fail to solve Uzbekistan's critical problems in time? Will there be a revolutionary situation in Uzbekistan? In his classic non-Marxian study of revolution, Crane Brinton found that the revolutions he examined tended to have certain common characteristics.[3] One was the structural weaknesses, economic and political, of the old regimes, which were characterized by inefficient government. He noted that "revolutions often come during economic depressions which follow on periods of generally rising standards of living." In Uzbekistan, the present disastrous situation follows a time of improving living standards in the earlier period of Brezhnev's rule. Karimov's program of action implicitly recognized the relevance of the Brintonian criteria to Uzbekistan, by attacking the structural weakness of the regime and the inefficient machinery of government.

Brinton also concluded that "actual misery" was less important as a determinant of revolution than "the existence among a group, or certain groups, of a feeling that prevailing conditions limit or hinder their economic activity." Karimov's speeches left no doubt that he was acutely aware of precisely this danger and is trying to head it off by opening up new avenues of economic activity.

In Brinton's view, the most reliable predictor of a revolutionary situation was what he called "the transfer of allegiance of the intellectuals" to "another and better world than that of the corrupt and inefficient old regimes." He noted the special role of intellectuals, from the American and French revolutions of the eighteenth century to the Russian and colonial revolutions of the twentieth. This "transfer of allegiance of the intellectuals" was frequently accompanied by demoralization of the old ruling classes, some of whose members went over to the revolution. At some point in the revolution, there would be "an attempted use of force by the government, its failure, and the attainment of power by the revolutionists."

The split in *Birlik*, many of whose members are intellectuals, reflects just such a "transfer of allegiance" on the part of those who did not wish to join in the rump *Erk* faction's plan to work within the system. (Ironically, as of mid-1991 the more moderate *Erk* had failed, just like *Birlik*, to gain recognition through official registration-- despite Karimov's professions of belief in democracy.[4] There are other signs of this phenomenon: as in other republics, intellectuals, such as the well-known poetess Gulchehra Nurullaeva, have been leaving the Uzbek Party in strength. Another member wrote to a newspaper on turning in his Party card after many years of membership to complain about how the Party had betrayed him: "Look at the miracle they've accomplished in twenty years without any slogans and ideologists in South Korea and Finland, not to speak of West Germany and Japan, and without any committees or 'isms.'"[5] Still another wrote, "They're saying that honest people are leaving the Party . . . That's what we've come to."[6]

To carry the Brintonian analogy a step further, Uzbekistan's nationalist proclamation of sovereignty from Moscow clearly fits his definition of a "territorial-nationalist revolution,"[7] its leaders members of the Uzbek elites (Brinton would call them "oligarchs") who pitted themselves against the power of the center. But if the "territorial-nationalist" revolution fails, possibly due to intervention by Moscow, or should succeed without relieving fundamental problems, there are also in Uzbekistan seeds of a popular "socioeconomic revolution," another type identified by Brinton. In that connection, it is worth recalling his belief that there is a common dynamic of revolutions, the tendency of the moderates who lead them in the early stages to be deposed by a more radical (and bloodthirsty) group. It is possible to imagine that such a situation might someday occur in Uzbekistan, with the leaders riding the crest of mob violence, of which we have already seen samples.

There can be no doubt that many of the elites who have led Uzbekistan's struggle for greater autonomy from Moscow came to be haunted by the fear that the situation will get out of hand. The threat of chaos, of a violent uprising of the hungry rural masses led by Islamic militants, possibly directed from outside, is a sobering one for those seeking orderly change. During the 1989 Ferghana riots, party secretaries were taken hostage and nearly murdered, an object lesson to members of the Uzbek establishment. Thus, the poet and Supreme Soviet deputy Erkin Vahidov, one of the leading nationalist reformers, was signatory to an open letter supporting an Uzbek government decree against unauthorized demonstrations.

Uzbek moderate reformers faced challenges by more radical leaders, who looked to the masses for support and were less concerned about the possibility of upheaval. When *Birlik* split, it was partly because the more restrained *Erk* group had became alarmed at where the *Birlik* leadership was headed. There were also signs of schism within the established leadership. During a June 1991 visit to Tashkent, an Uzbek official close to Karimov told the author that there had been a distressing resurgence of "Stalinism" in the republic. He was not more specific, but it was noteworthy that the capital was buzzing with rumors of feuding between President Karimov and Vice-President Mirsaidov, who was said to represent the interests of the Tashkent "merchant clan" (Russian *torgashestvo*). It was said that "compromising material" on Mirsaidov had been found, that the Karimov forces had planned to depose him at a recent Supreme Soviet meeting, but that the resistance of Mirsaidov's "merchant clan" supports had been too strong. In general, there was much talk of divisions within the Uzbek elites along "clan" lines, a phenomenon recognized by Karimov in the July 1991 interview cited above.

Dissatisfaction was being voiced everywhere. There was grousing about Karimov's failure to carry out reforms at a faster rate. His economic reforms, such as his vaunted redistribution of small amounts of land for private use, were described by a *Birlik* spokesman as trivial and incomplete. Lack of progress toward "saving the Aral" was another source of bitter comment. On the cultural front, a leading intellectual complained that "nothing" had been done to implement the Uzbek language law passed in 1989, that the situation in that area was a "disaster" (something of an exaggeration, to judge from the greater use of Uzbek in public places.) Karimov's authoritarian view of "democracy" was also a recurring subject of criticims, even though the openness with which criticisms were voiced seemed to reflect a considerably more democractic atmosphere compared with earlier days. As for co-operation with other republics of the region, a Karimov loyalist blamed the largest, Kazakhstan, for holding back. (On the other hand, Kazakhs interviewed a few days earlier in Alma-Ata had complained that Uzbekistan was too "backward.")

If, then, the present "territorial-nationalist" revolution were to become a socioeconomic one, corresponding to our second scenario, what could be the practical consequences? In all likelihood, there would be a chaotic situation, with total breakdown of government and widespread bloodshed. This would be accompanied by fragmentation of political authority, favoring the emergence of local warlords or "strong men" able to insure a kind of order. In his recent book *The Modern Uzbeks*, Edward Allworth recalls the importance in Central Asian history, particularly at times of trouble, of powerful individual leaders.[8]

It is noteworthy that Central Asian strong men of the past have tended to be secular, not religious. Yet one cannot rule out the possibility that a grass-roots socioeconomic revolution could pave the way for fundamentalist Islamic movements backed by other countries to seize power. In Uzbekistan, the secular elites are the best bulwark against such drastic revolutionary change.

There is in this a challenge for the West. A fundamentalist takeover in Central Asia would destabilize not only the immediate region but could upset the alignment of forces in the Middle East and South Asia. Obviously, the geographic and political remoteness of the region is only one of the factors that preclude direct intervention, even if that were to be judged in the Western interest. There are, however, significant practical steps that can be taken immediately to show support for moderate nationalists, whatever the climate in Moscow. One is for Western leaders to show through public statements that they are aware of Uzbekistan and the other republics and their problems, and to extend the hand of friendship, a hand that is sure to receive an eager welcome. Political conditions permitting, this could be followed up by other bilateral measures in areas like trade and educational exchange. It is incumbent on Western interest to seek direct ties with the new nations that are in the making, and will come into being— sooner or later.

Notes

1. *Rabochaya Tribuna,* July 3, 1991.

2. See Critchlow, "Will Soviet Central Asia Become a Greater Uzbekistan?" Radio Liberty *Report on the USSR,* September 14, 1991, p. 17.

3. Crane Brinton, *The Anatomy of Revolution,* New York (Vintage Books) 1965.

4. Author's interview with *Birlik* leader in Tashkent, June 22, 1991.

5. *Pravda Vostoka,* March 1, 1990.

6. *Pravda Vostoka,* April 8, 1990.

7. Brinton, *The Anatomy,* pp. 21-22.

8.   Edward A. Allworth, *The Modern Uzbeks: From the Fourteenth Century to the Present, A Cultural History*, Stanford (Hoover Institution Press) 1990.

Glossary

aktiv: Communist Party activists

amma (frequently *umma*): the body of Muslim believers

basmachi: participant in a guerrilla movement against the Soviet regime in the 1920s and 1930s; also used in Soviet media as a pejorative term, especially to describe the mujahedin who fought against the Soviet invasion of Afghanistan

bay: in pre-Soviet society, a rich man, usually one of power

fatiha: the opening verses of the Koran, especially when recited with special gestures

fetwa: religious decree issued by a Muslim leader

hadiths: legends about the life of the Prophet Muhammad, commonly regarded as sacred precepts

haram: forbidden in Islamic law, as the eating of pork

jadid: an adherent of jadidism (q.v.)

jadidism: turn of the century religious reform movement among Muslims of the Russian Empire, from *usul jadid*, the "new method" to be used in schools established by the jadids

kurbashi: a leader of the basmachi (q.v.) rebellion

meras (or *miras*): heritage, especially the cultural heritage of the Central Asian Muslim peoples

mufti: an authoritative Islamic religious leader

mujahedin: fighters for Islam

mulla: a teacher or interpreter of Islamic law, therefore a person of some authority in the Muslim community

shahid (literally "witness"): a person killed while fighting for Islam whose immediate entry into paradise is believed certain

shariat: Islamic law, based on the Koran, the hadiths, and other sources

Sufism: a mystical movement within Islam

Sunni: of the two main branches of Islam (Sunni and Shia), the one with most adherents (circa 80 percent); most Central Asian Muslims follow Sunni Islam

tekhnikum: school for technical training of workers

ulema: body of men learned in Islamic law and custom (plural of *alim*)

Wahhabite: member of a religious movement within Islam (*see* Chap. 10)

waqf: Muslim religious foundation, usually property-owning

Bibliography

Books in English:

Allworth, Edward (*ed.*), *Central Asia: 120 Years of Russian Rule*, Durham (Duke University Press) 1989.

Allworth, Edward A., *The Modern Uzbeks: From the Fourteenth Century to the Present, A Cultural History*, Stanford (Hoover Institution Press) 1990.

Bennigsen, Alexandre and Lemercier-Quelquejay, Chantal, *Islam in the Soviet Union*, New York, Praeger, 1968.

Bennigsen, Alexandre and Wimbush, S. Enders, *Muslim National Communism in the Soviet Union*, Chicago (Chicago University Press) 1979.

Brinton, Crane, *The Anatomy of Revolution*, New York (Vintage Books) 1965.

Cambridge History of Islam, Cambridge (Cambridge University Press) 1970.

Deutsch, Karl W., *Nationalism and Social Communication*, Cambridge (Massachusetts) 1966.

Fainsod, Merle, *How Russia Is Ruled*, Cambridge (Harvard University Press) 1956.

Fierman, William (*ed.*), *Soviet Central Asia: The Failed Transformation*, Boulder (Westview Press) 1991.

Frederick, Kenneth D. with Hanson, James C., *Water for Western Agriculture*, Washington, D.C. (Resources for the Future) 1982.

Glazer, Nathan and Moynihan, Daniel, P., *Ethnicity: Theory and Experience*, Cambridge, (Harvard University Press) 1975.

Heidenheimer, Arnold J. (*ed.*), *Political Corruption*, New York (Holt, Rinehart and Winston) 1970.

La Polombara, Joseph (*ed.*), *Bureaucracy and Political Development*, Princeton (Princeton University Press) 1963.

Lubin, Nancy, *Labour and Nationality in Soviet Central Asia*, Princeton (Princeton Univ. Press) 1984.

Matthews, Mervyn, *Privilege in the Soviet Union: A Study of Elite Life-Styles Under Communism*, London (George Allen & Unwin) 1978.

Pahlen, K. K., *Mission to Turkestan*, London (Oxford University Press) 1964. Edited by Richard Pierce.

Parks, George B. (*ed.*), *The Book of Ser Marco Polo, the Venetian*, New York (Macmillan Modern Readers' Series), 1927.

Bibliography

Pipes, Richard, *The Formation of the Soviet Union*, Cambridge (Harvard University Press) 1964.

Ramet, Pedro (*ed*.), *Religion and Nationalism in Soviet and East European Politics* (2nd edition), Durham and London (Duke University Press) 1989.

Report of Court Proceedings in the Case of the Anti-Soviet "Bloc of Rights and Trotskyites Heard Before the Collegium of the Supreme Court of the U.S.S.R., Moscow, March 2-13, 1938, Moscow (People's Commissariat of Justice of the U.S.S.R.) 1938 (in English).

Rossabi, Morris, *Khubilai Khan: His Life and Times*, Berkeley (University of California Press) 1988.

Rywkin, Michael, *Moscow's Muslim Challenge*, Armonk (Sharpe) 1982.

--------, *Russia in Central Asia*, New York (Collier Books) 1963.

Singleton, Fred (*ed*.), *Environmental Problems in the Soviet Union and Eastern Europe*, Boulder, Colo. and London (Lynne Rienner) 1987.

Tillett, Lowell, *The Great Friendship*, Chapel Hill (University of North Carolina Press) 1969.

Weinbaum, Marvin G., *Food, Development, and Politics in the Middle East*, Boulder (Westview Press) 1984).

Books in Other Languages:

Barthold, V. V., *Istoriya kul'turnoy zhizni Turkestana*, Leningrad (USSR Academy of Sciences Press) 1927.

Brockhaus, F. A. and Efron, I. A., *Entsiklopedicheskii slovar'*, St. Petersburg 1902.

Budagov, Lazar', *Sravnitel'nyy slovar' Turetsko-tatarskikh narechiy*, St. Petersburg 1869. (Re-published 1960 by the USSR Academy of Sciences.)

Istoriya narodov Uzbekistana, Tashkent 1947.

Istoriya Uzbekskoy SSR (in four volumes), Tashkent 1968.

Kappeler et al. (*eds*.), *Die Muslime in der Sowjetunion und in Jugoslawien*, Cologne (Markus Verlag) 1989.

Khodzhaev, Feizula (sic) et al., *Ocherki revolyutsionnogo dvizheniya v Sredney Azii, sbornik statei*), Moscow (Izdanie nauchnoy assotsiatsii vostokovedeniya pri TsIK SSSR), 1926.

Klimovich, L. I., *Islam* (second edition), Moscow 1965.

Narodnoe khozyaystvo (USSR Statistical Yearbook), Moscow (for various years).

Ozbek Sovet Entsiklopediasi (Uzbek Soviet Encyclopedia), Tashkent (various years).

Ramiz, Mannan (real name Mannan Abdullaev), *Khayaldan Haqiqatgha*, Samarkand-Tashkent (Uzbekistan State Publishing House) 1928. (In Arabic script.)

Safarov, G., *Kolonial'naya revolyutsiya*, Moscow (*Gosizdat*) 1921.

Saidbaev, T. S., *Islam i obshchestvo*, Moscow (*Nauka*) 1978.

Simon, Gerhard, *Nationalismus und Nationalitätenpolitik in der Sowjetunion*, Baden-Baden (Nomosverlag) 1986, pp. 17-18 and *passim*. Now available in English as *Nationalism and Policy toward the Nationalities in the Soviet Union*, Boulder (Westview Press) 1991.

Uzbekskaya SSR, Tashkent (Gosudarstvennoe izdatel'stvo Uzbekskoy SSR) 1963.

Weber, Max, *Wirtschaft und Gesellschaft*, Tübingen (J.C.B. Mohr [Paul Siebeck]) 1925.

Zlatopol'skiy, D. L. (ed.), *Natsional'naya gosudarstvennost' soyuznykh respublik*, Moscow 1968, pp. 5 *ff*.

Serial Literature:

Central Asian Survey.
Fan va Turmush.
Kommunist (Moscow).
Kommunist Uzbekistana.
Komsomolets Uzbekistana.
Literaturnaya gazeta.
Mushtum.
New Times (Moscow).
Obshchestvennye nauki v Uzbekistane.
Ogonek.
Oqituvchilar gazetasi.
Ozbekistan adabiyati va san"ati.
Ozbekistan Kommunisti.
Ozbekistan madaniyati.
Pravda
Pravda Vostoka.

Bibliography

Radio Liberty Research Papers. (Replaced in 1989 by *Report on the USSR.*)

Report on the USSR (Radio Liberty).

Sharq yulduzi.

Sovet Ozbekistani.

Yash Leninchi.

Zvezda Vostoka.

Index

Index